FEEL MY BIG GUITAR

FEEL MY BIG GUITAR

Prince and the Sound He Helped Create

Edited by JUDSON L. JEFFRIES,
SHANNON M. COCHRAN, and MOLLY REINHOUDT

University Press of Mississippi / Jackson

The University Press of Mississippi is the scholarly publishing agency of
the Mississippi Institutions of Higher Learning: Alcorn State University,
Delta State University, Jackson State University, Mississippi State University,
Mississippi University for Women, Mississippi Valley State University,
University of Mississippi, and University of Southern Mississippi.

www.upress.state.ms.us

The University Press of Mississippi is a member of
the Association of University Presses.

"Erotic Cities: Instrumental Anthropomorphism in Prince's Compositions" was first
printed in the *Journal of African American Studies*. It is reprinted here with permission of Springer Nature; all rights are reserved.

First printing 2023
∞

Library of Congress Control Number 2023935493
Hardback ISBN 978-1-4968-4525-2
Trade paperback ISBN 978-1-4968-4526-9
Epub single ISBN 978-1-4968-4529-0
Epub institutional ISBN 978-1-4968-4524-5
PDF single ISBN 978-1-4968-4528-3
PDF institutional ISBN 978-1-4968-4527-6

British Library Cataloging-in-Publication Data available

CONTENTS

SECTION II.
MUSICOLOGY AND INSTRUMENTAL EROTICISM

INTRODUCTION

JUDSON L. JEFFRIES, SHANNON M. COCHRAN, AND MOLLY REINHOUDT

PrincEnlighteNmenT, a term introduced in *Spectrum*'s Fall 2020 special issue on Prince, denotes how, through his music, Prince has over the years made us cringe as well as startled and informed us. On so many occasions, he turned conventional wisdom on its head, all the while giving us something to think about and challenged us to look and think beyond what we see and are told. Prince's music is a conscious-raising experience.

Although known for his seeming preoccupation with sex that manifests in his outrageous lyrics and stage antics, Prince was unquestionably a political animal. In fact, listening to a Prince album/CD is like taking a master class in the social sciences or the humanities. A close examination of Prince's catalog reveals that there are few works in which societal issues are not featured prominently. Aside from the politics of sex, gender, and sexuality, one can find topics ranging from international relations to abject poverty to drug addiction to the space race to the Cold War. When it came to the hot button issues of the day, Prince left few stones unturned.

Considered one of entertainment's more fascinating figures, Prince caught the eye of many outside of the music industry, even some who were universally considered most eccentric, case in point: when Andy Warhol spotted Prince and Billy Idol at a party in the mid-1980s, he wrote, "seeing these two glamour boys, it's like boys are the new Hollywood glamour girls, like Jean Harlow and Marilyn Monroe." Warhol was apparently so taken with Prince that he kept the twelve silk-screen prints he made of Prince in his personal collection rather than selling them, which was his custom with everything from wallpaper to his wooden Brillo boxes and Campbell's soup can cartons. Seldom did Warhol, a capitalist, allow sentiment or nostalgia to get in the way of making a buck.

Through his thirty-nine studio albums, Prince pulled back the veil of ignorance from the faces and eyes of many of his listeners—jolting us from the media-induced slumber to which many of us have succumbed—and in the process prodding us to question everyone and everything. Things are not always what they seem is the undercurrent one consistently finds in Prince's music.

This edited collection is our latest attempt, which began several years ago, to place Prince at the center of scholarly analysis with the express purpose of putting him in his proper cultural and political place in history. Since 2016, we have identified, recruited, and cultivated a small group of scholars that we believe was capable of producing some of the freshest, most intriguing, thought-provoking, and mind-bending work about Prince—an artist whose music exemplified those very characteristics. These scholars hail from an array of disciplines and, as a result, employ a unique blend of methodologies that have produced some rather dynamic perspectives—something we believe Prince would have very much appreciated.

Complementing the scholarly works contained therein are pieces written by other intellectuals as well as by laypersons. Prince's works touched and inspired so many that we believed it only appropriate that we provide space for those who endeavored to share memories of Prince in the form of a reflection. These personal reflections offer fans of Prince a great way to communicate to a wide audience what Prince and his music meant to them. For some, the opportunity is cathartic, medicinal, and fun—all at the same time. Then there are interviews of people who either knew Prince personally, worked with him, helped get him started, or interacted and/or watched him grow outside of music. These personal reflections and interviews grant readers a unique lens through which to view Prince in a light that enriches their understanding of the man.

This three-volume collection is divided into seven categories, examining a wide range of topics within Prince's oeuvre: In Vol. 1, readers are presented two themes, the first being *Influences and Rivalries (Real or Imagined)*. Chapter 1 begins with H. Zahra Caldwell's article, a comparative study of the lives and artistic output of James and Prince. In this work, the author discusses the American racial and social landscape that stood as a backdrop to their rise to stardom and the prominent role in which their hometowns of Buffalo, New York, and Minneapolis, Minnesota, played in their lives. The most thought-provoking aspect of Caldwell's work is her examination of the racialized treatment of Prince and Rick James by the press, audiences, promoters, and music venues and how those dynamics gave rise to their distinct sounds. The chapter's main goal is to unpack the parallels and impact of both artists in the late 1970s and 1980s as both men made historic and lasting imprints on the American musical landscape.

In "Haze and Rain: Exploring the Influence of Jimi Hendrix on Prince," Ignatius Calabria offers a comparative analysis of both guitar virtuosos, their playing style and personalities, shared qualities and influences, and key aspects of their music. Calabria maintains that both Prince and Hendrix demonstrated an uncanny ability to transcend the music and use the guitar as a mouthpiece for their immediate thoughts and feelings. When words were unnecessary, the guitar spoke volumes for both men. In chapter 3, Karen Turman follows with "Zoot Suits and New Jack Swing: Morris Day's Dandyism," bringing the discussion back to Minneapolis and the complement of Morris Day and The Time's look to Prince's own Dandyism. Closing the section is the Rev. Fred Mark Sheehan's essay examining the influence of Joni Mitchell on Prince. Chapter 5 includes an interview of Prince's first female bandmate, Gayle Chapman by Judson L. Jeffries. As someone who was there from the very beginning Chapman's viewpoint is unique as she talks about, among other things, her experience as the only female member of Prince's band. The section closes with an interview between Tony Kiene and Pepé Willie, Prince's first producer.

Theme II, *Musicology and Instrumental Eroticism*, shifts the discussion to musical analysis, beginning with Will Fulton's chapter on Prince's recordings from the 1980s. Fulton traces the development of Prince's 1980 solo recording process as a cottage industry, and how this extended to the development of vocal and instrumental character play as shown in "Let's Work," "Bob George," "If I Was Your Girlfriend," and "Adore." In chapter 8, Brian Jude de Lima further examines Prince's adoption of his electric guitar as an extension of his phallus, at times even "ejaculat[ing] onto the crowd." Sabatino DiBernardo provides a "lyrico-philosophical" examination of Prince's name change in chapter 9. DiBernardo argues that in an implied performative act of renaming himself, Prince successfully carried out an inaudible speech act that sought to undo the legal copyright to his musical production and performance of labor. His enigmatic semiotic gesture sought to sever "Prince" per se from himself and his record label without destroying the artist-subject Prince. Antonio Garfias rounds out volume 1 with a reflection that incorporates Prince's work into a long and winding life journey that he finds both mentally and intellectually illuminating.

In sum, this edited collection brings together a variety of scholarly articles as well as essays, reflections, and interviews to further our understanding of the enigma that was Prince. Several years in the making, we hope this work will add to PrincEnlighteNmenT and bring the full spectrum of Prince's life and work to the fore.

INFLUENCES AND RIVALRIES
(REAL OR IMAGINED)

Chapter 1

FIRE IT UP!

Prince, Rick James, Rivalry, Race, Punk Funk, and the Minneapolis Sound

H. ZAHRA CALDWELL

Following his back-to-back releases *Come Get It!* (1978) and "Fire It Up" (1979), Rick James embarked on a forty-two-week tour in the winter of 1979. It would round out in the spring of 1980. Prince, a young singer and musician on the rise, was added as an opening act last-minute. James watched footage of the singer and invited him on the road. He saw himself as helping an up and comer and immodestly reflected, "I thought the kid was pretty funky . . . he reminded me a bit of myself . . ."[1] At the time, his stardom far eclipsed that of Prince, the much less seasoned and exposed musician. James turned thirty about halfway through the dates, making him a full decade older than the fledgling Prince. This span was important musically as it placed James on the music scene as a professional musician during the latter half of the 1960s and throughout the 1970s. These were significant years in American music as well as in his musical and personal maturity. He had performed with rock, funk, and R&B bands all over the world by 1979. Prince shared these influences but had not yet slaved as a touring artist or spent as much time outside of Minneapolis. Because of the age difference and their dueling groove heavy approaches to Black music, the Fire It Up tour was billed "the Battle of the Funk" by promoters.[2]

The tour became legendary for many reasons, chief among them the rivalry that would arise between the two artists. There was trouble from the start. Egos on both sides hastened disaster. Despite graciously being invited on the tour, Prince never took the time to introduce himself to James. At the first concert date, James strode into the venue already disillusioned with the younger artist. Prince was playing the drums, which James described as "some bullshit beat."[3] He proceeded to sit down and played as a counter to

3

his new rival. Prince took a quick exit. Unfortunately, due to this immediate disdain they would share little more than a stage for the next six months. The first gig was in the south, an anchor audience for James as it was predominantly African American. Dez Dickerson, Prince's guitarist, explained that as musicians out of Minneapolis, they were used to small Black, mixed, and sometimes, predominately white audiences. He remembered, "For me, to come out on stage in a city like Shreveport, Louisiana, and see 18,000 African American faces was a powerful thing." It helped to further firm up Prince's R&B fan base. Dickerson added, "in light of the edgy 'punk meets funk rock' thing we were doing, we needed to capture the loyalty of that audience."[4] This is not to say that, as with most Black artists of this period, Prince's listeners were not already primarily Black.

It would seem that Prince and James had similar aspirations in sound and audience. However, as the tour moved forward, the onstage rivalry and backstage animosity only grew. Early in the tour dates James was told that Prince was adopting parts of his signature performance wholesale. James wrote in his biography, *The Confessions of Rick James: Memoirs of a Super Freak*, "Here's Prince doing my chants. Not only was he stalking the stage just like me, doing the funk sign, flipping the microphone and everything. The boy had stolen my whole show."[5] This could have been ignored but for the fact that Prince was the opening act. The resulting takeaway was that James was mimicking Prince. This was all very ironic as James was accused by some of stealing parts of the act of the original funkster, George Clinton, including his "rebellious terminology," chants, and keyboard accents.[6] This repletion may have pointed to actual cribbing or simply highlighted influences that were popular in the Black music at the time. In either case, the onstage sparring coupled with offstage dislike between the two camps. To make things much worse, James's heavy partying, drug use, and sexual exploits clashed with Prince's offstage purposefully distant aloofness and clean living.

Prince demanded monk-like discipline of his band. This included no drugs and little to no extracurricular activities. Dickerson recalled, "For all of the growing folklore about Prince and the sex crazed image, behind the scenes it . . . resembled *The Cosby Show*."[7] The bandleader was fixated on stardom and avoided anything he saw as a threat to that ambition. This may have worked in Prince's favor as he was often seen by critics as challenging James in his title as the "King of Funk" as they played night after night.[8] This tour and their rivalry was a prescient symbol for the roles the two would take in the 1980's musical landscape. Eventually, Prince's star was on the rise as James's began to fade. However, the first half of the 1980s would find both James and Prince at highs in their musical careers. The ensuing decades would unfold differently. Despite the contention in their relationship James and Prince had striking parallels in their personal backgrounds as well as their approach to musicianship, songwriting, production, and showmanship.

Considering this, I am interested in expanding the discussion on the sharply segregated music industry and racialized media treatment that produced, in part, the limitations on James's stardom and Prince's international success. I will discuss the American racial and social environment that stood as a backdrop to the stardom of Prince and James, their childhoods, their multilayered musical and personal influences, the impact of their home cities on their music, their work as businessmen and producers, as well as the media treatment that seemingly made one a global super star and left the other trapped in "Black music ghettos."[9] Significantly, this article will explore the racialized treatment of each artist by audiences, promoters, and venues of music promotion, such as MTV, and coverage of the press. Both made historic imprints on the American musical landscape of the 1980s and beyond. The article's main goal is to unpack the parallels and impact of both artists at the zenith of their, initially, dueling careers, in the late 1970s and 1980s. Although Prince's legacy will far exceed both James's and these decades, both artists belong in the canon of pivotal Black musicians.

THE PRINCE & THE SUPER FREAK: THE LITERATURE

The body of work written about both men is largely biographical. James has three biographies written about his life and music. *The Confessions of Rick James: Memoirs of a Super Freak*, written by James, is a detailed narrative of the singer's exploits living an outrageous lifestyle of excess. It seems to be written more for titillation than providing a thorough memoir. Two biographies were produced that pull heavily from *Confessions* adding some additional interviews and perspectives: *Glow* (2014) and *Super Freak: The Life of Rick James* (2017). Combined, the three texts provide a solid and wild life narrative but fail to contribute any reflective analysis of his contributions as an artist and producer. He also is discussed briefly in *Funk: The Music, The People, and The Rhythm of The One* by Rickey Vincent, in reference to his place in funk music's trajectory.

Literature on Prince, by contrast, is growing exponentially since his death. His posthumous biography, entitled *The Beautiful Ones*, is the only book about his life in his own words. It consists of transcribed and handwritten notes. For the sake of my topic, I will include some of the works here that I am in direct conversation with, largely books that focus on the same eras.

It would be hard to include an exhaustive list. *The Rise of Prince: 1958–1988*, is a biography of the artist that spans his early life until the pinnacle of his career in the late 1980s. *Prince and the Purple Rain Era Studio Sessions: 1983 and 1984*, by Duane Tudhal, and *Let's Go Crazy: Prince and the Making of Purple Rain*, by Alan Light, detail the creation of the *Purple Rain* album and movie, respectively. Other biographical examinations include *Prince: The Man and His Music*, by journalist Matt Thorne, and *Prince: Inside the Music and the Masks*, by Ronin Ro. *Dig if You Will the Picture: Funk, Sex, God, and Genius in the Music of Prince*, by Ben Greenman, mainly a myopic study of Prince's albums and individual songs as well as his persona, also adds to the bourgeoning post-death discussion of Prince and his larger meaning within American culture. Most recently, *I Wonder U: How Prince Went Beyond Race and Back*, by Adilifu Nama, is a needed look at Prince's engagement with race, masculinity, and sexuality and chronicles his career through those lenses. All of these books make an important contribution to the literature. However, as scholars and critics gain distance from Prince's death and the multiple eras in which he creatively produced, we can further contemplate his substantial bequest to modern American music. Considering their wide impact, this article will only add to a broader discussion of Prince and, significantly, James's many legacies.

BEGINNINGS

Mama, sit down for me please
Daddy, comfort her in this time of need
Your one and only son has got to get away
Before this ghetto life becomes the death of me . . .[10]
—RICK JAMES, "HOLLYWOOD"

Rick James penned "Hollywood" for his first album. The song has all the melancholy of Prince's "Purple Rain" and the pride of his "Baby I'm a Star." In it he describes his burning aspirations for stardom, but more he paints a picture of the lurking dangers of impoverishment and lack of access. James also centers the importance of family and specifically the influence of his mother in this song. Some of these experiences would echo within the life of a young Prince as well. James was born in Buffalo, New York, in 1948. Buffalo in the 1950s and 1960s, as experienced by James and his family, was a city which had not yet been subsumed by severe economic decline that would visit many urban centers in the coming decades. This fate awaited Buffalo in the ensuing years.

Bethlehem Steel Corporation and Chevrolet Motor Company, among other large corporations, still offered jobs to the Buffalo masses.[11] The third of eight children, James spent much of his youth on the city's predominately Black east side in the housing projects. His family first lived in all Black Willert Park Courts and, later, the newly desegregated Perry Projects.

Poverty and racial tension surrounded the single-mother-headed family. Despite this, James described his family as economically stable. He explained, "Mom kept eight children fed and clothed."[12] Mabel "Betty" Gladden had once been a dancer at the famed Cotton Club in Harlem and also danced for Katherine Dunham. But as she raised her children, she worked three jobs in Buffalo to stay afloat. She held down two as a house cleaner and her primary gig was as a numbers runner for the Buffalo mafia. This second occupation earned her the majority of her income and enabled her to support her large family.[13]

There was a booming underground economy, in which numbers running was just one lucrative hustle. James was exposed to this world via his mother's gig and often went on runs with her. He described assisting her with retrieving numbers slips that held that day's bet.[14] Musically, her occupation was a boon for James. Numbers runs would sometimes include bars and clubs with live music. Young James would sit in with the band: "I was only nine or ten, but the people who ran these Jazz and Blues joints never cared. They just loved to see us come in." He remembered his mother's "proud look when she'd watch her son kickin' on drums."[15] This early introduction to raw, live Black music and playing would help shape his gritty funk sound. He was talented from a young age. There are ways in which James's remembrances reflect an appreciation for his mother's ingenuity and her encouragement of his musical gifts. There are other ways, good and bad, that he would emulate her hustle. He skipped school to sing four-part harmony in a group he formed called the Duprees, performing in nightclubs and on street corners. He began honing his musical prowess on the streets of Buffalo. The city was also a stop on the Black nightclub circuit. His forays into New York City exposed him to the live music scenes there, including those in Greenwich Village, with its mixture of folk, rock, and jazz, and Harlem, with its rhythm and blues and more jazz. He, for example, fondly recalled seeing saxophonist John Coltrane at the Village Vanguard and soul singer Jackie Wilson at the Apollo on the same night as a teenager. All of this helped to form his musical roots.[16] It also led to lots of trouble with law enforcement.

James has defined himself as a "juvenile delinquent" for often having tangles with the police for stealing cars and other low-level offenses.[17] After dropping out of school he joined the naval reserve to avoid the Vietnam draft. Inadvertently, this life decision would deepen his wide-ranging musical adeptness. The compulsory discipline and rigid hierarchy were not a good fit for him. He went AWOL and fled to Toronto, Canada. He settled in the artistic Yorkville neighborhood. Artists such as Joni Mitchell, Kenny Rogers, Kris Kristofferson, and Simon and Garfunkel made the area a living and performance destination. James would become close friends with many of these later luminaries. He said of this time in his life, "I loved it all and felt like I was in the hippest college in the world."[18] It seemed to be a cross between the eclectic West Village and Berkeley. Here he was seriously exposed to musicians and genres of music such as rock, folk, and classical. It was also here that he teamed up with Neil Young, later of Crosby, Stills and Nash, to form the Mynah Byrds, a bi-racial R&B group with folk and pop influences. They were signed to Motown Records in 1966. Unfortunately, this return to the United States would end in James's five-month incarceration in the brig for desertion. This forced him to make some life choices. He rededicated himself to a life on stage and used this time to write music and reflect on his missed opportunities. More influential global wandering, training, and musical experimentation followed his release. Eight years later he ended up back at Motown and recorded his breakout album, *Come Get It!* (1978). By 1979, and the Fire It Up tour James had honed his skills as a musician in several different genres, cities, countries, and in front of different audiences.

In contrast to James's East Coast roots, Prince was raised in the upper Midwest in Minneapolis, Minnesota. His parents were both artists. His father, John Nelson (stage name Prince Rogers), was a jazz musician and songwriter, while his mother, Mattie Shaw, performed as a singer. His father, who migrated from Louisiana in 1948, formed the Prince Rogers Trio. He later met and married Shaw. Prince, their first child, would be born ten years after his father's arrival. In his posthumous memoir, *The Beautiful Ones*, Prince described a complicated childhood punctuated with both joy and sadness. He had fond early memories of his parents together as a couple. Prince attributed his passion for music and the modeling of musical genius to his father and his mother for being "nurturing and loving" when he was a young boy. The relationship was also fraught, tumultuous, and sometimes violent.[19] The ensuing strife in Prince's childhood home has been well documented in works about and interviews of him. The estrangement of the parents from each other (ending with a divorce in 1965) and finally, from him, left him without a family home by the time he was twelve. Asked to leave by his father and not welcomed by his mother's new husband he bounced from house to house between relatives and friends.

He described this time as difficult. He was unable to access his parents for emotional or financial support. According to the musician, he was often hungry and would sometimes stand outside of the local McDonald's to "smell stuff." He reflected to Neal Karlen, a *Rolling Stone* reporter, "I was very bitter when I was young. I was insecure, and I'd attack anybody."[20] Eventually he moved in with the family of Andre Anderson, later André Cymone, his good friend and future bandmate. This gave him stability and caretaking but still no dedicated family of his own. Because of this instability, he spent his youth on the North *and* South sides of Minneapolis, which both included the small Black enclaves of the city. Akin to Rick James, his turbulent adolescence marked him for life.

Perhaps due to the heavily racialized media coverage at the start of his career, as well as his insistence on presenting an ambiguous multiethnic background, more emphasis has been placed on the multicultural Minneapolis spaces that influenced Prince's music. Where James was consistently connected to urban, Black Buffalo, Prince is disconnected from the small but very present Black community and music scene that he was exposed to in Minneapolis. The city was very segregated socially and musically. It was also geographically isolated. This inadvertently worked for musical innovation and musical competition. Prince's father provided early entry into that world. John Nelson's primary instrument was the piano, although he played others. The Prince Rogers Trio played gigs around the city. In retrospect, and certainly at the time, many outsiders may not have appreciated the bourgeoning Black music scene that was attracting local and touring Black musicians.

This vibrant scene would be Prince's earliest musical exposure. First seeing his dad perform impacted him profoundly, "I went to watch one of his gigs when I was about 5. We were supposed to stay in the car, but I snuck out and went into the bar. He was up on stage and it was amazing." He recalled thinking, "These people think my dad is great."[21] By the early sixties there were many popular local musicians and groups playing the city such as Willie and the Bumblebees and the Valdons.[22] In her book *There's Got to Be Something Here: The Rise of the Minneapolis Sound*, music journalist and author Andrea Swensson outlines the major influence that Black musicians and singers had on Minneapolis's musical heritage. This was the one and same heritage that would shape Prince's sound. Much like hip-hop emerging in the Bronx in the late 1970s, these bands and musicians took inspiration from popular music but made something very much their own. For Prince, Minneapolis was a locus of musical invention and production. He understood his hometown as a unique musical mecca for good reason. And, contrary to media narratives of a dominant multicultural symbiosis in the city's live music productions, it had Black musicianship at its base. This reality was only heightened by Prince's own involvement in the substantial live music scene that he submerged himself in as an adolescent and teen. Playing live was more than a pastime; it was a sign of ultra-Minneapolis hipness. According to André Cymone, "The environment we grew up in, joining a band became the thing in Minneapolis. If you weren't in a band, you weren't really cool."[23]

As barely teenagers, Prince and Cymone formed a band with the moniker Grand Central and played throughout Minneapolis. Morris Day, drummer and later lead singer of the Time, joined the band and recalled the live gigging done by the group. They played high school dances, VFW halls and the local clubs. There were also "battles of the bands." Their biggest competition was Flyte Tyme, founded by Jimmy Jam and Terry Lewis, both later joining the Time and becoming renowned super-producers. Flyte Tyme included a three-part horn section, while Grand Central led with keyboards and guitar. Both groups preferred funk, although some top 40 was also a necessity for bookings.[24] A typical set by Grand Central included songs such as Earth, Wind & Fire's "Shining Star," "Tell Me Something Good" by Rufus and Chaka Khan, and "Fight the Power" by the Isley Brothers. Day explained, "In short, we were deep into fierce funk."[25] The local scene included popular Black acts who pushed each other toward perfection while the airwaves were ruled by white pop and rock with a dollop of R&B, soul and funk mixed in. Prince absorbed it all into his evolving musical persona. It is interesting that Prince's formative live playing centered around funk and R&B, as he would be increasingly distanced from these genres in media coverage as well as within his own personal narratives by the mid-1980s.

He decided to split from Grand Central in 1976, go solo, and leave Minneapolis briefly for New York. He thought that a move would help him gain exposure and get a recording contract. Despite the efforts of local musicians, Minneapolis was always behind the national musical trends. However, simultaneously, the isolation and freedom from trends would be the crucible for Prince's musical abilities and innovations. Only after returning home was he signed to Warner Bros. with a three-album deal, releasing his debut *For You* in 1978. It was written, produced, and performed, including each instrument, by Prince. The innovation out of Black Minneapolis would reshape American music. Like Rick James, Prince found creative inspiration in his hometown. Although they hailed from smaller, less heralded cities, they used these spaces as incubators for their own particular sound. Each city, Buffalo and Minneapolis, functioned as a key element in the development of Rick James's eventual "Punk Funk" and Prince's funky Minneapolis derived multicultural, multi-genred fusion.

1981: THE MAVERICKS, THE MUSIC, AND THE MEDIA

Rick James appeared on the *Merv Griffin Show* on October 15, 1981. After a performance of "Super Freak" with his Stone City Band he sat down on the couch opposite the host. His most recent album, *Street Songs,* had gone triple platinum.[26] James, over time, crafted what he termed "Punk Funk." He liked the idea of funk music with more influences and more edge. He said, "We created the name because if . . . we really made a dent in the music world, we'd do it before Joe Blow titled us. 'Cause Joe Blow is quick to take our music and put names to it . . . bebop, jazz, blues, disco . . . all that silly shit."[27] James had only a few days before being the first funk or R&B act to sell out the 20,000 seat Philadelphia Spectrum for two consecutive nights.[28] This was achieved within a matter of hours and notable because the Jacksons performed at the venue a month prior to his first show.

He strutted off the stage in a one armed black and white sequined jumpsuit as he ended his performance. Griffin's bizarre questioning of this mega star began with his braids. "Can you get us a braid?" The host was curious if there was "a head braider in the band?" James was gracious and professional throughout the interview, in spite of the belittling and racialized questioning. Griffin continued, but shifted the discussion to James's mother, "Your mother is famous. She used to run numbers!" The artist's response shook off the insult: "Yes, she did." He added endearingly, "She supported eight kids on her own." His best efforts to turn the interview in a different direction were thwarted. The multi-millionaire performer described his rural mansion and his interest in polo. Griffin seemed surprised. The topic was turned only when Griffin, cutting James off, announced, "Let's talk professionally now. Let's get Kal Rudman to jump in . . . he loves Rick James!"[29] Rudman, who was awkwardly sitting on the other side of the couch, began to point out how successful James was, quoting album and concert sales. Rudman, who had been a radio personality and music journalist, functioned as a music expert on Griffin's show regularly. Griffin, who had been known to invite an interesting cross section of guests, was very clearly out of step with the times and needed the assistance. Regrettably, in this instance, Rudman's presence worked to further silence James and posit him as an object within his own narrative and original musical productions. In essence, Rudman embodied the "Joe Blow," that James had been concerned about. This scenario seemed to signal that James, one of the top selling Black artists, could only gain national validation when his success was cosigned by two middle aged white men. His experience on this show was symbolic of the eighties media's racialized and antagonistic engagement with African American artists.

Prince made his first major television appearance on *American Bandstand* with Dick Clark on January 26, 1980. Dressed in skin tight gold pants, pink shirt, and his hair feathered and pressed and curled, Prince's performance contained the raw energy for which he would become known. "I Wanna Be Your Lover" was the lead off song. The appearance was one among many that he would make in the months that followed, after *Prince*, his second album, gained traction. What made it memorable was the awkward interview with Clark, the show's host. Dez Dickerson has even suggested that it was planned and staged by Prince.[30] It was brief but painful. Clark introduced Prince's set by emphasizing his age of nineteen to the audience. He was actually twenty-one but took off two years for dramatic effect. After the first song, Clark conducted the standard *American Bandstand* two-to-three-minute interview. His initial comment was about the unlikelihood of music such as this coming out of Minneapolis. Clark then turned, again, to Prince's young age. The artist seemed offended and was vague and sometimes silent when asked questions such as "how long ago did you shop demos?" In response, he put up four fingers. To the question of "how many instruments do you play?" Prince said, "thousands." Clark would later say, "I've always said that was one of the most difficult interviews I've ever conducted, and I've done 10,000 musician interviews."[31] This is hard to imagine, but many writers have dissected this interview because it was Prince's first major national broadcast and televised interview. The interpretations have focused on Prince's purposeful building of his celebrity mystique.[32] I believe that, layered on to this understanding, should be one that considers Prince's navigation of the racialized landscape of the media and music business. He was making a conscious attempt to contest the erasure that befell Black musicians and Black musicianship as well as gain control over the trajectory of his image and artistry. Unlike James's encounter with Merv Griffin, Prince, with his frustrating elusiveness, was able to move himself from object to subject.

Witnessing the mainstream's treatment of Black musicians, even those who were wildly successful like James, it is little wonder that a just signed Prince told a music executive, "Don't make me black."[33] Despite misleading interviewers with his talk of mixed parentage and visions of a multi-racial, amalgamated city of origin, Prince was Black. He understood himself to be Black and, even in overwhelmingly white Minneapolis, had been subsumed in Black life, had Black parentage, and was reared in Black spaces. His decisive distancing, while understandably suspect to the loyal Black audience and larger Black community, was, in his mind, a necessity of capturing white listeners. This declaration, circumventing Blackness, came from the minimizing, and dismissing of Black artists. His words to the executive were instructive rather than a repudiation: "Don't make me black." His first five albums incorporated strands of new wave, rock, and pop but kept funk at their center. The mainstay of his audience was Black until the release of 1984's *Purple Rain*. In fact, according to Jimmy Jam, the First Avenue club made famous in the film was chosen by Prince because it was one of the only fully integrated clubs in Minneapolis. It had welcomed Black bands, such as Grand Central, when they were turned away from others.[34] Via this venue, a somewhat false picture of the city's supposed interracial unity through music was broadcasted, all while it was picked up as an important symbol in media treatments of Prince.[35]

By 1981, the year of the Griffin performance, Rick James had released five of his own albums as well as produced one album for Teena Marie, his label mate at Motown, and two Stone City Band records. Prince, meanwhile, was on his fourth: *Controversy*. The start of the decade was fruitful for the two artists as individuals. Yet, generally, the economic and social realities were constricting for African Americans as the decade unfolded. The year 1981 also marked Ronald Reagan's election to the presidency and the start of his first term in office. Much of white America reacted to the gains made through the civil rights and Black Power movements with a severe backlash to racial progress. Reagan, a Republican, rode the rising tide of conservatism and placed thinly veiled racist policies at the center of his agenda. The results for African Americans were what historian Daniel Lucks dubbed a "new nadir." He contends that Reagan's administration "compiled the worst civil rights record of any president in the modern era."[36] The social safety net that many poor Black and white communities relied on for assistance was villainized and dismantled. Civil rights gains were also decidedly reversed. This spiral was heightened by the skyrocketing incarceration rates of African Americans due to an overreaching, racially coded "War on Drugs." It is, of course, impossible to separate the experiences of Black artists from the larger Black community in this moment. The 1980s brought a familiar but distinct set of challenges for Black music and Black artists.

The late 1960s and 1970s seemed to have the promise of some integration within music. Major Black musicians, sticking to their Black musical styles, had huge crossover audiences. By the mid-1970s, Black and white concert-goers mingled at Earth, Wind & Fire, Stevie Wonder, Aretha Franklin, and Sly and the Family Stone performances. The mixing here did not amount to a unified racial nirvana, but was a far cry from strictly separate or racially partitioned shows of the previous decades. Unfortunately, behind the scenes at music companies the narrative for artists still relied on apartheid like systems. This ultimately retrenched extreme segregation in music and radio and led to its resurgence in the eighties. The first label to establish a "Black music" department was CBS in 1972. By 1980, it had a roster of 125 acts. Warner Bros., who signed Prince, began its Black music department not long after CBS.[37] What accompanied the opening of these departments was further under-valuing of Black artists, many of whom had come from underfunded Black labels that did not have the money for promotion and payouts that larger labels possessed. This undervaluing, underpaying, and under marketing only deepened by the 1980s and coupled with the pronounced white backlash, created an environment in which achieving wide-ranging Black success was near impossible. The 1980s would be witness to fewer major Black artists than the previous decades. Rick James and Prince were focused on formulas to become one of the chosen few.

One ingredient for musical stardom in the 1980s was a brand-new medium: the music video. It would become one of the main sources of music consumption and a dominant vehicle for music sales and distribution. Music Television (MTV) became the foundation of this new way to consume and enjoy music. The cable-based channel was the premier place to have music videos played, and, at the outset, often had to convince performers to make them. The popularity of the channel was near instantaneous, and it wielded power. Previously unknown white groups, like Human League, became over-night sensations and were "suddenly selling out without any radio play" after their videos were put into heavy rotation.[38] Regrettably, MTV became an extension of the segregated record and radio industries. James's and Prince's diverging encounters with the channel would shape their own futures and that of other Black artists on MTV. James was one of the first and most outspoken artists to rail against what he saw as racism in yet another facet of the divided music industry.

At MTV's inception James was surpassed only by the Rolling Stones in concert sales, yet Motown (his label) could not get his videos played.[39] His magnum opus, *Street Songs*, spent twenty weeks at number one on the R&B chart and reached number three on the pop chart. It spawned the hits "Super Freak," "Give it to Me Baby," and the duet "Fire and Desire." 1982's *Throwin' Down* was another smash album for the singer. He produced videos for several of the hit songs, including "Give it To Me Baby," although many art-ists were not yet doing so. None of this earned him airplay on MTV. He explained to an interviewer, "They're catering to white people . . . It's taking black people back 400 years."[40] James surely had his own career interests in mind with his public feud with MTV. However, he was no less correct in his observations about the music industry and its bearing on artists. He pointed out to CBS reporter Sam Ford;

A lot of white kids put on MTV and say where's Stevie Wonder? Where's Marvin Gaye? Where's Rick James? . . . This isn't the *Wizard of Oz*. There are Black people here and we make music and we spend thousands . . . and we're not doing it because we enjoy it. We're doing it because it's part of the art. We're being excluded from the art."[41]

They were also being excluded from the profits of wide exposure. MTV executives insisted that video choice was based solely on its fit within their all rock format, although they played artists such as Hall and Oates, ABC, and Culture Club, each playing R&B and soul based music. Another glaring issue was the implication that rock belonged to and was spawn from white America. All of this in spite of the Black modern and foundational, inimitable contributions to rock and roll.

In a 1983 CBS news special, "MTV Discriminates Against Black Artists," key record executives from Black companies and Black music departments, including Solar, Motown and CBS criticized the channel for completely blocking access to their artists.[42] Within their rosters were established popular acts such as Shalamar, the Whispers, Marvin Gaye, and in the case of CBS, super group Earth, Wind & Fire. Singer David Bowie joined his voice with James's and condemned the lack of Black performers. In a much talked about interview on the network, Bowie took VJ Mark Goodman and MTV to task. He pushed, "I'm just floored that there are so few Black artists" and noted that racism was "rampant through American media."[43] Goodman insisted that there were no decisions made along racial lines and but tellingly explained, "We have to try and do what we think not only New York and Los Angeles will appreciate but also Poughkeepsie [N.Y.] or pick some town in the Midwest . . . that would be scared to death by Prince . . . or some other Black faces."[44] Goodman's limp responses did not appease an unmoved Bowie who had tried to move the conversation to larger American racial inequality. The discussion had turned to a myopic denial of interpersonal racism, avoiding the structural racism and racialism that permeated the 1980s.

MTV responded to the criticisms by first adding Prince's funk laced "1999" and then Michael Jackson's decidedly R&B "Billie Jean." Prince's changing image centered utopian multi-culturalism and gender non-conformity while his music incorporated more crossover styles such as rock and pop. Aside from his race, he was a good fit for MTV, but he was in light rotation in off hours at first. There were many white music lovers who could not name Black artists outside those with the very biggest followings such as Stevie Wonder, but now, thanks to MTV they could name Prince. This recognition only heightened when MTV began airing the video for "Little Red Corvette."

It seemed the heavier the rotation the higher the record and concert sales. Keyboardist Monte Moir said of the influence of MTV and the 1999 tour: "It was 90 percent black until 'Little Red Corvette' came out . . . all of a sudden it shifted, drastically. It got to be half and half, if not 60–40 white. By the end of that tour, depending on what city, you could see that real crossover was possible."[45] Prince *never* lost his Black audience, but some Black media outlets began questioning his changing image. When commenting on Prince's album *Controversy*, Philip Harrigan, entertainment editor for *The Pittsburgh Courier*, asserted, "Prince seems to have forgotten (or doesn't care) that the audience that had thrust him into musical prominence is primarily Black, and though he may be extending into rock, the way his current rock output is presented leaves something to be desired . . ." This reporter also reasoned that ". . . for all of his considerable talent, [he] appears destined for obscurity for his radical eclecticism."[46] Little did he know that the "eclecticism" he critiqued would be the very basis for his ascendance.

Jackson, who also had dreams of true crossover, had been trying to get a video played from his album, *Thriller*. Although the single had been number one for two months and the album was also at the top of multiple charts, Jackson's label, CBS, had to threaten to pull all their artists and videos if the network did not capitulate.[47] "Billie Jean" was later joined by a fourteen-minute video for the single "Thriller," which was so popular it was played on a nightly schedule. Even as *Thriller* went on to be the best-selling album of the decade, in no small part because of its exposure on MTV, Jackson brought unprecedented traffic to the channel. In their book, *I Want My MTV*, the authors devote a chapter to Jackson's outsized impact on music television entitled, "I'm Not Like Other Boys: Michael Jackson Saves a Struggling Network from Itself."[48] Like Jackson, the Black talent that was finally let on to MTV were not upstarts but household names long before being featured, unlike many of the white singers and groups. It should be noted that despite MTV's resistance, these artists brought legitimacy and widened the channel's audience and profits. Those chosen to be aired saw a bearing on sales and exposure.

Alternately, this did create a further separation in music. Much of American music history had been oriented around "race music," in other words, Black music, as apart from mainstreamed white music. Though not absolute, if a white audience wanted to listen to a Black artist they mostly had to "crossover" to them. They had to seek out the Black radio station or buy the records as they were presented. The 1980s brought with it, thanks in part to MTV, both an emphasis on Black acts that were palatable and "acceptable" to whites in image and sound, as well as a more solid partition between white and Black artists. Whitney Houston, one of the other few Black singers to ascend, described the pressure to conform to white mainstream cultural expectations, via record company demands, as one of the factors that led her to self-destructive behavior, such as heavy drug use.[49] In his case, the campaign against the racism on MTV left Rick James not only blackballed by the channel but sequestered to Black radio and marketed to Black audiences, although he had been poised for crossover mainstream success.

In 2011, a flurry of media coverage and interviews marked the thirtieth anniversary of MTV. In many ways, it was incredible, though expected, that over thirty years later many who were in key positions at the network still had a hard time recognizing the impact of structural racism on MTV in its heyday.[50] They treated the media channel as if it stood outside of societal norms and white, eighties backlash. More significantly, for the purposes herein, they failed to acknowledge the long-term consequences that this facet of the music industry, in tandem with several others, had on Black musicians and Black music. They let only a few utilize the network as a vehicle while they stunted the careers of other Black artists and cemented the racialized musical landscape.

1985: THE FALL OF PUNK FUNK AND THE RISE OF A GENRE-DEFYING ICON

Nineteen eighty-nine would be a pivotal year for Prince and James. The intervening years since the Fire It Up tour had seen each keep up a grueling pace. They produced an album a year, sometimes two. Although James's professional career began long before Prince's, their solo debuts were in the same year, 1978. Prince was on his sixth album by 1985 as James released his eighth. The sparring musical output and resulting hits made them competitors and rivals but also with kindred ambitions. While their own production was at a breakneck speed, each created and acted as producers for multiple groups and solo artists. In addition to assisting Teena Marie on her first album, with whom he had a fruitful musical relationship, James immersed himself in side projects. He helped to revive the careers of the Temptations by writing, producing, arranging and singing on the hit single, "Standing on the Top." They had been an inspiration to him as a musician and were also labelmates. The song was released on his *Street Songs* album and, *Reunion*, the album marking the Temptations first Motown recording in several years. It reached number six on *Billboard* and signaled the fleeting return of the Temps to the charts.[51]

James, like Prince, had visions of building a stable of artists under his leadership. He wrote and produced two albums for singer Val Young for Motown Records and had produced albums for his Stone City Band. James also accused Prince of stealing his idea for a sexy girl group: "I wanted four chicks—a Valley girl, a classy vamp, a leather queen, and a Rick James bitch."[52] He created the Mary Jane Girls and the lead singer, Joanne "JoJo" McDuffie, was a former back up in his group. Prince was hard at work with his group Vanity 6, led by Vanity. The misogyny implicit in both groups' construction did not deter audiences. They scored hits. Vanity 6 with "Nasty Girl" and "You Drive Me Wild" and the Mary Jane Girls with "In My House," "All Night Long," and "Candy Man." Prince and James also had competing male groups: the Time and Process and the Doo Rags, respectively. The Time would have much more staying power with Morris Day as the lead, and have a string of successful albums. Meanwhile, in 1985, James produced and wrote "Party All the Time" for comedian Eddie Murphy, scoring him his only hit. Prince was busy helping to produce and record Sheila E.'s critically acclaimed debut album, *The Glamorous Life* and its popular lead single of the same name. Prince also added to his collective with a group named the Family and released their debut on his Paisley Park label.

James and Prince used these years to hone their performance style as well. Of course, James was the senior in this arena and had long pushed his performances to a place he felt Black artists had not yet gone. He has described his concerts as akin to Kiss, a popular seventies rock band, in the sense that it was an extreme production that he hoped to rival glam rock's shock and awe entertainment. He achieved this in various ways.[53] He always dressed in distinct performance outfits, covered himself in glass glitter, had as many as twenty people on stage, including his full band, sometimes included pyrotechnics, and occasionally passed out joints. Incorporating these elements into his show inched him closer to what he saw as rock star like; not a realm of music celebrity normally reserved for Black performers. He rebelliously challenged the status quo. Likened to James, Prince's early eighties productions were decidedly and purposefully stripped down. Comparatively, he had few musicians on stage. James would have had access to a larger budget being the bigger star, initially. Regardless, Prince showed little interest in James's glitzy brand of performances. There was plenty to look at in Prince's show. The musicians wore risqué attire and there were always plenty of points of interest, including great musicianship, but Prince was the absolute center of his show. He did most of the dancing on stage and kept the viewer's attention with his energy, singing, instrumentation, and sheer will.

Prince was hard at work on something that would differentiate him from his contemporaries, including James: a film. *Purple Rain* was based on a series of notes he had written. Those notes were transformed into a script and that script into a movie. It was based in Minneapolis and pulled on some of Prince's personal and professional experiences, though it was not biographical. This undertaking was audacious. His popularity remained very niche for the music business. He had a firm following but was widely marketed to the Black funk and wider Black audience—even as his music evolved. Rick James remained a fixture in the Black press and on Black radio through the mid-1980s. *Purple Rain* changed all of that for Prince. It became a critical commercial breakthrough. The film was at first released to small art house theaters but was quickly moved to larger venues because of its popularity. It was accompanied by a soundtrack, single, and video that all rose to number one on multiple charts and ruled the summer and fall of 1984.[54]

For much of his new, wider audience, Prince seemed to appear overnight. *Ebony*, a decades old magazine targeting the Black middle class, did not put Prince on the cover until after the film's release. The five-page spread treated him as just discovered. Although writer Lynn Norment acknowledged his "musical genius" and that the artist had put out six albums, five of which went gold, she referred to "his rapid rise to fame." The young writer must have known better even if her readers did not. The children reading *Ebony* knew exactly who Prince was. He filled the pages of their favorite Black teen music magazines such as *Right On!* and *Black Beat.* By the time *Purple Rain* premiered, Prince had appeared on no less than five covers of *Right On!* alone, beginning with his second album in 1979.[55] Howard Bloom, a music publicist in the 1980s, reflected: "It made absolute sense to me . . . before anybody knew who Prince was I read the black charts . . . that phenomenon of going platinum when you were buried on the black charts, that says something."[56] Prince had been recording and touring for years. He had captured a wide fan base, had videos on MTV, but the rigidly segregated 1980s musical landscape kept his genius isolated on the Black charts. It is hard to imagine that but for *Purple Rain*, Prince may have met the fate of so many other uber talented Black performers.

For Rick James, the outcome of 1980s stardom would be far different. He released his final charting album in 1985, entitled *Glow.* It garnered him a hit in the title track and a popular video. There was also the success of his groups, particularly the Mary Jane Girls. By this time, however, James had made missteps. He did not evolve with the times, and, at the same time, his music lost some of its identity. Funk was not sought-after. The demise of punk funk and his collective was hastened by his drug addiction. Much has been made of James's excessive drug use and his stalled career. He openly discussed his heavy smoking of marijuana and his use of cocaine with inter-viewers, at concerts, and with friends and fans. It became a part of his star text. One of his most beloved hits, "Mary Jane," was a not so veiled reference to the drug and reached the third spot on the R&B charts. His 1982 album *Throwin' Down* was an undercover reference to snorting cocaine. Drugs and drug use were very much an open part of music culture.

Band members discuss, however, a sudden personal transformation as he began to freebase cocaine (crack), which would be his undoing along with so many others in the eighties.[57] It would be impossible to argue that his drug addiction did not badly affect his career, however, I believe this is another juncture in which race must be considered. I am focusing specifically on James in the 80's as a decade. Even in the depths of his drug use he was in good company. Many of his white contemporaries suffered from comparable addictions. Steven Tyler, lead singer of the rock band Aerosmith, was so overwhelmed by addiction that he nearly destroyed the band and took to wandering the streets for heroine in the early 1980s.[58] He became friends with James through a shared love of music and cocaine. They would eventually spend two stints in rehab together. According to keyboardist Levi Ruffin, during one stay the two were caught indulging in an ounce of cocaine. [59]

Tyler, like many other musicians, was able to return to making music and had multiple hits with an acute and ongoing drug problem that stretched past the eighties. It is no small irony that Aerosmith's career was revived by Run DMC's remake of "Walk This Way." Yet another example of undervalued Black music saving the white mainstream. Singer songwriter Neil Young, former band mate of James, also battled alcohol addiction and was as outspoken on his heavy marijuana use. With a habit which, according to him, spanned forty years, he too was able to sustain his career.[60] Tyler and Neil are still making music and touring in the modern day, decades after the decadent eighties. Discussions of their body of work do not pivot on their well-known drug use. The list of addicted performers in the 1980s, Black and white, is far longer. Yet, James drug use was and is deeply inscribed in his narrative. This outcome can be seen with other Black performers of the era such as Alexander O'Neal and even the iconic Whitney Houston.

Certainly, James descended further into drugs and ruin later in his life. He was convicted of violent felonies, including kidnapping and assault, and had nine different drugs in his system when he died of a heart attack in 2006.[61] This exploration neither erases nor dismisses these facts. It is also true that celebrity and fame are fickle and elusive. We are forced to ponder, nonetheless, what separated James from similarly addicted and troubled white musicians. It seemed that media and industry forgiveness was in short supply when it came to the excesses of Black musicians. The point here is to consider how race and racism operated, and operates, in regard to white and Black celebrity and addiction. Whiteness was supported even in the throes of drug addiction as it added to the fragility of Black artistic success. For James, in a less forgiving, more segregated 1980s, this became an important element in the fall of punk funk.

CONCLUSION: BABY, I'M A STAR!

There's gotta be a better life
Take a picture sweetie, I ain't got time 2 waste
Oh, baby I'm a star
Might not know it now . . .[62]
—PRINCE, "BABY, I'M A STAR"

I vividly remember watching *Purple Rain*. We had a system for our suburban movie theater, one person would go in and pay, then prop the door for whoever they came with. We could watch movies multiple times with little money. I lost count of the number of times I saw the film. It was striking to me for many reasons. First, I *loved* Prince and, second, being a know-it-all-thirteen-year-old, I was exasperated by the lack of hipness of my white counterparts. My cousin and I side-eyed the newly-christened, over-hyper Prince fans. To our mothers' chagrin, we had long had half clothed posters of the purple one plastered all over our bedroom walls. We loved the new album, but also acknowledged it was a bit different and more mainstream than his previous records. We had been sneaking listens to them since we were in single digits. What we did not and could not have understood is that we were witnessing the crossover of a soon to be Black global superstar. There was Michael Jackson and now there was Prince. As the hit song from the film indicated, baby—Prince was a star. His imagining of stratospheric stardom stretched far beyond our underground icon positioning of him. He became one of the very few chosen African American artists to ascend to super stardom in the 1980s. This status is and was nearly as hard to obtain and elusive in any population. However, for artists occupying Black bodies, it is an even more impossible reach.

Upon James's death, Jason King, professor of the Clive Davis Institute of recorded music, implores us to revisit James as an ultra-savvy professional on the defensive, constantly struggling for industry and personal recognition in the midst of embattled circumstance: As the '70s morphed into the '80s Motown was running out of gas, black music was under attack from reactionary rock fans and ignored (pre-*Thriller*) by MTV, the Purple-clothed upstart from Minneapolis was being hailed as the next post-Stevie genius; and, by the end of the '80s, baggy-panted hip-hoppers started sampling his copyrights but not paying up.[63]

In 1984, the rock magazine *Creem* put together a compendium special issue that featured the most notable R&B, Soul, and Funk (read Black) performers of the moment. The cover consisted of the three reigning musicians: Prince, Jackson, and James. If this cover had been composed just a year later, James would not have been featured. He was erased quickly from the top of the charts and magazine covers. The segregated eighties, like all the decades before it, exacted a price for all of these artists. It is not surprising that the handful of Black artists who touched or achieved the upper echelon of success in the era met insurmountable personal challenges. Their names alone read like cautionary tales: Whitney Houston, Michael Jackson, and Prince as well.[64]

Prince was the more talented and more sustaining artist than James, but he as well died of an accidental overdose of fentanyl laced Vicodin, pain medication resorted to after decades of pushing his body to its limits.[65] There were musical and professional costs too, including, for example, his fight for the rights to his masters. The era in which he began his trek to icon status had pressured him to choose between the Black audience and the white mainstream. He refused to split himself into two. Rocker Lenny Kravitz reflected on conversations that he had with Prince in which they discussed rock and race: "'Ain't no black folks in my audience' and it's like, where are they? This is our music, this is rock and roll, we created this!"[66] Prince was well acquainted with this frustration. More than simply misplaced historical memory, tremendous Black musical contributions are subsumed by entwined racialized systems of inequity. By comparing and contrasting the lives and creative productions of Prince and James in the racially charged 1980s, we can see the crooked trajectory that was erected for African American performers and its tangible obstacles to recognition and longevity. Prince and James, together, had experienced the compartmentalization of Black music and each challenged it, making new spaces, in the process, for the countless Black artists who likely refused limitation and definition.

Notes

1. Rick James, *The Confessions of Rick James: Memoirs of a Super Freak* (Phoenix: Colossus Books, 2007), 165.

2. Per Nilsen, *DanceMusicSexRomance: Prince, the First Decade* (Richmond Hill: Firefly Publishing, 2001).

3. James, *Memoirs*, 166; Rick James and David Ritz, *Glow: The Autobiography of Rick James* (New York: Atria Books, 2014), 209.

4. Dez Dickerson, *My Time with Prince* (London: Pavilion Press 2003), 95.

5. James, *Memoirs*, 166.

6. Geoffrey Himes, "Uncle Jam: Fulfilling the Promise of Funk." *The Washington Post*, November 21, 1979, B4.

7. Dickerson, *My Time*, 98.

8. Nilsen, *DanceMusicSexRomance*, 65.

9. Palmer, R, "The Pop Life."

10. Rick James, "Hollywood," *Come Get It!*, Motown Record Corporation, 1978.

11. Deindustrialization would come to Buffalo by the 1970s. The steel industry, a main economic engine in Buffalo, collapsed in 1973, causing many of the steel mills to close. James's mother's income also tumbled with the closures as people had less disposable income for nightlife and numbers. Peter Benjaminson, *Super Freak: The Life of Rick James* (Chicago: Chicago Review Press, 2017), 5.

12. James, *Memoir*, 9.

13. James, *Memoir*, 9–10.

14. Benjaminson, *Super Freak*, 4. The numbers were an underground illegal betting franchise that predated the current lottery system in many states. A set of numbers were chosen by a player. These set of numbers, if they matched that of the "banker," could win the player who placed the bet a sizable return on their original bet.

15. James, *Memoirs*, 17.

16. James and Ritz, *Glow*, 37–38; Benjaminson, *Super Freak*, 9.

17. James, *Memoirs*, 31.

18. James and Ritz, *Glow*, 65.

19. Prince and Dan Piepenbring, *The Beautiful Ones* (New York: Spiegel and Grau, 2019), 97.

20. Neal Karlen, "Prince Talks: The Silence Is Broken," *Rolling Stone*, September 12, 1985, 28.

21. Prince, *The Beautiful Ones*, 189.

22. Andrea Swensson, *Got to Be Something Here: The Rise of the Minneapolis Sound* (Minneapolis: University of Minnesota Press, 2017), 7–9.

23. Ericka Blount Danois, "Minneapolis Music Pioneer André Cymone Speaks for the First Time in Twenty-Seven Years," *WaxPoetics*, October 29, 2012, https://www.waxpoetics.com/blog/features/articles/andre-cymone/.

24. Morris Day and David Ritz, *On Time: A Princely Life in Funk* (New York: Da Capo Press, 2019).

25. Day and Ritz, *On Time*.

26. At that time, a platinum album equated a sale of one million albums or a sale of two million singles.

27. Dave DiMartino, "Rick James: Stone City Burns," *Creem*, December 1981.

28. James, *Memoirs*, 192; Kal Redman cites these sales on Griffin.

29. *The Merv Griffin Show*, "The Hit Makers," season 19, episode 177, directed by Dick Carson, aired May 19, 1981, in broadcast syndication.

30. Matt Thorne, *Prince: The Man and His Music* (Chicago: Bolden, 2016), 53.

31. *American Bandstand*, season 23, episode 11, January 26, 1980, in broadcast syndication; Ben Greenman, *Dig If You Will the Picture: Funk, Sex, God and Genius in the Music of Prince*, (New York: Henry Holt and Company, 2017), 29.

32. Writers such as Ben Greenman in *Dig if You Will*.

33. Anonymous, "Oral History: Prince's Life by People Who Knew Him Best," *Star Tribune*, June 7, 2019, https://www.startribune.com/the-life-of-prince-as-told-by-the-people-who-knew-him/376586581/.

34. Alan Light, *Let's Go Crazy: Prince and the Making of Purple Rain* (New York City: Atria Books, 2014), 4.

35. In fact, the stark and historical racial segregation that led to Prince's sound has been sadly spotlighted in the 2020 death of George Floyd at the hands of a white policemen and subsequent protests in the same city.

36. Daniel S. Luck, *Reconsidering Reagan: Racism, Republicans, and the Road to Trump* (Boston: Beacon Press, 2020), 13.

37. Nelson George, *The Death of Rhythm & Blues* (New York: Pantheon Books, 1988), 134.

38. Ben Fong-Torress, "Why MTV Is Shaking the Music Industry," *San Francisco Chronicle*, San Francisco, 1983, May 1.

39. Richard Harrington, "Race Lines on the Radio: What Color Is Pop?" *The Washington Post*, 1982, K1.

40. Fong-Torress, "Why MTV . . ."

41. Sam Ford, "CBS Evening News." In *MTV Discriminates Against Black Artists*. Vanderbilt Television News Archive #292079, 1983.

42. Ford, "CBS Evening News."

43. Staff Writer, "David Bowie Accusing MTV of Racism in '83: Read the Interview Transcript." *LA Times*, Los Angeles, 2016, January 12.

44. Staff Writer, "David Bowie."

45. Dave Hill, *Prince: A Pop Life*, (New York: Harmony Books, 1989).

46. Philip Harrigan, "The Prince Controversy Continues," *The New Pittsburgh Courier*, 1981, November 14.

47. Craig Marks and Rob Tannenbaum, *I Want My MTV: The Uncensored Story of the Music Video Revolution* (New York: Plume Penguin Group, 2011), 173.

48. Marks and Tannenbaum, *I Want My MTV*, 172–88.

49. Mark Seal, "The Devils in the Diva," *Vanity Fair*, May 8, 2012, https://www.vanityfair.com/hollywood/2012/06/whitney-houston-death-bathtub-drugs-rehab.

50. John Petkovic, "MTV Looks Nothing Like the Video Channel That Roared," *Cleveland*, 2011, https://www.cleveland.com/tv/2011/07/at_30_mtv_looks_nothing_like_t.html. Marks, *I Want My MTV*, 165–72.

51. Benjaminson, 182–83.

52. Ritz, *Glow*, 245.

53. DiMartino, *Stone City*.

54. Lynn Norment, "Prince: The Story Behind His Passion for Purple and Privacy," *Ebony*, November 1984.

55. Cynthia Horner, "A Close Encounter with Prince," *Right On!*, June 14, 2018 1979, https://rightondigital.com/2018/06/14/exclusive-princes-first-interview-with-right-ons-cynthia-horner/.

56. Light, *Let's Go Crazy*, 57

57. *Mike Judge Presents: Tales from the Tour Bus*, "Rick James Part 2," season 2, episode 3, aired November 16, 2018, Cinemax.

58. Steven Tyler and David Dalton, *Does the Noise in My Head Bother You?: A Rock 'N' Roll Memoir* (New York: Ecco Press, 2011), 230.

59. *Mike Judge Presents: Tales from the Tour Bus*, "Rick James Part 2," season 2, episode 3, aired November 16, 2018, Cinemax.

60. David Carr, "Neil Young Comes Clean," *New York Times Magazine*, September 19, 2012.

61. Anonymous, "Coroner: Rick James Died of Heart Attack," *Billboard* (September 17 2004), https://www.billboard.com/articles/news/66447/coroner-rick-james-died-of-heart-attack.

62. Prince, "Baby, I'm a Star," *Purple Rain*, side 2, track 3, Warner Bros., 1984, vinyl LP.

63. Jason King, "I'm Rick James: 15 Hours of the Funk Supernova's Best Songs." *NPR*, February 4, 2015, https://www.npr.org/2015/02/04/383558326/i-m-rick-james-10-hours-of-the-funk-supernova-s-best-songs.

64. Jackson's troubles are well documented in the media. This coverage includes his troubled life, the ebb and flow of fame, financial and legal troubles, as well as allegations against him of sexual abuse.

65. Merrit Kennedy, "Prince Died with 'Exceedingly High' Level of Fentanyl, Report States," *NPR*, March 27, 2018, https://www.npr.org/sections/thetwo-way/2018/03/27/597249429/prince-died-with-exceedingly-high-level-of-fentanyl-report-states.

66. Bryan Hiatt, "Prince's Lost *Rolling Stone* Interview: 'I Don't Think About Gone,'" *Rolling Stone*, April 22, 2016, https://www.rollingstone.com/music/music-news/princes-lost-rolling-stone-interview-i-dont-think-about-gone-227347/.

Chapter 2

HAZE AND RAIN

Exploring the Influence of Jimi Hendrix on Prince

IGNATIUS CALABRIA

Guitarists of all styles and genres share some common traits. We love our instrument. Passionately. We cradle and caress it. We dote on it. Sometimes we name it. We see our guitar as a companion in life. Our guitar is forgiving and shows unrequited devotion. When not connecting with its master, it sits and waits. Both Jimi Hendrix and Prince loved their guitars dearly and dedicated many private hours to exploring the intricacies of this popular instrument. While many play guitar, only those who invest the time and energy learn how to make it speak for them. Hendrix and Prince did not just play the guitar, they bonded with it. While attached, man and instrument invite the audience to observe and enjoy a display of delicate, erotic, and even violent behavior. The guitar is loved, abused and worshipped in the hands of its owner. It is a remarkable relationship. Both guitarists exhibited an ability to rise above the music and use the guitar as a mouthpiece for their immediate thoughts and feelings. When words failed, the guitar spoke clearly for both Prince and Jimi Hendrix.

When listing the greatest rock guitarists of all time, however, one tops the chart while the other lags behind. The winner, for those who have "never been experienced," is Jimi Hendrix, according to a professional poll conducted by *Rolling Stone* who placed Prince at thirty-three.[1] Not many would immediately think of Prince as a guitar virtuoso, except maybe colleagues or his legions of diehard fans. But then why has Prince been repeatedly considered not only the successor to Hendrix as history's greatest rock guitarist but the greatest rock guitarist *since* Hendrix?[2] How is this determined and is this a sound and accurate title? What are the grounds of this statement beyond opinion and what facts might persuade someone to agree? I have decided to compare the two musicians side by side, deconstruct keystones of their music, careers, guitar style and personalities, discuss the significance of any shared qualities and influences, question if it is fair and accurate to name Prince the greatest rock guitarist since Hendrix if not his successor, and will reveal more significant topics that this debate presents. Allowing age before beauty, I will start with Hendrix.

James Marshall Hendrix was raised in the predominately Black Central District in Seattle, Washington, in a broken home. He was shifted from house to house and raised by his dad. His absent mother, who died when he was sixteen, left a lasting impression on him, creating a constant need for female companionship and a ready source of songwriting and poetry. Intrigued by guitar, teenage Jimi quickly learned radio hits by ear, formed bands in high school, and realized music was more than a hobby during his brief tenure in the army. After his discharge for "homosexual tendencies" and stranded in Tennessee, Hendrix was basically forced to make a living as a musician, which was fine with him.[3] Time was on his side, and this is when he sprouted roots in what would become a foundation in the blues that would weave into the essential fabric of his music and that would be the means of his most sincere expression and emotional outpour. The very essence of Jimi Hendrix, the vital lifeblood surging through his music, was the blues.

Not so with Prince. Yes, Prince played the hell out of the blues when given the opportunity, but I would not call him a blues guitarist by a long shot and I would not say that his guitar style is rooted in this genre. Guitar is present in the Minneapolis Sound but not blues-centric and not immediately on the forefront, often locked into the rhythm section and repeating phrases and licks with a clean tone sometimes accentuated by effect pedals like wah, chorus or delay. Hawkins and Niblock write, "Dominated by keyboards and rhythm guitar parts, with brash synthesizers substituting for the horn section, the Minneapolis sound comprised a rhythmic underlay that was less syncopated than funk and clearly influenced by new wave."[4]

While the Minneapolis Sound is easily deconstructed, the roots of Prince's guitar style are difficult to pinpoint because there are many and his guitar style changes to accommodate the song. Like him and his music, his guitar playing was constantly evolving. One song will feature a metal riff, the next pure funk, the next, straight jazz, and the next something totally, well, Prince. And it's all good, really, *really* good. Consider the introduction of the simple masterpiece "Kiss," which he released with the Revolution on the 1986 studio album *Parade*. It's the simplest thing in the world. He just strums a seventh chord in sixteenth-note rhythm on beats one and two and stops on three while rolling the wah pedal from heel to toe. The drums kick in on beat four, and it's time to hit the dance floor. It's absolutely infectious and grabs you right by the ear. How did he decide to open "Kiss" with this simply but absolutely perfect little lick? Perhaps it's all the song needed to get going, for it's really the *song* that is incredible, not the intro. Just as Michael Jordan the athlete made the name legendary, the song makes the lick amazing. Through the years, his constant development and growth as a guitarist produced his eclectic style, totally unique to him as a person and musician and making his style of guitar playing just as mysterious, complex and fascinating as he was.

Prince, as a musician and entertainer, wasn't any specific *anything* which enabled his enormous body of music, dynamic career and continued success. His gender and sexual interests even seemed blurred and curious at times; he was handsome, beautiful, perpetually horny and unabashedly naughty. Like Hendrix, he appealed to both men and women as a musical hero as well as an object of envy, longing and desire. In a word, he was and still is captivating. This is a quality Prince did share with Hendrix and is not immediately guitar-related in a musical sense, unless you try to pinpoint exactly what made each guitarist so attractive and why. It's complicated and it involves gender. For lack of a better term and if I may carefully tread on thin ice, Hendrix was more "macho" than Prince.

Hendrix did not live long enough for this to pan out to much. For the masses he is happily frozen in history as an innovative, macho, electrically charged guitar god with lines of women waiting outside his bedroom. But Prince isn't. It's fascinating because Prince *played* like the macho guitar god he was, but he wasn't immediately recognized as one. What does it mean exactly to play like a macho guitar god? One must yield their axe with ease and confidence and conjure sounds previously unheard from man. He will be the admiration of fellow guitarists and the subject of lustful desire by all women. But sing with a delicate falsetto? It doesn't quite add up. Did Hendrix sing with falsetto? The serious fan would say yes as heard in his later recording "Drifting" released on the posthumous album *The Cry of Love*. Would Hendrix consider himself macho? Tough? I'd say no. Remember, he was a hippie. He believed in Flower Power and was timid and shy by nature. He wrote beautiful poetry about angels, waterfalls, and rainbows . . . but would sometimes smash his guitar in a fiery cloud of violent chaos after licking his lips at pretty girls and humping and grinding his guitar in some kind of sexual ritual. As Waksman writes, "Hendrix's music cannot be considered separate from his physicality: his style of virtuosity was itself highly phallocentric."[5] I supposed every bad boy has his soft side? Was Prince like this? Yes, but in a different way. While Hendrix tested the morals of his female fans, Prince invited them to "come be naughty with me." There is a difference. And I think Prince also saw women as equals both personally and professionally, often hiring and working alongside women. If Hendrix worked with women, I'm afraid to say the relationship would have often led to the bedroom.

So, is it possible to say a major difference between the two guitarists, and a difference that kept Prince off the top of the Best Rock Guitarists list, was their treatment of women and therefore their male image? How many women are on that list? Men dominate the rock world and more specifically the list of guitar slingers for many reasons. It's again complicated and perhaps out of scope of this essay, but essential to this comparison. It may be best to leave it as this: Prince had a different place for women in his music than Hendrix did. This kept him from becoming an immediate guitar god in a time when eighties hair bands (macho bad boys with teased hair and full makeup wearing belly shirts?) were dominating the stage. It's ok to say this. Times were different in the sixties and people are different. Did any of this matter to Prince? No. Did it affect his career? Respecting women and welcoming them to his stage as band members only furthered his success. But what does this say of the rock music industry? Is rock male-dominated? Sexist? Sometimes. In this comparison, the topic is only relevant to help clarify some differences between the two performers who at first glance seem to have some strong similarities, some physical, emotional, and some related to their personalities and how they chose to portray themselves to the public.

Both Prince and Hendrix transformed from enigmatic, soft-spoken sophist offstage to band-leading showman while in the spotlight. They were both aware of the power of the elusive, masterfully slipping from the grasp of categorization and concrete definition, speaking quietly and carefully when giving interviews and keeping their complex personalities concealed. The reasons for this may vary. To corner oneself as an artist is to dedicate oneself to one thing, a move Hendrix and Prince would never make. In addition to the possibility of losing the dedication of fans and fellow musicians, this would also require the pop stars to upkeep these beliefs and values which would only add more unwanted stress and strain to an already exhausting profession. Bob Dylan eventually used silence as the only controlling way to preserve himself as a person as opposed to a product. Marshall writes:

> Given the inescapability of stardom, the only option would seem to be silent . . . if one's stardom is contested, and one's statements are open to constant misinterpretation, then saying nothing would seem the only eloquent solution. But while silence *could* result in the complete dissolution of stardom—the public could get bored, move on to the next thing—it is the public that decides if this happens, not the star. If the public maintains an interest, then the star remains a star.[6]

Whether remaining elusive and coy preserved their humanity or their stardom, both Hendrix and Prince maintained the public's interest during their lives, a more impressive feat for Prince considering his much longer career and his demanding role as front man and bandleader from the very beginning. While Hendrix learned how to lead a band and work an audience during his post-army years as a sideman touring the Chitlin' Circuit, Prince assumed this leadership role right away.[7] And while Hendrix tried several monikers before eventually settling on simply "Jimi Hendrix," Prince Rogers Nelson was given his stage name at birth, a convenient birthright for the rising star if anything. Prince experienced a similar upbringing to Hendrix in Minneapolis, but they blossomed at different stages in their lives and had very different musical beginnings.

Prince matured at an early age and was quickly dedicated to music, exploring many instruments at an age when Hendrix was tinkering with guitar but also living the mischievous life of an unsupervised teen in a big city. At this stage, he played plenty of guitar but, unlike Prince, had no work ethic and no agenda. I chose Hendrix's immersion in Nashville as a major life-altering time of musical growth specifically because he claimed this was where he "learned to play, really."[8] This period took place in the late months of 1962, making Jimi twenty years of age. By twenty, Prince was already working on his second record.

This introduces several important character traits that are significant to Prince's early and immediate success, which he carried with him for decades and that fueled his musical proliferation: professionalism, focus, dedication and a constant interest in future endeavors. At an age when Jimi was sprouting the roots of his guitar style and literally struggling to survive let alone score a record contract, Prince was already a Warner Bros. recording artist with his huge career on the horizon. He would make an album almost every year, leading into the mega-fame of *Purple Rain*. From 1978, when he released his debut *For You*, to 1984 and the release of *Purple Rain*, Prince already accomplished more than some might hope to achieve in a lifetime (while unshaken by the global domination of Michael Jackson's *Thriller* in 1982 and answering with his mainstream breakthrough *1999*). This was only what I would call the seedling years of a momentous time of musical cultivation, growth, and reinvention that produced a whopping thirty-nine studio albums, hundreds of singles and music videos, and many more recording, composing, and production credits. This early period exceeds the whole of Jimi Hendrix's career, as his recording years span from 1967 to 1970, during which he produced only three studio and one live album. While their output appears lopsided when examined side by side, Hendrix stands out as he innovated on the electric guitar in ways no one, including Prince would achieve.

Prince, however, never really dedicated himself to one instrument as Hendrix did, never aspired to reveal unexplored potential in the electric guitar, and unlike Hendrix, his music is not consistently guitar-centric. It seems he learned, mastered, and performed all instruments needed to compose or produce a record, modeling himself after one of his great influences, Stevie Wonder. In this way, Stevie Wonder would seem a figure that influenced Prince's approach to recording, mixing, and producing, leaving a much larger impression on his overall music and career than Hendrix could have as a guitarist. Prince cast a much larger net of focus; he explored all borders of music, pioneering the Minneapolis Sound of synth-pop/funk/rock in the process. Hendrix was focused on the electric guitar and was determined to conjure the cosmic sounds that teased his imagination from it with the help of his fellow engineers and technicians.

We will never hear what Hendrix was attempting to emulate, but it is clear that guitar noises and sounds that were commonly perceived as nuisance came close enough. While guitarists like Pete Townshend, John Lennon, and Jeff Beck experimented with guitar feedback in the studio and on stage, Hendrix learned how to generate, control, and musically integrate the tones produced from guitar feedback into recordings and live performances. "Look Over Yonder," a posthumous release found on *South Saturn Delta* (1997) shows how thoughtfully Hendrix used feedback, even recording multiple tracks to create thick, howling harmonies manipulated only with the whammy bar and a wah pedal. The tones were not random or accidental, but intentional. He was one of the first to preserve his discoveries on a record, while everyone in his wake had to give it a try.

Musical use of feedback is a trademark Hendrix technique that Prince kept in his deep, cavernous bag of tricks, as heard in this simply awesome Hendrixesque solo on "Let's Go Crazy." It starts at 3:05 but jump to precisely 3:12 and you'll hear a cadenza begin with a wonderfully screaming string bend, complete with wah-enhanced treble and the natural, gradual distortion created from two slightly out-of-tuned but bending-into-tune notes that would have made Jimi grin. This is followed by a barrage of nimble-fingered blues runs, whammy dives and a classic full-band blues coda. If specific evidence is needed to confirm Hendrix's influence on Prince's guitar playing, compare the "Let's Go Crazy" solo to the first minute or so of Jimi's "Woodstock Improvisation." It is about four and a half minutes of searing, beautiful, captivating guitar based on his instrumental "Bolero" and found between "Purple Haze" and "Villanova Junction" on *Jimi Hendrix: Live at Woodstock*

(1999), a record carefully pieced together by Hendrix's loyal recording engineer Eddie Kramer and producer/Hendrix scholar John McDermott. It is doubtful Prince ever heard this recording in the late seventies, but it seems he did enough work as a student of Hendrix to impressively capture a sliver of his sound on "Let's Go Crazy," intentional or not.

Was Prince influenced by Hendrix as a guitarist? To a degree, absolutely. But his lyrical style and phrasing reminds me of other, more delicate guitarists like Carlos Santana. A good example is his solo on "Why You Wanna Treat Me So Bad?" at 2:49 featuring big, singing bends followed by pure Prince virtuosity at 3:04: a series of jaw-dropping scalar runs that would only make sense in this song and ends with an Allman Brothers-type harmonized guitar melody. As a masterful vocalist, it makes sense that Prince was a fan of Santana whose expressive style is rooted in Latin harmony in addition to blues. While Hendrix relied heavily on the minor pentatonic scale and some respective modes to solo and compose, Santana often crafted his melodies and compositions from minor and major pentatonic, harmonic and melodic minor scales. Specifically, these minor scales have a different scalar construction that make a huge difference as heard on Santana's "Africa Bamba," "El Farol" or "Samba Pa Ti" and allow thoughtful, colorful, straining melodies that remind me of such memorable solos on "Purple Rain," or the often-admired moment of Prince guitar mastery on "While My Guitar Gently Weeps," performed at George Harrison's 2004 induction into the Rock and Roll Hall of Fame. This solo is colorful, heartfelt, and awe-inspiring, but the only Hendrix influence present is purely visual: the moves, the drama, the intensity.

Hendrix inspired Prince's stage performance, as seen in the simple handling of the instrument during this and many other solos. Prince observed and borrowed these musically timed arm extensions and body arches and made them part of his show, adding to the dramatic outpour of soul and feeling that made his concerts incredible. Another epic moment is his performance at Super Bowl XLI on February 4, 2007. "Purple Rain" in the pouring rain? Pure Prince. But again, Hendrix is seen, not heard. Is Prince therefore more accurately a disciple of Santana?

Not necessarily. Four songs after "Why You Wanna Treat Me So Bad?" on his self-titled album sits "Bambi" which is only timid and innocent in title. "Bambi" bursts open with a heavily distorted guitar intro teasing the main Black Sabbath-like riff. Stabilized by his impeccable falsetto, the verses allow some breathing space between the hard-rocking choruses and harmonized multitrack guitar bridge. He eventually rewards us with the much-anticipated guitar solo beginning at 3:16. He quickly locks into tempo, raises the intensity with some repeated phrases, ups it further with bigger and higher bends, and cascades down with some impressive scalar runs. It triumphantly rocks just as much as one might hope and sounds like no one in particular, just him. It's just an awesome solo. While these are early examples, later songs like "Live 4 Love," "Walls of Berlin," and "Dreamer" show clear evidence of his interest in metal guitar with speedy, scalar flat-picking, heavy distortion, delay, and chorus effects. We can't gloss over the musical presence of metal guitarists of the early 1980s like Yngwie Malmsteen, Steve Vai, and Joe Satriani, from whom I hear likely inspiration in these songs from the 2000s that feature the progressive, modern guitar sound found in many late recordings.

If Hendrix didn't dominate Prince's guitar playing, i.e., if you can't hear Hendrix when you close your eyes and listen, then why has Prince been considered the greatest guitarist since Hendrix? The successor? Sadly, the visual similarities, not always the actual music, connect the dots for some people. The elephant in the room is the fact that they were both Black rock guitarists. In more detail, they were both thin, light-skinned, handsome, Black rock guitarists. Throw in some colorful, flowing garments and ban-dannas, and they really start looking alike! Most people can rattle off a few household Black *blues* guitarists like perhaps B.B. King, John Lee Hooker, or Buddy Guy. And some may even know some Black jazz guitarists like Wes Montgomery or Grant Green. But Black *rock* guitarists, especially in Hendrix's time, were sparse. Either way, sharing skin tone is no justification to equate their music.

To call Prince the greatest guitarist since Hendrix, in my opinion, is shal-low, ignorant, and lazy. It is a feeble attempt to connect two African Ameri-cans for the wrong reason. Similar statements have been made connecting Hendrix to other Black guitarists like Lenny Kravitz and Gary Clark Jr., who have a totally different style and sound. I remember Lenny Kravitz emerg-ing to fame with his 1993 release "Are You Gonna Go My Way," right around the time Hendrix made a resurgence. Good timing for the both of them, and as a teenage Hendrix fan I was personally excited to have an exciting, living guitarist to admire regardless of color. But what about Kenny Wayne Shepherd? Jonny Lang? Not Black, but they sounded more like Hendrix than Prince! I've never heard any attempt to connect Mike McCready of Pearl Jam or Dave Frusciante of the Red Hot Chili Peppers (RHCP) to Hendrix, but musically, his influence is indisputable. A good example is Pearl Jam's 1992 release "Yellow Ledbetter." Any Hendrix fan would agree that the similari-ties to Hendrix's "Little Wing" almost sound intentional. McCready seems to dedicate this slow, haunting ballad to his idol, paying homage to one of his most admired teachers. We hear clear Hendrix influence in Frusciante's guitar work on the RHCP 1991 release "Under the Bridge" where he embellishes the verses with nimble accents and articulations on chords similar to Hendrix's melodic rhythm playing on "Castles Made of Sand" and "Bold as Love," both found on his 1967 studio album *Axis: Bold as Love*.

Sometimes it's better to shut your eyes and open your ears. The music is all you need. And besides, Hendrix influenced all guitarists during and after his time anyway because he changed the approach to the instrument and opened completely unknown doors. He shared his discoveries and showed his colleagues what you could do with existing tools of the trade, including the whammy or tremolo bar, simple effect pedals like fuzz and chorus (rotating speaker effect of the Univibe pedal), and excessive overdrive and volume. His genius and innovation lie in his acute awareness and attentiveness to the potential of existing technology but used in different combinations and in unconventional ways. The significance is that his discoveries were immediately made accessible to every electric guitarist with basic gear. This is key. Stanley Jordan treats the guitar fretboard like a keyboard, but he needs a custom-made guitar with low action and sensitive pickups to achieve his sound and to play in his style with the tapping technique. To a lesser degree is Rage Against the Machine's Tom Morello who sometimes rubs the strings of his guitar with his hands to solo as a DJ scratches a record. But you can't just pick up a random guitar, plug it in and solo in this way; alterations and special gear is needed. Hendrix, on the other hand, preferred a standard Fender Stratocaster, Marshall amplifiers, and a handful of effect pedals that were not exactly made available in retail music stores at the time but didn't require custom designs and machinery. His sound was very much in his head and hands.

Hendrix also made it ok to be a guitar hero in a time when masters like Eric Clapton and Jeff Beck couldn't rise above their stiff British social norms and publicly pour themselves out as Hendrix did. While Clapton and Beck pushed the advance of blues rock and progressive guitar playing, respectively, they were at first strictly guitarists in a band, not yet the frontman. Yes, Hendrix sharpened his chops as a sideman, but he was not yet mainstream while doing so. Another later guitarist, however, more rightfully deserves the esteemed honor of a possible Hendrix successor than Prince, and for more concrete reasons. More specifically, another guitarist possessed characteristics similar to Hendrix as a player and manipulated the guitar in a similar way as he, making his influence more distinct than what is heard in Prince's guitar work.

Stevie Ray Vaughn (SRV) was much more a Hendrix protégé than Prince. SRV handled the guitar like Hendrix. He played with a passionate urgency similar to Hendrix, as if he knew his time with us was very limited. While Prince always appeared calm, collected, and calculated, Hendrix and SRV both experienced abrupt fame and success that required a frenzied and exhaustive touring schedule. Both struggled with depression and substance abuse, and Hendrix specifically with legal issues and business pressures that contributed to already mounting and overwhelming stress and anxiety. Perhaps both Hendrix and SRV, therefore, desperately used the guitar as a means to vent a mounting inner pressure that urgently needed release. I believe Prince shared a similar relationship with the instrument, but the music was far different, and as mentioned above, Prince seemed in better control. Rather than a valve or vital release, Prince treated the guitar as one of many tools in a collection, an instrument needed to complete his music. Also, in contrast to Hendrix, Prince used many other creative methods, including producing, mixing, and acting during the lifespan of his career. It's difficult to tell during a live performance what moves and expressions Prince staged and what are spontaneous reactions to the moment.

SRV was decidedly and consistently a blues guitarist, even more so than Hendrix in some ways. While the blues was the glue of his music, he stretched these limits thin and often ventured far from home. SRV stayed closer to the traditionally clean Texas blues form and sound and was more grounded than Hendrix on stage. Like Prince and countless others, he borrowed many moves Hendrix brought to the American pop stage, like the behind-the-head and back or through-the-leg-playing but kept his songs tighter and more polished than Hendrix during live performances. His solos were more planned and calculated. He seemed to control his energy better than Hendrix and was more disciplined and efficient as a player. When Hendrix searched on stage, SRV was moving on to his next song.

While a masterful student of Hendrix, SRV lacked the innovation on the electric guitar that Hendrix pioneered. SRV learned how to unlock the instrument to his imagination and play with no limitations while attracting millions of devoted fans and spearheading a blues revival in the 1980s, but no discoveries were made. He, like so many others, stood on Hendrix's shoulders and reaped the benefits. Unlike Prince, however, Stevie Ray clearly stated his gratitude to his idol and kept several Hendrix originals, including "Voodoo Child (Slight Return)" and "Little Wing" in his live repertoire, even preserving them in the studio with his own very distinct and personal interpretation.

The only known credit to Hendrix found in Prince's catalog is a rare recording of his twelve-bar blues "Red House" renamed "Purple House" (for obvious reasons) and is found on the 2004 album *Power of Soul: A Tribute to Jimi Hendrix*. "Purple House" is what a tribute recording should be; his version of the celebrated artist's work, and Prince pays homage in the way he did best. The classic blues feel is intact with some rich backing vocals and Prince's expected, searing solo boldly shining in its own inimitable way. This may be the only recording of Prince playing Hendrix. He quickly dismissed rumors of a Hendrix tribute tour in early 2016 for speculative reasons, some say to debunk the constant parallels between the two.

As detailed, Hendrix's innovations on the electric guitar had a huge effect on all resulting guitarists. His influence is part of every rock guitarist's foundation, and his contributions to American music should be crystal clear. Prince's overall contributions to pop music require more unpacking since his career spanned some thirty-eight jam-packed years. To better appreciate his contributions, it's important to observe him from all sides.

It's easy to locate artists that were heavily influenced by Prince as a musician, performer, and pop icon: Madonna, Beyoncé, Questlove, Justin Timberlake, D'Angelo, André 3000, Beck, Frank Ocean, etc., etc. The list is long and varied. His music paved the way for 1990s R&B, inspired many hip-hop artists to embrace the drum machine, and helped push the advance of house and modern dance music. It's also easy to locate Prince's influence on pop culture. He was a straight man in full makeup who sometimes dressed in bikini bottoms, if clothed at all. He could have had the same hair stylist as Oprah Winfrey during the 1980s. He was a malleable figure representing the ideals of his music which were often love, current events, and a funky good time. And with Prince as the master of ceremonies, all seemed welcome regardless of color, creed, or sexual identity. Hendrix longed to include a more diverse fan base like Prince, but his concerts were often dominated by a white audience, and he was sometimes criticized for playing "white music." When writing of Sly and the Family Stone, Vincent says, "They were not divested from their Black audience as Jimi Hendrix was, nor were they bound to it as James Brown was. Sly and the Family Stone, for a brief period, put forth an entirely new concept of integration."[9] Vincent's words reveal a refreshing comparison to Sly, another of Prince's huge influences (not only musically but socially and politically) and give light to one of Sly and the Family Stone's greatest contributions to music: inclusion. Carrying these values with him as a musician and producer, it is therefore not surprising that Prince left the impression he did in the pop world. Also, not surprisingly, his committed fan base was large and diverse. What might be unknown to some is the impression he left on the music industry. When someone was involved in their career as deeply as Prince, and experienced continued success through the many adaptations and lifespans he endured, the role stretches beyond that of "musician."

As Prince learned the legal ropes of the music business, he became more active in fighting for his legal rights and jolted the whole industry in the process. Disagreements with Warner Bros. in the early 1990s led to Prince dropping his name and assuming the now-legendary glyph. Later, he was one of the first musicians to pull their material from Spotify and patiently waited to regain the rights to his music after his contract with Warner Bros. expired in 2014. During the early 2000s, he released free albums at concerts and brought these often-unaddressed issues to the forefront, inspiring artists like Taylor Swift to read the fine print of their contracts as well as the writing on the wall. Adding to his numerous titles, this was "Prince: The Savvy Business Executive," and many modern musicians such as Kanye West and Radiohead have since practiced similar supervision over the release of their music, specifically via the internet.

As Hendrix generously constructed a platform for all succeeding guitarists by staying firm to his musical goals and vision, Prince inspired not only countless musicians but also motivated many to reassess the production and distribution of their music by staying firm to one of his fundamental career needs: control. Hendrix learned the value of this principle as he worked to restructure his band and broaden his sound toward the end of his life. Additionally, his long-gestating recording studio, Electric Lady Studios, finally opened in Greenwich Village. He was free to jam, record, and mix at his will without the stress of ever-mounting fees and constricting schedules.

Hendrix's studio was a much-needed sanctuary to explore his cosmic creativity, not unlike Prince's Paisley Park. Waksman writes, "If Hendrix on stage was a near-mythic presence who both drew upon and signified a complex history of racial representations, Hendrix in the studio was someone else, an almost insular figure who could lose himself in the seemingly endless sound possibilities afforded by electric technology."[10] What is rarely discussed is the great accomplishment that owning and building Electric Lady Studios was for Hendrix as a Black male in the late '60s. Waksman continues, "With the opening of the studio in 1970, Hendrix had achieved a degree of artistic control inaccessible to most African American musicians of the time."[11] While often seen as a victim or casualty of his own success, Electric Lady Studios represented a bold step in the right direction for him financially, creatively, and professionally.

Sadly, Hendrix barely enjoyed his custom-built, state-of-the-art studio and died several weeks after the opening party. The chokehold of the music industry that Prince was always able to dismantle had a firm grip on Hendrix, partially contributing to his demise. Forming the Jimi Hendrix Experience was a whirlwind endeavor taking place in a faraway country and rapidly orchestrated by new, strange faces. He barely knew his own band-mates. Prince maintained control in the beginning, recording all vocals and instruments, and toured extensively but stayed in the US until 1981. Hendrix recorded in London and toured Europe almost immediately, which quickly led to his American debut, superstardom, merciless schedule, understandable exhaustion, depression, frustration, excessive drug use, and his early death in London at age twenty-seven. Thankfully, Prince learned to manage him-self right away. Maybe he also knew to surround himself with good people, learning from the tragedies of some unfortunate predecessors like Hendrix. It appears Prince was constantly scanning his surroundings for not only musical inspiration and guidance but on-the-job training from anyone with any wisdom in the business and was most likely keen to eliminate anyone who wasn't on his side.

I could easily imagine a ten-year-old Prince gazing at a Hendrix record jacket and seeing the possibilities for his life as a musician in front of him. In a time of extreme racism and civil unrest in the United States, I'm sure he was excited and inspired to see a Black male succeed in the pop music business to such a degree. Still, I'm also sure Hendrix was one of many early role models, Black, white, or in between. A significant difference between say, Sly or Stevie Wonder as an influence on Prince is what Hendrix meant to Prince as a Black rock guitarist. During his lifetime, Hendrix was very much an oddball, and critics and colleagues often didn't know what to make of him, one journalist even labeling him "The Black Elvis" in a desperate and failing attempt to pinpoint his identity.[12] I'm sure Prince experienced similar struggles from those trying to corner his persona. Interestingly, fans often had nothing to figure out; they admired, indulged, and followed.

The most significant connection between Jimi Hendrix and Prince was not their African American heritage, their guitar solos, their wardrobe, or their showmanship but their extraordinary roles as musical innovators. One used six strings to abruptly and permanently alter rock music, sending shock waves still felt to this day. The other steadily made music that would inspire others to create new genres of music, testing and expanding the categories of American music. Both made history. Their passion and allegiance to their art made their enormous contributions to American music possible. Their belief in the power of what was new and different and their courage and confidence to blaze new trails made them pioneers. It's impossible to replace anyone. Rather than attempt to connect two brilliant musicians based on appearance, I encourage people to listen and learn but also to explore and compare their lives and careers; the music speaks eloquently and leads to more worthy discoveries.

Notes

1. *Rolling Stone*, "100 Greatest Guitarists," *RollingStone.com*, December 18, 2015, https://www.rollingstone.com/music/music-lists/100-greatest-guitarists-153675/.

2. Jack Hamilton, "Why Prince May Have Been the Greatest Guitarist Since Hendrix (and Why That Shouldn't Seem Like a Surprise)," *Slate*, April 28, 2016, https://slate.com/culture/2016/04/why-prince-was-the-greatest-guitarist-since-jimi-hendrix.html.

3. Charles R. Cross, *Room Full of Mirrors: A Biography of Jimi Hendrix* (New York: Hyperion Books, 2009), 93.

4. Stan Hawkins and Sarah Nibloc, *Prince: The Making of a Pop Music Phenomenon*, (London: Ashgate, 2011), 5.

5. Steve Waksman, *Instruments of Desire: The Electric Guitar and the Shaping of Musical Experience* (Cambridge: Harvard University Press, 1999), 188.

6. Lee Marshall, *Bob Dylan: The Never Ending Star*, (Cambridge: Polity Press, 2007), 129.

7. Charles Shaar Murray, *Crosstown Traffic: Jimi Hendrix and the Post-War Rock 'n' Roll Revolution* (New York: St. Martin's Press, 1989), 37; Preston Lauterbach, *The Chitlin' Circuit and the Road to Rock 'n' Roll* (New York, W.W. Norton & Co., 2011).

8. Jimi Hendrix, *Starting At Zero: His Own Story* (New York: Bloomsbury, 2013), 31.

9. Rickey Vincent, *Party Music: The Inside Story of the Black Panthers' Band and How Black Power Transformed Soul Music* (Chicago: Lawrence Hill Books, 2013), 85.

10. Waksman, 169.

11. Waksman, 169.

12. Cross, 211.

Chapter 3

ZOOT SUITS AND NEW JACK SWING

Morris Day's Dandyism

KAREN TURMAN

In his posthumously published *Journaux intimes* (1897), French poet and art critic Charles Baudelaire describes the Dandy as "[aspiring] to be sublime without interruption; he must live and sleep before a mirror."[1] The quintessential Baudelairean Dandy sought the total sublimation of his existence through a constantly deliberate and self-conscious alignment of style, artistic production, and social rebellion. One century later, Prince Rogers Nelson would sing on the hidden track "Prettyman" on his album *Rave Un2 the Joy Fantastic* (1999): "In the early morning when I'm feeling nice, I walk by the mirror and kiss it twice."[2] A "prettyman" in front of a mirror, Prince himself epitomized the contemporary equivalent of the evolved dandy figure with his countless traffic-stopping fashions and complete commitment to his style and aesthetic at all times. A fierce fashion-forward rock-star aesthetic with no reprieve, Prince's ever-evolving, and never-subservient style was studded throughout his forty years in the limelight with bejeweled canes, asymmetrical tailored suits, ruffled New Romantic blouses, and brocade-covered high heels. While his personal style was second to none, one may argue that his semi-fictitious rivalry with the larger-than-life Morris Day, whose character's conception was created by Prince himself to provide a source of competition and keep him on his proverbial toes, aimed to compete, not only for the love of the female protagonist and the impeccably dressed audiences at the clubs in his films but on the fashion stage as well. No one in the Prince universe is more synonymous with both the metaphoric and literal mirror than Morris Day, both on and off the cinematic stage in *Purple Rain* (1984)[3] and *Graffiti Bridge* (1990),[4] as well as the performance stage on tour with Prince and the Revolution. While Prince himself exemplifies the dandy figure, this article will explore the definition of dandyism through a cultural history perspective, examining the stylistic relevance of one of the most celebrated of Prince's side projects, the Time.[5] Through sociocultural and historical analysis of Black dandyism, the zoot suit, and the dance aesthetic and roots of New Jack Swing, this article will dissect the philosophical underpinnings of sartorial rebellion as a profound statement of power and assertion of agency in the character Morris Day's caricature of dandyism.

What is a dandy, exactly? Popular media tend to recognize the dandy as an elegantly dressed person who may distinctively accessorize or manipulate the traditional cut of a three-piece suit.[6] But dandyism goes beyond the superficial sartorial level when we acknowledge the power of clothing and image through historical contextualization of the dandy figure. Author of *Slaves to Fashion: Black Dandyism and the Styling of Black Diasporic Identity*, Monica L. Miller describes it as "not just about the clothing, but also the pointed deployment of gesture and wit . . . often a critical response to changing circumstances."[7] She analyzes the emergence of iconic dandy figures at moments of historical change in social hierarchies. The figure of the dandy, according to Miller, is one who critiques previous norms and comments on the future potential of those identities. For Miller, "the dandy's clothing and person is semiotic" since they both interpret and are interpreted, and they are at once questioning and questioners.[8] Although white scholars credit England's George "Beau" Brummel at the turn of the nineteenth century as the first dandy, Miller travels back to the eighteenth century and analyzes the cultural turmoil related to political changes stemming from slavery, imperialism, equality, and revolution.[9] When outlining the origins of dandyism, she focuses on the powerful figure of the Black dandy in England, whose sartorial gestures of wit questioned the social order and hierarchy by using their own objectification and taking agency over it. She begins with a study on Julius Soubise, who was taken from Jamaica as a child to England to become an enslaved servant to the Duchess of Queensberry in 1764. It was fashionable during this period for elegant ladies to keep young Black children as personal servants, often dressed extravagantly in silk turbans and other finery. Soubise was given the most elaborate clothing, a quality education, music lessons and was integrated into the Duchess's household as a luxury item himself. He was known for wearing diamond-buckled red shoes and, as he matured, would push social boundaries to the extreme in public spaces. For example, he would reserve the most expensive box at the opera and would venture ostentatiously through the public park surrounded by a team of white footman. Soubise's dandyism is exemplified through the radical public displays of his lavish tastes as a grown man, making a statement on his childhood as an enslaved living caricature of the deeply troubling fashion of "exotic children."

Miller then traces the roots of dandyism across the Atlantic to the eigh-teenth-century colonial era African American festivals, nineteenth-century cakewalk performances and minstrel shows, twentieth-century queer culture in Harlem, New York, and beyond.[10] The distinction between Black dandy-ism and European dandyism lies in the meaning of subversion through fashion in a white supremacist society: clothing was often a signifier that would determine the survival of oppressed people in a racist society. Showy, attention-seeking dress that often contributed toward the subversion of soci-etal norms represented a deeper and more radical social statement when practiced by people of color.

In contrast, European dandyism was popularized by the aforementioned George "Beau" Brummel, England's first "celebrity," at the turn of the nine-teenth century, then crossed the English Channel and adapted to French society where writers Honoré de Balzac,[11] Jules Amédée Barbey d'Aurevilly, and, subsequently, Charles Baudelaire theorized the dandy as a subversive figure emulating aristocratic artifice. In *The Painter of Modern Life* (1863), Baudelaire defines the dandy as spiritual and stoical in the attention to detail regarding an all-encompassing sartorial style and way of life: the dandy figure cultivated his life as a work of art itself.[12] The dandy is not to be confused with the "fop," a term dating to the seventeenth century that pejoratively refers to a man who pays excessive attention to fashion at the risk of appearing foolish. Rather than exhibiting ostentatiously flamboyant style, the European dandy was known for paying close attention to his look while playing on subtle details that broke away from the fashion trends or traditional cuts of the three-piece suit and its accessories. According to twentieth-century French theorist Roland Barthes, for dandies in nineteenth-century Paris, "it was the *detail* . . . which started to play the distinguishing role in clothing." In his essay "Le Dandysme et la mode," Barthes cites "the knot on a cravat, the material of a shirt, the buttons on a waistcoat," and "the buckle on a shoe" as illustrating social differences and class hierarchy, all pointing to the new ambiguous values of "taste" and "distinction."[13] In other words, dandyism is exemplified by a person wearing an elegant suit with subversive styling as an expression of social rebellion and empowerment.

Prince's rebellious looks evolved from an androgynous trench-coat- and bikini-briefs-clad rude-boy in 1980 to a look that was slightly more reminis-cent of a dandified suit with the addition of a tuxedo shirt and waistcoat (still no pants) in 1981. He then began sporting fully matched and tailored New Romantic suits in 1982 that would provide a blueprint for the most iconic Prince look as solidified in 1984's *Purple Rain*: high-waisted black pants with asymmetrical front button closure, white ruffled blouse, and purple trench coat with a silver-studded right shoulder.[14] While Prince's own fashion was rapidly evolving into a look that aligned well with this manipulation of the classic three-piece suit, he invented rival band, the Time, with frontman Morris Day, longtime friend and drummer from one of his first bands, Grand Central. In Day's 2019 memoirs, he describes Prince's motivation behind creating the Time, for which he wrote, produced, and played all instruments on the recorded albums, with Day's vocals on top: "It's one thing to compete with your peers, it's another thing to create competition from within your own camp" . . . this was "ego-merging . . . Prince saw me as an extension of himself. I was his creation. That was OK with me since, as a creator, Prince was master."[15] In line with the control that Prince maintained over the band, echoing famously authoritarian band leaders such as Cab Calloway and James Brown, he also dictated their sartorial aesthetic. During his 2017 interview with Questlove Supreme, producer and former member of the Time Jimmy Jam states how the whole band was required to dress in this style by Prince, who wanted them to have a cool aspect that showed both respect and class by dressing well.[16]

Dressing elegantly has often been associated with femininity, and as such, androgyny and gender expression are also related to dandyism. Barbey d'Aurevilly outlines in his essay, *Du Dandyisme et de George Brummel* (1845): "Twofold and multiple natures, of an undecidedly intellectual sex, their Grace is heightened by their Power, their Power by their Grace; they are the hermaphrodites of History, not of Fable."[17] The connections between queerness, androgyny, and dandyism became further pronounced within the Black community of New York City during the Harlem Renaissance in the late 1920s. In her essay, "Harlem's Queer Dandy: African-American Modernism and the Artifice of Blackness," Elisa Glick underscores the necessity to recognize "the dandy's hypermasculinity (and anti-feminism) in order to privilege his effeminacy as a form of gender rebellion."[18] As Niblock and Hawkins remind us in their book, *Prince: the Making of a Pop Music Icon*, "many considered Prince the gayest and queerest performer ever to hit mainstream pop" due to "his blurring of binary distinctions throughout all his work."[19] While Prince's gender expression aligns clearly with this fundamental aspect of dandyism, how does the hypermasculine Morris Day character fit into this dichotomy?

As his fictional nemesis and comedic foil, Morris Day's character represents the exaggerated, macho yet refined extension of Prince as a caricature of the dandy. The misogyny in *Purple Rain* and its sequel, *Graffiti Bridge*, particularly in the treatment of the female characters by antagonist Morris Day, remains in line with Baudelaire's definition of the dandy in the nineteenth century. In her article, "Self Construction and Sexual Identity in Nineteenth-Century French Dandyism," Deborah Houk reminds us that, while the dandy figure is known for his effeminate gesture and fastidious attention to his elegant appearance, he does not "generally hold women in high regard."[20] In his *Journaux intimes* Baudelaire demonstrates this virulent misogyny in his statement that women represent the contrast to the dandy because he views them as naturally beautiful and thus abominably vulgar creatures.[21] While Prince's character, the Kid, is not free from any misogynous reprimands during *Purple Rain*—the prank in which he tells Apollonia to "purify [herself] in the waters of Lake Minnetonka" and subsequently leaves her temporarily on the chilly shore of a different lake, for example—much of the problematic content in both films comes from Day's fictional villain. Arguably the most infamous example of the character Morris Day's misogyny is the scene in which he reacts to a former lover's laments by ordering his sidekick Jerome to throw her into a nearby dumpster in an alley. The misogyny surfaces again in *Graffiti Bridge* when Day's character forces Robin Power to shed her glamorous cape to provide clean passage to the club entrance, and peaks during the controversial drugging of love-interest Aura (Ingrid Chavez) to "seduce" her in *Graffiti Bridge*. As Day mentions in his memoirs, Prince manifests in Day's character as an "extension of himself"; we see Prince play with cartoonish exaggerations and hypermasculine stereotypes in the context of Day as Prince's alter ego while also distancing himself from the behavior of the films' villain. Despite the deconstruction of gender expression exhibited in the dandy figure, Morris Day's character exemplifies the inherent complexity in the dandy's ostensible appropriation of aspects of traditional feminine appearance while exhibiting hypermasculine behavior.

This caricature of the dandified figure ultimately allowed Day to steal the spotlight as the outrageously entertaining yet misogynous villain in both films. In the opening montage of *Purple Rain*, the viewer catches a first glimpse of Day in preparation for his night out. Unlike the Kid, whom we never see out of his dandified trappings, Day is caught vacuuming in boxers, an undershirt, and a do-rag, indicating the level of work entailed to embrace dandyism fully. After this unusual scene of masculine domesticity, Day is never spotted without his impeccable suit, Stacy Adams wingtips, and various dapper accessories, including canes, scarves, suspenders, rings, cuff links, silk handkerchiefs, and even a handy mirror that materializes with the ever-present and delightful Jerome Benton, who might be himself considered the ultimate accessory to Day's dandy. Originally a roadie for the band, Benton earned his spot as Day's personal valet by improvising the mirror bit during a rehearsal of the song "Cool," complementing Day's authentic comedic persona, complete with mockingly aristocratic voice register, turns of phrase, and subtle gesture, all characteristics of the nineteenth-century dandy.[22] Although Benton later both toured and performed onstage with Prince and the Revolution in addition to playing the unforgettable sidekick Tricky to Prince's Christopher Tracy character in *Under the Cherry Moon* in 1986, Benton remained an integral member of the Time alongside brother Terry Lewis.[23]

The Time's general uniform is most closely aligned with the zoot-suit aesthetic. The zoot suit exemplifies radical dandyism, especially in its origins, wearers, sociocultural implications, and the various interpretations of its semiotics. In her book on zoot suits, Kathy Peiss summarizes the look as:

> The long killer-diller coat with a drape shape [V-shaped] and wide shoulders; pants with reet-pleats [large, sharp pleats], billowing out at the knees, tightly tapered and pegged at the ankles; a porkpie or wide-brimmed hat; pointed or thick-soled shoes; and a long, dangling key-chain . . . created by African American men, . . . associated with racial and ethnic minorities [in particular Latinx men] and working-class youth, celebrated in the world of jitterbug, jive, and swing, condemned by government authorities seeking to conserve precious textiles for the war effort."[24]

Bandleader Cab Calloway first defined "zoot" as "exaggerated" in his seminal *Hep Cat Dictionary* (1938), the first dictionary published by an African American and the official jive language reference at the New York City Public Library.[25] Later, Malcolm X would famously describe the zoot suit in his autobiography, defining the drape-shape as "a long coat that pinched [his] waist and flared out below [his] knees" and providing the measurements of his first pair of "sky-blue pants thirty inches in the knee and angle-narrowed down to twelve inches at the bottom," and later his second pair of sharkskin gray pants with "cuffs so narrow [he] had to take off [his] shoes to get them on and off."[26]

In his essay, "The Riddle of the Zoot: Malcolm Little and Black Cultural Politics during World War II," Robin Kelley points out that "Zoot suiters appropriated, even mocked, existing styles and reinscribed them with new meanings drawn from shared memory and experience" and that ultimately "one of the central attractions of the zoot suiters was their collective refusal to be subservient."[27] The nineteenth-century definitions of European dandyism would most likely exclude the zoot suit due to its excessive flamboyance. For example, Baudelaire practiced dandyism himself by wearing pink gloves with his usual all-black ensemble, recalling Barthes's analysis that the subtle details of the look could engender subversive sociocultural meaning. However, I believe the zoot suit is an important example of Black dandyism. In its creative appropriation of traditional colonial products and the audacity behind the young working-class men of color who sported the look in public, taking up space both visually and materially, the zoot suit proved a way to express cultural pride and reject the imposed fashion codes of white society. Up until this point, for over a century, men's fashion was purposefully understated, intending a sign of power with no need for flashy display to garner attention: "inconspicuousness became the hallmark of the well-dressed man" by early 1800.[28] Conversely, young men of color, between the Great Depression and World War II, started to collectively break this rule with their loud and outrageous suits—the wider the shoulders and pants, the better.

The Time, with their vivid monochromatic or pin-striped suits, wide-shouldered and long double-breasted coats, wide-legged and high-waisted trousers with tapered ankles, and wingtip shoes, were known for their energetic choreographed numbers, including the mirror gag and musically coordinated high fives. Peiss speculates that the emergence of the original zoot-suit aesthetic coalesced with the development of the lindy hop dance craze on the floor of the Savoy Ballroom in Harlem, New York, because zoot suiters, like the Time, were known for their dance skills.[29] The lindy hop, or jitterbug, was a new dynamic partner dance developed by African Americans and evolved from West African dances, the Charleston, and other vernacular jazz dances. The original form of swing dancing, the lindy hop required athleticism and agility at extremely fast tempos from the dancers because it was practiced to big band swing music. The roomy cut of the jackets and wide-legged pants allowed for mobility in the dance where other suit cuts would not last through the evening of dancing, while the tapered or pegged ankles of the pants prevented the leaders from tripping and getting entangled with their partner in the circular and acrobatic moves of the dance. Among the rare extant video clips showcasing the lindy hop during this era, one of the best examples of both the lindy hop and the zoot-suit style can be found in the 1941 *Hot Chocolate: Cottontail* soundie starring Duke Ellington and members of the Whitey's Lindy Hoppers dance team, the most famous lindy hoppers at the time: Anne Johnson, Frankie Manning, William Downes, Frances "Mickey" Jones, Willa Mae Ricker, Al Minns, Billy Ricker, and Norma Miller.[30] The high-waisted pegged pants are prominent among the male dancers, and Ricker, Minns, and Manning each sport a "sack" jacket, a coat so wide and long it would only touch the shoulders.[31] This consumer-driven look was originally made to order or semi-custom tailoring. However, many people simply improvised the style and shape by combining old clothes, hand-me-downs, and clothing bought a size or two too large.[32] In fact, half a century later, Manning was recruited as a choreography consultant and also performed with Miller in the stunning lindy hop dance sequence in Spike Lee's *Malcolm X*.[33] Kelley analyzes the meaning of Malcolm Little/ X's embracing of this intersection of clothing, language, movement, and cultural signifying: "for Malcolm [Little/ X], the zoot suit, the lindy hop, and the distinctive lingo of the 'hep cat' simultaneously embodied [the] class, racial and cultural tensions [within urban Black communities]."[34] More than a passing dance craze, the lindy hop was a bold physical assertion of Black identity and corporeal agency in the face of Jim Crow politics. More than a dance costume, the zoot suit was a radical statement signifying membership to a specific community.

Much like the original zoot suiters, members of the Time would at first shop in thrift stores to find these styles, which Prince required them to wear at all times, both on and off the stage, which we also see depicted in the characters of the Time in *Purple Rain* and *Graffiti Bridge*. Over-the-top frontman Day tended to be the flashiest member of the Time with his iconic shiny gold and black brocade jacket. It evolved from a suit coat on the covers of both *The Time* (1981) and *What Time is It?* (1982) albums, to a velvet-trimmed smoking jacket in the *Graffiti Bridge* promotional photos.[35] He dons a black and white zebra-print monogrammed version of this look when lounging at home in *Graffiti Bridge*, and he subsequently sports a similar look in black and burgundy during the "Shake" performance at his Pandemonium nightclub. This juxtaposition of the smoking jacket looks in both private and public settings further demonstrate Baudelaire's statement that "the dandy lives and sleeps in front of a mirror"[36]: Day dresses up even while wearing his bedclothes at home. Contrary to the iconic vacuuming scene in the opening montage of *Purple Rain*, we only see Day in his dandy looks in his private residence behind the public sphere during *Graffiti Bridge*. Day plays with this merging of public and private life by bringing his glamorous intimates to the stage and further demonstrating the constant performativity inherent in dandyism.

The audacity behind the flamboyant sartorial performance of wearing the zoot suit in public spaces sparked many debates surrounding its symbolic meaning at the time. Peiss's analysis of the exaggerated nature of the garment unlocks a multifaceted enigma surrounding its meaning—specifically, who is talking about the zoot suit and their agenda. Interpretations ranged from a "masking of masculinity," considered by some as effeminate and a deviance of gender and sexuality,[37] to symbolizing youthful dissatisfaction,[38] to a means of self-expression available to minority and underprivileged youth.[39]

Langston Hughes saw zoot suiters as "depression's kids," and interpreted the trend as an exciting way for them to "go to extremes" in fashion when they finally had a little money to spend and in turn formed community amongst themselves.[40] Conversely, due to the pressures of respectability politics during Jim Crow, many middle-class Black people rejected the fashion in an attempt to align themselves with dominant white cultural and moral practices.[41] In addition to the alleged criminality associated with the look, the media denigrated the zoot suit as an antipatriotic symbol of fascism due to the supposedly wasteful amount of fabric used in its confection during a period of wartime rationing. This is notably portrayed in Disney's Donald Duck wartime propaganda cartoon for the US Treasury Department, "The Spirit of 43," in which "Zootie" the zoot-suited duck resembles a hepcat with a Hitler mustache and a bowtie in the shape of a swastika.[42] This contradicts the reality of the zoot-suit trend taking shape in Europe, where versions of the drape were also worn by Zazous in France and Swing Youth in Germany, both youth countercultures in opposition to the Nazis.[43] This vilification of zoot suiters in the United States is of course directly linked to racism against young people of color. This is especially true for Black and Mexican American men, though Filipino and Japanese men also sported the look. Luis Alvarez provides a comprehensive analysis of the intersections of race, gender, and class issues at play in the historical context surrounding the zoot suit in his seminal book, *The Power of the Zoot: Youth Culture and Resistance During World War II*.[44]

The erroneous causality of the zoot suit as engendering violence and crime was famously exacerbated on June 4, 1943, when fifty US sailors, armed with makeshift weapons, left their naval base to raid Los Angeles with the intention of inflicting harm upon young Mexican American men. This was one of many race riots, labeled as such, that erupted during the summer of 1943, including in Harlem, New York, Detroit, Michigan, and Beaufort, Texas. The zoot suit often worn by the Mexican American youth was deemed the cause for what the media labeled as the Zoot Suit Riots which represented a culmination of violence resulting from increasingly intensifying tensions between zoot suiters and servicemen in Los Angeles since the 1930s.[45] Additionally, the sexual threat of zoot suiters on the home front endangering the wives and girlfriends of servicemen overseas was a common trope at the time. Police reports from the five days of violence show that many of the ninety-four injured civilians were not even wearing zoot suits, but all were Mexican American. Blamed for igniting the riots, scores of Mexican American youth were arrested compared to only two servicemen. The zoot suit at the time was associated with criminality and deviance by the racist media in a way to condemn the radicalized other as unpatriotic. However, Chicano scholars, artists, and writers would reappropriate the Mexican American zoot suiter, also called *pachuco/a*, by the 1960s and 1970s as a symbol of pride for the Chicano community: "They embraced the *pachuco* as an example of ethnic assertion and Chicano power, with his dress, language, and music [exemplifying] early strategies of resistance to discrimination, invisibility, and assimilation."[46] This was exemplified in Luis Valdez's 1978 play and subsequent 1981 film, *Zoot Suit*,[47] in which the zoot suiter hero is exalted for standing against white American discrimination.

In addition, the same year that the riot occurred in Los Angeles and one month before the 1943 riot in Harlem, Cab Calloway and the Nicholas Brothers appeared in dandified dress in *Stormy Weather*.[48] This vehicle for a star-studded cast of all Black performers featured musical numbers depicting the history of jazz dance and African American culture and music from the turn of the century through the second world war. With tap dance legend Bill Robinson, singer Lena Horne, and jazz pianist Fats Waller at the helm, the climax of the film centered on a show-stopping performance by both the bandleader Cab Calloway and acrobatic tap duo, brothers Harold and Fayard Nicholas. This legendary performance constitutes a true pinnacle of jazz dancing while exemplifying Black dandyism and the reappropriation of dress as a means of empowerment. During this final performance for Black soldiers before shipping out overseas, the film featured Calloway in an iconic zoot suit in the opening number, followed by the penultimate piece, "My, ain't that something." Calloway exemplifies the role of frontman with the flashiest zoot suit on the stage, complete with billowing pants, bowtie extension to the shoulders, extra-wide lapels, and watch chain that practically touches the floor. Peiss points out that this scene, with a chorus of zoot suiters symbolically moving in harmony against a backdrop of the "American Dream" with a suburban house surrounded by a white picket fence, explicitly countered the antipatriotic associations surrounding the article of clothing and its wearers.[49]

Although the Time had been wearing zoot suit-inspired fashions during the early 1980s, the zoot suit appeared more prominently in popular culture, specifically in music videos and movies, in the late 1980s and early 1990s.[50] Before the iconic zoot suits worn by Denzel Washington and Spike Lee in *Malcolm X*[51] homage was paid to these jazz-era styles in music videos such as MC Hammer's retro jazz-era inspired "Turn this mutha out"[52] from 1988 and the zoot-suited Paula Abdul and her animated tap-dancing partner, MC Skat Kat, in "Opposites Attract" from 1989.[53] Janet Jackson's second and third albums were noticeably sprinkled with zoot-soot aesthetics throughout:

first, Janet Jackson's *Control* video,[54] produced by Time members Jimmy
Jam and Terry Lewis in 1986 with the original band members performing,
as well as zoot-suited dancers in the "When I think of you"[55] video directed
by Julien Temple from the same album.[56] Jackson's most jazz-era inspired
video in which she herself sports a black and white pin-striped zoot suit
throughout the entirety of the song "Alright" (released 1990) off the *Janet
Jackson's Rhythm Nation 1814* album, was also directed by Temple and produced by Jam and Lewis. Circling back to *Stormy Weather,* Jackson chose
to pay homage to the aforementioned zoot-suit icon Cab Calloway and the
legendary Nicholas Brothers with separate cameos in the music video. This
throwback to Calloway's patented dynamic onstage presence and eccentric
showmanship exemplifies Miller's definition of the dandy's use of wit and
gesture, reiterated in Day's presence both on and off the stage throughout
Purple Rain and *Graffiti Bridge.* Day's first look in *Graffiti Bridge* is a yellow
and burgundy ensemble inspired by the zoot suit and reminiscent of Calloway's famous yellow look featured in "Alright," complete with an embroi-
dered cape and two-toned shoes. And much like the white suburban youth
who swarmed to co-opt the dance craze of the jitterbug and the zoot suit
style trend (none of whom were targeted or arrested during the 1943 Zoot
Suit Riots in Los Angeles), white culture yet again appropriated the zoot suit
during the Neo-swing craze in the mid- to late 1990s, as shown in movies
such *The Mask*[57] and *Swingers.*[58]

While the zoot-suit aesthetic was resurfacing in mainstream popular culture during the late 1980s and early 1990s, popular dance and music trends
also reflected this throwback to the big band swing era. As aforementioned,
swing dancing enjoyed a resurgence of mainstream popularity at this time,
but within the rapidly growing musical genre of hip-hop, a new take on this
blend of jazz-age rhythms and movement was introduced slightly earlier
with New Jack Swing in the late 1980s and early 1990s.[59] The song "Nasty" on
Jackson's first album, *Control,* produced by Jam and Lewis, is often credited as
the inspiration for singer, songwriter, and producer Teddy Riley's creation of
the New Jack Swing sound.[60] Innovative mixing of styles and specifically the
use of the swing beats on drum machines with R&B vocals on top defined
this new music genre.[61]

Along with the unique sound of New Jack Swing came both a sartorial and kinetic aesthetic: zoot-suit-inspired styles were often featured or
referenced in the clothing worn, and the dance moves exhibited a similar
quality of movement to the Charleston, lindy hop, and other vernacular jazz
dances from the 1920s to the 1940s. The grounded movement, supple bent-
kneed stance, loose and relaxed posture, constant pulse, and repeated kicks

in various patterns and formations exemplify the general form of both these jazz dances and New Jack Swing moves. Originating with jazz music and culture, these dances have direct lineage to the roots of West African dances passed down through generations of African Americans and their enslaved ancestors who retained the movement and rhythms. The Charleston was popularized in the 1920s and featured partnered or solo movement with constant pulsing with inward-pointing toes on the even beats, kicks and inward-pointing heels on the odd beats. The specific 1920s partnered Charleston with the loose ankles and fanned footwork evolved to the "mashed potato" step during the 1960s and eventually resurfaced in New Jack Swing dance moves, one of the most famous examples of which is featured in *House Party* during the dance battle scene with rappers Kid 'n Play.[62] The two dancers face each other and execute the 1920s Charleston basic step with added toe touches and spins to face the back. The constant pulsing, loose posture, relaxed kicking, and even the fanned footwork are direct references to the 1920s Charleston basic step. In addition, Play sports a teal zoot-suit-inspired look with black and white tie and matching two-toned shoes, exemplifying the intersection of music, dance, and style in Black culture, as a (sub)conscious echo of zoot-suit culture in urban Black and Latinx communities from the swing era. The continuous homage paid to the style of the zoot suit era in addition to the dance references that hark back centuries to West African dance movements via enslaved ancestors, point to the *power of the zoot*, to quote the title of Alvarez's book, and its profound connection to these dances. The unapologetic joy exhibited through the dancers performing these moves is, in fact, in line with radical resistance in the same way as wearing the zoot suit itself is emblematic of the audacious claiming of public space and agency over one's body in an oppressive society.

Through a cohesion of style (clothing and accessories), gesture (dance and movement in public space), and wit (language, actions, visual subtleties), semiotics and performative signifying define dandyism. The dandy questions authority by wearing an elegant suit with subversive styling as an expression of social rebellion and empowerment and a tool for questioning racial, sexual, gendered, national, and class categories. And while European dandies were often dismissed as mere "fops," despite the distinction, the semiotic meaning behind dandyism practiced by people of color in the US was often interpreted by white America as a violent act of subversion that merited a violent response. A Black person wearing any kind of elegant clothing in a white supremacist society is already subversive because luxuries in such a society are reserved for white people. The Black dandy takes this a step further by wearing exaggerated luxury, ensuring that the rebellious act gets noticed for what it is—a deliberate radical act of subversiveness to the white supremacist status quo.

The look behind Morris Day and the Time, as curated by Prince himself, not only represents these core values of dandyism but also pays homage to a legacy of social and political rebellion through its adaptation of the zoot-suit aesthetic. In the same vein as the original dandy, Julius Soubise, whose claiming of public space and assertion of agency through sartorial rebellion has echoed throughout communities of color for over three centuries, we have seen time and again the intentional use of style as a socio-political statement that remains relevant today. In June of 2020, hundreds of Black dandies led by stylist Gabriel M. Garmon marched through the streets of Harlem to protest police brutality in the wake of George Floyd's murder in Minneapolis.[63] Ian Reid's images of this protest march remind us of one of the first civil rights protests in the United States in which clothing was a focal point, the Silent Parade in Harlem in 1917, organized by the NAACP to protest anti-black violence. From Soubise in the eighteenth century to the swing era during WWII to Prince and the Time in the 1980s to the Black Lives Matter protests today, why is this aesthetic so enduring, and why are there always new ways to do this now timeless personal art form? As Miller states, the dandy often surfaces during changing circumstances in history "as a mode of creative appropriation, . . . [that is not] just a strategy of social critique but, as we have seen, a mode of survival."[64] Reid's images of the 2020 Black Lives Matter protesters in Harlem remind us indeed that, while progress has been made, the world we see today ultimately still resembles the world we see today, demonstrating the effectiveness and semiotic meaning of Black dandyism. As outlined by Malcolm X and Prince scholar Zaheer Ali, many of Prince's actions, especially into the 1990s, explicitly reflected his espousal of the Black radical tradition of resistance. Ali reminds us that Prince helped fund Lee's *Malcolm X* in 1992, a film that not only represented one of the most iconic zoot suiters but, more importantly, told the story of one of the most radical freedom fighters in our history.[65]

Notes

1. Charles Baudelaire, *Journaux intimes*, my translation (Project Gutenberg, 2004), chap. 3, http://www.gutenberg.org/files/13792/13792-8.txt.

2. Prince Rogers Nelson, "Prettyman," Track 18 on *Rave Un2 the Joy Fantastic*. Recorded 1999. NPG Arista, compact disc.

3. *Purple Rain*, directed by Albert Magnoli, (1984; Burbank, CA: Warner Bros., 2004), DVD.

4. *Graffiti Bridge*, directed by Prince, (1990; Burbank, CA: Warner Bros., 2005), DVD.

5. Karen Turman, "'Prettyman' in the mirror: Dandyism in Prince's Minneapolis," *Prince and Popular Music*, Eds. Alleyne, M. and K. Fairclough-Isaacs (New York: Bloomsbury Academic, 2020): 45–55.

6. Most notably the iconic Herb Ritts photo shoot with Prince as a Pop Dandy, in George Kalogerakis, "Prince in Vogue : Portraits of an Icon," *Vogue*, 21 Apr. 2016. Accessed Jan. 5, 2021: https://theico006Eicprince.wordpress.com/2017/01/31/prince-in-vogue-portraits-of-an-icon/

7. My paraphrasing from her Dec 18, 2018 interview on the *Dressed: The History of Fashion* podcast: https://www.iheart.com/podcast/105-dressed-the-history-of-fas-29000690/episode/black-dandyism-a-cultural-history-an-30315508/.

8. December 18, 2018, interview, *Dressed*.

9. Monica L. Miller, *Slaves to Fashion: Black Dandyism and the Styling of Black Diasporic Identity* (Durham, North Carolina: Duke University Press, 2009).

10. The Dandy figures in minstrel shows emerging during the late 1820s were offensive archetypes that mocked newly freed Black men who started to dress more elegantly, depicting them as extravagantly effeminate in dress while also exhibiting mythologized and threatening hyper-heterosexuality.

11. Honoré de Balzac, *Treatise on Elegant Living*, Translated by Napoleon Jeffries (Adelaide, Australia: Wakefield Press, 2010).

12. Charles Baudelaire, *The Painter of Modern Life and Other Essays*, Trans. and Ed. By Jonathan Mayne, (New York: Phaidon Press, 1964).

13. Roland Barthes, "Le Dandysme et la mode," *Language and Fashion*, Translated by Andy Stafford, Eds. Andy Stafford and Michael Carter (London: Bloomsbury, 2013), 62.

14. Jim Sherrin created the patterns for Prince's suits during this era which would serve as a blueprint for Prince's fashions throughout the 1980s and 1990s.

15. Morris Day, *On Time: A Princely Life* (Cambridge, MA: Da Capo Press, 2019).

16. Questlove, host, "Episode 035 feat. Jimmy Jam Pt 1," *Questlove Supreme*, iHeartRadio, June 7, 2017, accessed May 2020, https://www.pandora.com/podcast/questlove-supreme/ep-035-feat-jimmy-jam-pt-i/PE:308146.

17. Jules Amédée Barbey d'Aurevilly, *Dandyism*, translated by Douglas Ainslie (New York: PAJ Publications, 1988), 78.

18. Eliza Glick, "Harlem's Queer Dandy: African-American Modernism and the Artifice of Blackness," *MFS Modern Fiction Studies* 49, no. 3 (Fall 2003), 438.

19. Sarah Niblock and Stan Hawkins, *Prince: The Making of a Pop Music Icon* (Farnham, UK: Ashgate Publishing, 2011), 26.

20. Houk, Deborah, "Self Construction and Sexual Identity in Nineteenth-Century French Dandyism," *French Forum* Volume 22, Number 1 (January 1997), 60.

21. Baudelaire, *Journaux intimes*, chap. 3.

22. The Time, "Cool," written and produced by Prince, recorded and released 1981, track 4 on *The Time*, Warner Bros, vinyl.

23. *Under the Cherry Moon*, directed by Prince (1986; Burbank, CA: Warner Bros., 2005), DVD.

24. Kathy Peiss, *Zoot Suit: The Enigmatic Career of an Extreme Style* (Philadelphia: University of Pennsylvania Press, 2011), 2.

25. Artes & contextos, "Cab Calloway's Hepster's Dictionary: A Guide to the Language of Jive (1938)," *Artesecontextos*, last modified May 3, 2017, accessed January 4, 2021, https://artesecontextos.pt/2017/05/a-guide-to-the-language-of-jive/.

26. Malcolm X and Alex Haley, *The Autobiography of Malcolm X: As Told to Alex Haley* (New York: Grove Press, 1965), 59, 66.

27. Robin Kelley, "The Riddle of the Zoot: Malcolm Little and Black Cultural Politics during World War II," *Malcolm X in Our Own Image*, ed. Joe Wood (New York: St. Martin's Press, 1992), 160, 171.

28. Peiss, 18.

29. Peiss, 19.

30. Hot Chocolate ("Cottontail") RCM Productions (1941). *Youtube.com*, uploaded June 20, 2017, accessed January 4, 2021, https://www.youtube.com/watch?v=PvU48WBP3hc

31. In Manning's 2007 autobiography, *Frankie Manning: Ambassador of Lindy Hop*, he explains that the men were wearing the sack jackets in the soundie due to the cold temperatures on the soundstage where they were filming (182). The drape is prominently worn in many images of lindy hoppers such as depicted in Cornell Capa's 1939 photo of a couple dancing at the Savoy Ballroom in Harlem, New York.

32. Peiss, 27, 31.

33. The vivid description of the dance scene originated in *The Autobiography of Malcolm X*, co-authored by Alex Haley (New York: Grove Press, 1965), 65–67. Both Manning and Miller discuss their positive experience with the conception of this sequence in the film but critique the cinematic liberties taken with the final product in their respective autobiographies, pages 234–37 in *Franking Manning: Ambassador of Lindy Hop*, and page 244 in Miller's *Swingin' at the Savoy: The Memoir of a Jazz Dancer*. Miller later compares the dance sequences in Debbie Allen's *Stomping at the Savoy*, for which she earned an Emmy as choreographer, as more accurately depicting the dance and atmosphere in the ballrooms at that time.

34. Kelley, 159.

35. Many of these early 1980s photos of the Time can be found in photographer Allen Beaulieu's book, *Prince: Before the Rain* (St. Paul, MN: Minnesota Historical Society Press, 2018).

36. Baudelaire, *Journaux intimes*, chap. 3.

37. Ralph S. Banay, "A Psychiatrist Looks at the Zoot Suit," *Probation* 22 (February 1944): 84–85.

38. S.I. Hayakawa, "Second Thoughts," *Defender* (June 19, 1943): 15.

39. J. V. D. Carlyle, "The Psychological Implications of the Zoot Suit," *MAR 11* (July 1943): 36.

40. Langston Hughes, "Here to Yonder," *Defender* (June 19, 1943): 14.

41. See Evelyn Higginbotham's seminal book, *Righteous Discontent: The Women's Movement in the Black Baptist Church, 1880–1920* (Cambridge, MA: Harvard University Press, 1993.

42. Just Toons, "Spirit of 1943," Walt Disney Productions, 1943, *YouTube.com*, uploaded July 23, 2017, accessed May 2020, https://www.youtube.com/watch?v=cL4exKyk7oE.

43. As depicted in the 1993 film, *Swing Kids* (Buena Vista Pictures), for example.

44. Luis Alvarez, *The Power of the Zoot: Youth Culture and Resistance During World War II* (Berkeley, CA: University of California Press, 2008).

45. In the fifth chapter of *The Power of the Zoot*, "Zoot Violence in Los Angeles," Alvarez outlines many of the reports of violence between Mexican American youth and servicemen leading up to the riots of 1943, 157–68.

46. Peiss, 186.

47. *Zoot Suit*, Valdez, Luis, dir. screenwriter. 1981; Universal Pictures. Amazon, streaming.

48. *Stormy Weather*, Andrew, Stone, dir. 1992; Twentieth-Century Fox Film Corp. Youtube .com, streaming.

49. Peiss, 94.

50. Other lesser-known references to zoot suits appearing in popular culture during this time include the aforementioned *Zoot Suit* niche film by Valdez and the band, Kid Creole and the Coconuts.

51. *Malcolm X,* Spike, Lee dir. 1992; Burbank, CA: Warner Bros., 2005. DVD.

52. MC Hammer, "Turn This Mutha Out," Track 1 on *Let's Get it Started*, Capital-EMI Records, 1988, compact disc, music video available online: https://www.youtube.com/watch ?v=co6tF_mC2zY.

53. Paula Abdul, "Opposites Attract," written and produced by Oliver Leiber, track 3 on Forever Your Girl, recorded 1988, Virgin Records, compact disc. Music video available online: https://www.youtube.com/watch?v=xweiQukBM_k.

54. Janet Jackson, "Control," Written by Jackson, James Harris III and Terry Lewis, Track 1 on *Control*, Recorded August 1985, A&M, compact disc. Music video available online: https://www.youtube.com/watch?v=LH8xbDGv7oY.

55. Janet Jackson, "When I Think of You," written by Jackson, James Harris III and Terry Lewis, Track 6 on *Control*, Recorded 1985, A&M, compact disc. Music video available online: https://www.youtube.com/watch?v=EaleKN9GQ54&list=RDsC3SEDWdNsA&index=6.

56. Because this article's focus is primarily on men as dandies and zoot suiters, the gender dynamics at play with women dandies and *pachuas* merit further study. Paula Abdul's zoot suit-inspired look in "Opposites Attract" and, more prominently, Janet Jackson's multiple appearances in zoot suits and other traditionally masculine forms of dress throughout the 1980s and early 1990s deserve attention that is beyond the scope of this current study. For more discussion on women zoot suiters, see Catherine S. Ramirez's seminal book, *The Woman in the Zoot Suit: Gender, Nationalism, and the Cultural Politics of Memory* (Durham, NC: Duke University Press, 2009).

57. *The Mask*, directed by Charles Russell, 1994, New Line Cinema, 1997, DVD.

58. *Swingers*, directed by Doug Liman, 1996, Lionsgate, 2002, DVD.

59. While swing dancing and lindy hop, as the original form of partner-dancing to big band swing music, were not as prevalent in mainstream culture between the 1950s and 1980s, the dance culture was still regularly practiced and performed in various communities such as in Harlem, NY, and Los Angeles. Most notably, Norma Miller and Mama Lu Parks both continued to organize, develop, and train dancers for performance troupes during this era while many social dance venues remained open and cultivated small local dance communities. For more information on Miller's extraordinary life in showbusiness, refer to her autobiography, *Swingin' at the Savoy: The Memoir of a Jazz Dancer*, coauthor Evette Jensen (Philadelphia: Temple University Press, 1996).

60. Janet Jackson, "Nasty," track 2 on *Control*, written by James Harris Jackson III and Terry Lewis, recorded 1985, A&M, compact disc. Music video available online: https://www.youtube.com/watch?v=-s1fHtIVqiQ.

61. Nelson George, *Hip Hop America* (London: Penguin Books, 1998) 115–18.

62. *House Party*, Reginald Hudlin, dir. 1990; New Line Cinema, Youtube.com, 2020. Streaming.

63. Chioma Nnadi, photography by Ian Reid, "In Harlem, a Group of Black Men Pays Their Respects to George Floyd in Impeccable Style," *Vogue*, June 6, 2020, accessed Jan. 7, 2021. https://www.vogue.com/article/george-floyd-100-black-men-memorial-harlem-gabriel -garmon-james-felton-keith-bradon-waight-tiffany-rea-fisher-harold-waight.

64. Miller, "Fresh-dressed like a million bucks," *Artist/ Rebel/ Dandy: Men of Fashion*, Eds. Kate Irvin and Laurie Anne Brewer, (New Haven, CT: Yale University Press, 2013), 153.

65. Zaheer Ali, ""Slave 2 the System: Prince's Labor Activism & the Black Radical Tradition," *Purple Reign: An Interdisciplinary Conference on the Life and Legacy of Prince*, Salford, UK, Presentation, https://www.youtube.com/watch?v=uZ12lLE5quc.

Chapter 4

CLOUDS, COLORS, AND THE WONDER OF U

The Influence of Joni Mitchell on Prince

FRED MARK SHAHEEN

Maybe I've never really loved. I guess that is the truth. I've spent my whole life in clouds at icy altitudes.
—JONI MITCHELL (FROM "AMELIA")

CLOUDS

In "All I Want," the opening track to her album *Blue*, Joni Mitchell sings, "I am on a lonely road, and I am traveling . . . looking for something. What can it be?" In another song originally intended for the same album, she sings, "I get the urge for going/When the meadow grass is turning brown/And summertime is falling down and winter is closing in." "Urge For Going" is a song about things on the move—seasons, lovers, birds—all of them "going" in their appointed time. Joni observes the movement and the changes, and she describes them with poetic precision. "I get the urge for going," she sings in the opening verse, "but I never seem to go." In her most famous song, "Both Sides, Now," from her album, *Clouds*, she uses clouds as a metaphor for love and life: "So many things I would have done, but clouds got in my way." Joni comes to the realization that what we see of things are merely illusions, and we never really know the thing itself: "I really don't know life at all."

Often when we're looking up at clouds in the sky, we think we can discern shapes and forms of things—people, animals, etc. But looking away for a moment and then returning our gaze to the sky, we can't see the thing anymore. Then we understand it was never there, and the only realities are movement and experience. This is what the artist does: using a medium—color, paint, words, music—she recounts her experience of the movement of clouds.

In "Clouds," from Prince's *Art Official Age* (2014), it is another kind of cloud that gets in the way. The song champions experience over technology, and advocates for romance in real time: "Never underestimate the power of a kiss on the neck when she doesn't expect." Despite "this brand new age" in which we are accustomed to doing everything "quick, fast in a hurry," Prince insists on face-to-face engagement, an experience that all the tech in the world cannot replicate: "We're getting high on something that doesn't require clouds."

Arguably the most prolific pop and rock musician of his era, Prince was also its most protean. Over four decades, he was constantly inventing and reinventing himself, giving meticulous attention to every detail of his art—the music, the image, the performance, the words, and even the colors and fonts used on album covers. Prince's own prolific body of work includes not only thirty-nine albums released under his own name but dozens by satellite acts (the Time, Sheila E., Madhouse, the Family, Jill Jones, and others) in which he writes, produces, and performs the music. A handful of musical figures loom large over Prince's formation—Stevie Wonder (the studio virtuoso), James Brown (the showman par excellence), Sly Stone (the integrating bandleader), and Jimi Hendrix (the guitar god). Not as immediately obvious, but no less significant is Joni Mitchell, the musician, the songwriter, the painter. Prince was inspired by Joni's use of color as a means of expression in both the literal and figurative sense. She also influenced Prince's use of space and silence in his musical arrangements. At times both Joni Mitchell and Prince connected brilliantly with audiences—she is a nine-time Grammy Award winner; he has been awarded multiple industry awards, including several Grammys and an Oscar (for *Purple Rain*), and sold over 130 million records worldwide. Both artists have been inducted into the Rock and Roll Hall of Fame. Even when their work wasn't well received (*Mingus, Under the Cherry Moon*), neither artist deemed it a failure; neither Joni Mitchell nor Prince defined artistic success solely in terms of commercial sales or critical recognition.

> I am a lonely painter. I live in a box of paints.
> —Joni Mitchell, from "A Case of You"

The first few times you hear "River" (from Joni Mitchell's *Blue*) the musical notes from "Jingle Bells" prepare you to be carried off as if on a float in a holiday parade. "It's coming on Christmas, they're cutting down trees, they're putting up reindeer and singing songs of joy and peace," the singer announces. But it's not in the right key for "Jingle Bells," and the imagery takes a different turn. "River" is no Yuletide carol. The twist is subtle, so much so that it feels natural. The singer wants to get away: "I'm going to make a lot of money, then I'm going to quit this crazy scene," she elaborates, a reference to the music business. She wishes she had a river, not to float down, not to carry her home, but rather "that I could skate away on." In this scenario, the river does not flow but is solid ice; the protagonist is looking for a way to *escape* rather than a passageway home. All of this during Christmastime, when people typically long to come together with the people they care for the most. The sentiment is bittersweet, and the irony is heightened by the "Jingle Bells" motif reprised at the coda.

IT'S A LONG WAY FROM CANADA

The singer knows about icy rivers. Roberta Joan Mitchell was born in Alberta, Canada. At age twelve, after several moves around western Canada—her dad was a lieutenant in the Royal Canadian Air Force—the family settled in Saskatoon, the largest city in the province of Saskatchewan. From her youth, Joni was chiefly interested in painting but also developed a love of country music. Her first instrument was the ukulele. From there, Joni taught herself guitar from the Pete Seeger songbook. Two musical favorites early on were Edith Piaf and Miles Davis. Hailed as the most important and influential female recording artist of the late twentieth century, and one of the greatest songwriters ever, Joni Mitchell claims that her notable musical career was the result of serendipity: "I stumbled into it by accident," she says. "I was very, very serious about my art and not very serious about my music."[1] Eventually, she relocated to the United States and recorded her first album, *Song to a Seagull*, in 1968. The quintessential singer-songwriter artist, Joni Mitchell's catalog includes nineteen studio albums and embraces elements of music from her early years—folk, rock, pop and jazz. Her fourth album, *Blue* (1971), is her most universally acclaimed album; and her sixth, *Court and Spark* (1974), is her most commercially successful.

MOOD INDIGO

"It don't snow here, it stays pretty green," continues Joni Mitchell in "River," the "here" meaning sunny California, where this song and all the songs on *Blue* were recorded. The weather is but one reason for her longing to skate away. Another is a failed romance: "Now I've gone and lost the best baby I ever had,"

she says about one who "loved me so naughty, made me weak in the knees."
"River" is an eloquent expression of melancholy, that craving for the comfort
and solace of isolation. In a later song she would sing, "There's comfort in
melancholy, when there's no need to explain" ("Hejira"). The color blue (indigo
in particular) is captured visually in the album art. Of the many tools in Joni's
paint box, indigo blue is her most potent and expressive. "Blue, songs are like
tattoos," she sings on the title track. "I've been to sea before. Crown and anchor
me or let me sail away," she continues, touching again on the motif of escape.
Blue is a color associated with loneliness and solitude: indigo, in particular,
with "intuition, perception and the higher mind,"[2] the perfect symbolic color
for Joni's fourth record, a seminal singer-songwriter album.

> You meant the world to me, but now you're gone and I'm so blue.
> —Prince, from "So Blue"

Prince utilized the "blue as loneliness" motif on his debut album from
1978. But he was in the third decade of his career when he produced what
may be called the closest spiritual cousin to Mitchell's *Blue* in his catalog:
his solo piano and voice album, *One Nite Alone . . .* , originally released in
2002. Included on the album was Prince's cover of "A Case Of U," another
song from *Blue*. The title track, the album's opening cut, begins with a lyrical
conflation of color and sound: "In a pale blue spotlight, a figure spins around.
And a voice calls out to you, 'baby, do you like the sound?'" That sound is a
sparse arrangement of Prince's voice accompanied by his piano and a few
other instruments and sound effects. Although Prince had recorded a whole
album with sparse instrumentation before, *The Truth* (1997) employs primarily acoustic guitar with a few embellishments. The blue mood and sound of
One Nite Alone . . . is the closest he comes to paying homage to Joni with
an entire album.

For Joni, a painter, color is literally her medium of expression. Moreover,
her own artwork adorns the covers of a majority of the albums in her catalog.[3] Prince drew and designed, using cut-and-paste, the cover of his *1999*
album; his hand-drawn art also adorns the cover of his 1991 single, "Gett Off."
But Prince uses color in the figurative sense, almost like a painter would.
Color features extensively in the artwork and motifs of his albums and their
accompanying tours: easter egg pastels (*Around the World in a Day*), black
and white (*Parade*), peach and black (*Sign o' the Times*), gold (*The Gold Experience*), lemon yellow (*Diamonds and Pearls*) and orange (*Emancipation*). The
most famous color associated with Prince, of course, is purple. A combination
of red and blue, Prince's signature color, evokes passion and royalty. In two

of his best-known songs, purple conveys the end of the world. "The sky was all purple, there were people running everywhere," he exclaims in "1999" and in the title track to his hit album and film, "I only want to see you bathing in the Purple Rain." In these instances, the color of the sky (blue) mixes with blood (red) to make purple. The blood suggests destruction, and in Prince's biblically literate worldview, that destruction signifies redemption.[4] Prince has prefaced performances of "Purple Rain" with a discussion of his music bringing people together from different backgrounds. At the United Center in Chicago, at one of three benefit concerts in late September of 2012 (a Presidential election year) Prince said it was time for red (Republicans) and blue (Democrats) to come together and create one color, purple. For "Gold," a similarly styled anthem from the early 1990s, Prince adopted a different, brighter color to convey the message that "all that glitters ain't gold." One part of the song speaks about people living in "ocean of despair" and includes this typically Prince-like couplet: "They're unhappy each and every day/But hell is not fashion/so what you trying to say?" That line recalls Joni Mitch-ell's observation in "Blue": "Everybody's saying that hell's the hippest way to go/but I don't think so." And she adds, "but I'm gonna take a look around it though." Blue, the color, is an apt description of the most pivotal album in Joni's catalog. Simply put, *Blue* sounds like blue. In like manner, Prince's "Gold" twinkles and shimmers for seven and a half minutes with layers of keys and a load of reverb that make it the aural equivalent of beholding the beauty of that precious metal; a true "Gold Experience."

Coming from the land of snow, I guess I'm kinda used to cold.
—Prince, from "White Mansion"

Minneapolis is so cold it keeps the bad people out.
—Prince to Oprah Winfrey (1996)

An apocryphal story circulated online shortly after his death purporting that Prince had inspired the main song from Disney's *Frozen*. The claim was that the Purple One had met with the film's producers, who were looking for a strong musical number with a classic pop feel to it. Prince reportedly described what it was like growing up in Minnesota, telling them that he thrived there despite the loneliness and harsh winters and—wait for it—the cold never bothered him anyway. Thus was born the lyrical punchline to the Grammy and Academy Award-winning song, "Let it Go." The story—which the superfan in me kind of hoped was true—made the rounds on social media before being denied by the film's producers. In the aftermath of

Prince's death in 2016, some seemed uber-zealous to assert his influence on popular culture, even fabricating a connection to the most highly acclaimed and lucrative film of the era. Nevertheless, a key takeaway from the "Prince inspired *Frozen*" hoax is this: Prince, like the enchanted Elsa in the film, grew up bearing the blessing/curse of a unique and potent gift, and both of them cultivated that gift in solitude. Isolation, particularly self-imposed, can lead to loneliness and loneliness to despair; in some, such as the kid born Prince Rogers Nelson, it can also inspire and foster intense creativity.

Prince was born in Minneapolis in 1958. Both his parents, John L. Nelson and Mattie Shaw, were musicians. Nelson led a band called the Prince Rogers Trio. From his father, Prince learned the hard work and discipline required for making music, particularly the demands of learning your instrument and performing for an audience. He was also exposed to the exciting side of show business when the senior Nelson brought his son onstage at a James Brown gig: "I saw some of the finest dancing girls that I had ever seen in my life!"[5] Prince revealed this in an interview for MTV in 1985. The thing that impressed the young Prince most was the control Brown had over his dancers. Or, as he put it, "over his apples and his oranges."

From the heart of Minnesota, here come the Purple Yoda.
—Prince, from "Laydown"

After John and Mattie separated, Prince was often left to fend for himself at home. He taught himself to play piano at age seven. By his midteens, he could also play guitar, bass, and drums. Prince could hear a song and instantly play it back. "In high school, he retreated into himself quite a bit," observed Rev. Art Erickson, who supervised youth activities Prince was involved with at Park Avenue Methodist Church in Minneapolis. "He would eat lunch alone and became very reflective."[6] Prince was the lonely kid, seemingly shy, who found expression in the ability to learn music and make his own. Aside from his sense of humor, "sometimes sophisticated verbal stuff, other times pure pranks,"[7] music was the way he communicated. "In high school, Prince was absorbed in his music," said Jon Bream. However, "he wasn't much for sharing his music. But he'd pay attention to the music of other students . . . that seemed to be his style—always absorbing."[8] As talented and committed to learning as he was, Prince was dead serious about making music his profession. "I'm about to be a star," he told Ronnie Robbins one day in 1976. Robbins replied, "I know you are."[9] He was also determined, having seen James Brown, to control every aspect of his art, even wanting to produce himself once he had a recording contract. Once, at age eight, Prince was to learn piano from a teacher who lived across the street from his mother. He refused to go back after one lesson. The reason: "She wants me to play what she wants me to play, and I want to play what I want to play."[10] In a strikingly similar episode, when seven-year-old Joan Anderson presented her first composition to her piano teacher, she received a slap on the wrist "for playing by ear." Her teacher scolded her: "Why would you play by ear when you can have the masters under your fingers?" Relating the story now, Joni says she realized then, "I didn't have any masters I wanted to follow."[11]

God, Joni, And U.

This writer has a confession to make. When I first noticed the references to "Joni" in the credits of early Prince records, I had no idea who she was. I really didn't know much about Prince either. There he was, staring out at me from the cover of *Controversy*, looking dead serious about something. Behind him, the headlines screamed: "Do You Believe In God" (a statement, not a question), "Love Thy Neighbor," and on the back, simply "Joni." In the credits of his previous album, *Dirty Mind*, Prince had thanked "Joni" alongside "God" and "U." My unseasoned sensibility gave me a hunch that if Prince was deeply religious, he might also be an admirer of Joni Eareckson, the evangelical Christian author (who also happened to be a paraplegic). I was mistaken. Whoever Joni was, though, Prince was making her front-page news when no one else was.

Don't play me, I already do in my car.
—Prince, from "Don't Play Me"

In 1981, the year in which albums by REO Speedwagon, Foreigner, and Pat Benatar dominated the *Billboard* charts, Prince certainly stood apart as different. So different that it seemed as if he came out of nowhere. Journalist Neal Karlen put it this way: "Everyone came out of a tradition. [Prince] came out of no tradition."[12] Even so, it was possible to see some of his influences (R&B, funk, new wave) on the surface. In a review of *Controversy*, one journalist referred to Prince as a "young RJIT—Rick James In Training." *Rolling Stone*, in a four-star review of the album, noted the influences of Funkadelic and Jimi Hendrix. But how exactly did Joni Mitchell, a white, female, country- and folk-inspired singer-songwriter from Canada, fit into the equation? Apparently, Prince really admired her, but aside from that fact, how important was Joni Mitchell in the big picture? Who was playing her in 1981? Prince's attitude and philosophy would be this: It does not matter how significant or popular an artist is as long as that artist is significant and popular to you. It would be another year until Joni made a "comeback" and returned to pop music with her album, *Wild Things Run Fast* (***½ in *Rolling Stone*). *Blue*, her fourth album, has been considered a definitive artistic statement; it was her best album up to that point. After reaching a commercial high water mark three years later with *Court and Spark*, Joni took a left turn artistically and began exploring what we would now call "world music" but at the time was not even a recognized genre. *The Hissing of Summer Lawns* (1975) and *Hejira* (1976) followed a musical path that left some of her followers behind. Excursions into jazz with Herbie Hancock, Pat Metheny, and Weather Report bassist (and fellow Canadian) Jaco Pastorius; a collaborative effort with Charles Mingus shortly before his death; a double album with one song taking up an entire side ("Paprika Plains" from *Don Juan's Reckless Daughter*)—such moves fed Joni's artistic muse, but at the time alienated a good portion of her listeners. Time has caught up to *Hissing* and *Hejira* and vindicated both. They are to her catalog what *Around the World in a Day* and *Parade* are to Prince's catalog precisely a decade later: one-time commercial and critical letdowns that now rank among the artists' most highly regarded albums, particularly for the wealth of deeper cuts. Notably, the cover art of both *Hejira* and *Parade* make effective use of black and white.

FUNK IS SPACE

Prince contributed songs for two tribute albums: one to Jimi Hendrix (*The Power of Soul*) in 2003, and the other to Joni Mitchell (*A Tribute to Joni Mitchell*) in 2007. Uncredited, he contributed guitar to "Edith and the Kingpin" on Herbie Hancock's Grammy-winning album, *River: The Joni Letters*, from 2007. He also selected "A Case of You" for a collection of Joni songs curated by other artists in 2005. People like Hendrix, James Brown, and Sly Stone are low-hanging fruit on the tree of Prince's musical influences. Joni Mitchell, no less significant an influence, requires more reaching. It is worth noting that Prince has drawn inspiration from Joni's "difficult" period. He had used a phrase in Joni's "Coyote" (from *Hejira*) as the title of a ballad, "When We're Dancing Close and Slow," on his second album, *Prince*. That song showcases a peculiar hallmark of Prince's balladry—a sparse beat embellished with discreet synths to create a unique quivering effect, which critic Jon Pareles had praised, drawing attention to his "ear for floating tempos."[13] The effect is utilized on other songs such as "The Beautiful Ones," "Condition of the Heart," and "When 2 R In Love." His penchant for minimalist arrangements certainly owes a debt to Ms. Mitchell. And also to Miles Davis, whom both he and Mitchell admired. The legendary jazz trumpeter was an advocate for knowing that the notes a musician does not play are just as important as the ones he does. On his *A Piano & a Microphone* tour in 2016, Prince told anecdotes about growing up with a musician father and shared that one of the things he learned from him was the importance of that minimalist approach: "Funk is space," he would say and then demonstrate by pounding a funky groove on the keys. In 1996, while playing back a preview of his *Emancipation* set, Prince revealed to Anthony DeCurtis of *Rolling Stone* his inspiration for the sparse arrangement on "Let's Have a Baby": "Bass, piano and silence. Joni Mitchell taught me that. If you listen to her early stuff, she really understands that."[14] Joni's most developed and effective use of space and silence is on *Hejira*, on which she collaborates with jazz musicians, most notably bassist Jaco Pastorius. He creates rolling colorful bass lines that serve as a counterpoint to the melody. The result is music that is more impressionistic than immediate; more of a challenge to penetrate initially but ultimately more rewarding too.

> He's driven like an artist. His motivations are growth and experimentation as opposed to formula and hits.
> —Joni Mitchell on Prince[15]

Prince told journalist Neal Karlen in 1985 that Joni Mitchell's *The Hissing of Summer Lawns* was "the last album he loved all the way through." Prince was coming off the success of his watershed *Purple Rain* (his sixth album) and was discussing with Karlen critical and commercial responses to his then recently released follow-up, *Around the World in a Day*. Like Mitchell after *Court and Spark*, Prince did not take commercial appeal into consideration much and did not seem too concerned about not selling as many records. "The same people who bought *1999* bought *Around the World in a Day*," he reasoned. At the time, both albums had sold close to three million copies, compared to nine million for *Purple Rain*. "I'd rather have people buy my music because they like it and not just digging it because it's hip," he continued, suggesting that he placed greater emphasis on making art that pleased himself than on multi-platinum sales.[16] Joni Mitchell, on her live album *Miles of Aisles*, her follow-up to *Court and Spark*, jokes from the stage about the pressure on musicians to repeat their own success that a painter does not face: "Nobody ever said to Van Gogh, 'paint a Starry Night again, man!' You know? He painted it and that was it." Significantly, Prince essentially said he did not want to make another *Purple Rain*. "Do you know how easy it would have been to open *Around the World in a Day* with the guitar solo that's on the end of 'Let's Go Crazy'?" he asks rhetorically. "I don't *want* to make an album like the earlier ones."[17]

In that same conversation with Neal Karlen for *Rolling Stone* in 1985, Prince spoke about his bandmates: "Lisa (Coleman) is like my sister. She'll press two notes with one finger, so the chord is a lot larger . . . she's into Joni Mitchell too."[18] Wendy and Lisa were themselves unabashed admirers of Mitchell, something that is reflected in the music that they made together with Prince, as well as on their own albums following their time with him.[19] Indeed, the mutual admiration of Mitchell shared by Prince and his Revolution bandmates Lisa Coleman and Wendy Melvoin—as well as Wendy's twin sister and one-time fiancée of Prince, Susannah—can be heard most tellingly on songs he recorded during their time together: "Sometimes It Snows in April," Starfish and Coffee," and "The Ballad of Dorothy Parker," the latter being one song in his catalog that name-checks Joni. In the recently unearthed "All My Dreams," from the same era (it was originally recorded for *Parade*), Wendy announces, "Lisa, I'm going to hand you the brush and you're going to paint the side of the train," at which point Coleman proceeds to do the aural equivalent of just that with the piano keys. It is a striking example in Prince's music of sounds imagined as colors. During that same prolific era (*Parade, Sign o' the Times*), Prince offered Joni Mitchell a song, "Emotional Pump." She turned it down, thanking him and saying it was probably a hit for someone else. Joni did not think she could sing it. Despite the song's musical merit—a spare, pounding Linn drum beat over a strong melody and hook, it's not hard to see why Joni did not connect with it. A sample of the odd (but not for Prince) lyrics: "I want you not just sexually/ Not just sexually/But in a way like a mother wants a child." In the sparse, demo-like "Why The Butterflies?" from 1983, the piano chords and phrasing owe a debt to Ms. Mitchell. One later-period Prince song that unmistakably bears Joni's influence is "Reflection," released digitally in 2003 (and later on *Musicology*) in which he gets nostalgic (briefly) for the laid back scene of his adolescence, specifically 1977, the era of *Don Juan's Reckless Daughter*: "Two sevens together, like time indefinite." Significantly, when Prince performed the song for the *Tavis Smiley Show*, he chose to have Melvoin accompany him. It was the first time the two had performed together in seventeen years.

It's hard to see green when there's so much blue.
—Prince's character (The Kid) in *Graffiti Bridge*

Prince once described his songwriting in terms of painting and revealed that he visualizes the sounds as colors. "Sometimes I'll be walking around and I'll hear the melody as if it were the first color in the painting," he said to Robert L. Doerschuk in an interview for *Musician* describing "The Holy River" (1997).[20] "If you believe in the first color and trust it, you can build your song from there," he continued. Of another track from *Emancipation*, "Soul Sanctuary," he said, "I'll have a color or a line in mind, and I'll keep switching things around until I get what I'm hearing in my head. Then I'll try to bring to Earth the color that wants to be with that first color."[21] Discussing his creative process using the "sounds as color" metaphor is certainly befitting the Prince mystique. In the 1997 *Musician* interview, Prince elaborated further on the process of songwriting, shifting the imagery from a color palette to a delivery room: "It's like having a baby, knowing that this baby wants to be with you. You're giving birth to the song."[22] Prince had compared his songs to children before, but here he is extending that metaphor and speaks of creating songs in terms of giving birth.

"Little Green" is another key song from Joni Mitchell's *Blue*. In it, the singer addresses the difficult subject of losing a child. In Joni's specific case, it meant having a daughter but giving her up for adoption, something she would allude to later in "Chinese Cafe/Unchained Melody" from *Wild Things Run Fast* (1982): "My child's a stranger. I bore her but I could not raise her." The narrative in "Little Green" is rich with nostalgia and imagined longing for an experience that now ultimately belongs to someone else: "There'll be crocuses to bring to school tomorrow . . . there'll be icicles and birthday clothes and sometimes there'll be sorrow." Here, Joni associates the titular color with the newness of life: "Just a little green like the color when the spring is born." Significantly, it's that same "green" that fuels her longing to get away in "River." Lyrically, despite the emotional difficulty of the situation, the speaker holds everything together with optimism and dignity: "You're sad and you're sorry but you're not ashamed." And she exhorts the daughter she does not know to "have a happy ending."[23] In November of 1996, Prince became a father for the first time, but the son born to him and his wife Mayte only lived for weeks. Prince was reticent to address the loss of their child, and only made an oblique reference to the tragedy in a song: "If you ever lose someone dear to you, never say the words 'they're gone. . .' they'll come back." Significantly, in that same song, he coins a phrase, "Chelsea afternoon," an intended nod to Mitchell's artistic influence on the acoustic guitar-driven singer/songwriter approach of the parent album, *The Truth*.[24]

SUBTERRANEAN BY YOUR OWN DESIGN

Fast-Forward: 1991. It's Thanksgiving week, and Joni Mitchell is setting the music charts on fire, in spirit at least. Prince Nelson and Prince Be of P.M. Dawn—both unabashed devotees of Ms. Mitchell—have scored number-one hits on the *Billboard* Hot 100, nearly back-to-back. While Prince and the NPG's "Cream" was in second place after two weeks at the top spot, "Set Adrift on Memory Bliss" by P.M. Dawn, in its rapid ascent toward the peak, was bumping up against it at number 3.[25] The catchy "Set Adrift" was loaded with pop culture references, some current and others more obscure, all of them *tres* cool at the dawn of the 1990s. For their breakthrough hit, P.M. Dawn sampled the beat from Dennis Edwards' 1984 song "Don't Look Any Further" and the main hook from Spandau Ballet's 1983 hit "True"; they name-dropped actress Christina Applegate (from *Married With Children*); and they quoted, of all things, Mitchell's "The Boho Dance" from *The Hissing of Summer Lawns*, a generally under-appreciated album in her catalog, but one which Prince Rogers Nelson claimed to truly admire. "Joni, help me, I think I'm falling . . ." P.M. Dawn would sing two years later in another top-ten hit ("Looking Through Patient Eyes"), taking their cue from Prince's interpolation of "Help Me" in "The Ballad of Dorothy Parker," a song in which Joni's hit from *Court and Spark* is purported to be the protagonist's favorite. Another song on P.M. Dawn's 1993 release *The Bliss Album . . . ?* samples "I Had A King" from Joni's first album.

Prince was fairly straightforward in his devotion to Joni, as was P.M. Dawn in their love of Prince. The group covered Prince's "1999" as part of their "Fantasia's Confidential Ghetto" medley on their album *Jesus Wept*. Prince Be, asked by *Rolling Stone* in 1993 if he had ever met "a feather that could crack a nut," replied, "Once. His name was Prince. And he was funky." Such tribute by triangulation prefigured somewhat of a Joni Mitchell revival in the early 1990s. Her 1994 album, *Turbulent Indigo*, had been her best-reviewed work in decades and was awarded two Grammys, including one for Best Pop Album. After several years of underwhelming appeal, including a string of albums released on the Geffen label, Joni Mitchell once again had critical and commercial clout. The following year, "Big Yellow Taxi" from *Ladies of the Canyon* (1970) appeared on the soundtrack to *Friends*, the most popular television sitcom of the decade, alongside hits from Hootie and the Blowfish and the Rembrandts. In another telling example of Joni's being tapped into the cultural zeitgeist, in late 1997, Janet Jackson scored a number three R&B/hip-hop hit with "Got 'til It's Gone." The main hook of the song, produced by one-time Prince protégés Jimmy Jam and Terry Lewis, was an interpolation of the aforementioned "Big Yellow Taxi." Taking the lead from their musical mentor, Prince's disciples did not hesitate to publicly acknowledge both their love for Joni and her influence on their own work.

RAISED ON ROBBERY

"I don't think Prince is an innovator. He's a great hybrid," Mitchell told *Rolling Stone* in 1991 when asked about the Minneapolis superstar.[26] Prince had the talent to absorb his influences, then turn around and produce something from them that sounded fresh and original. Prince's love and appreciation for Mitchell has cropped up over the years, sometimes in unexpected places. In the unreleased track "Lust U Always," Prince says that his fourth-grade teacher's name was "Joni." The name of Prince's fictional boss in "Raspberry Beret," his 1985 hit, is "Mr. McGee," and is lifted from a song, "Paprika Plains," that comprises an entire side of Joni's *Don Juan's Reckless Daughter*. In his film, *Under the Cherry Moon* (1986), the cover of *Hejira* can be seen on display in Christopher's bedroom, alongside records by Miles Davis (*You're Under Arrest*) and Sheila E. ("Sister Fate" twelve-inch single). The title of the third album by the Time, a Prince satellite act, is a borrowed lyric ("Ice Cream Castle") from Joni Mitchell's signature song, "Both Sides, Now."

The influence of Joni on Prince, even through his associated musical acts, often hides in plain sight. Moreover, Prince has done a number of things over the years that pay subtle tribute to Joni. His seductive pose on the inside sleeve of *1999*, his fifth record, shows the artist lying on a bed poised with canvas and paintbrush, his backside partially showing under the cover. Joni Mitchell, inside the gatefold of her fifth record, *For the Roses*, is photographed standing on a rock naked, her bare bottom exposed. On the same Prince album, his band, the Revolution, is credited (backward) only on the hand-drawn artwork by Prince himself, but not on the spine or record label. Joni Mitchell has drawn or painted a number of her album covers, and on her 1974 live album, *Miles of Aisles*, also a double, her band, the L.A. Express, is credited *only* on the cover art and in Mitchell's own hand.[27] The "Oh, say can you see?" in Prince's 2004 single, "United States of Division," sounds like it comes straight out of Joni's "Don Juan's Reckless Daughter."[28] And the "Amen" at the end of "The Sacrifice of Victor" from Prince's 1992 album bears an uncanny similarity to the vocal coda at the end of Joni's "Rainy Night House" from *Ladies of the Canyon* (1970). Compare also the following: "Tell those girls that you've got Joni, she's coming back home" (Joni, from "Blue Motel Room"); "If anybody asks you, you belong to Prince" (Prince, from "Private

Joy"); "I met a woman, she had a mouth like yours" (Joni, from "A Case of You"); "Excuse me but I need a mouth like yours" (Prince, from "Let's Pretend We're Married"). Even in burglary, Prince was meticulous.

Despite his expressed devotion to Joni, Prince's covers of her songs were rare. In 1990 on the *Nude* tour, Joni's "Blue Motel Room," the playful, saucy blues from *Hejira*, was performed on at least one occasion. In 2002, Prince and the band spent hours rehearsing "Twisted," the 1959 Annie Ross song covered by Joni on *Court and Spark*, but only played it at one gig on that tour. Moreover, Joni herself is known to have guested onstage with Prince at least once, at a show in Denver in 1986. Prince's most well-known Mitchell cover is "A Case of You," which he played for the first time live in 1983 (at the hometown gig where "Purple Rain" made its debut) and released on *One Nite Alone . . .* some nineteen years later. The latter version was also contributed to a Joni Mitchell tribute album in 2007. An early version of the song had surfaced on an intimate cassette recording and circulated unofficially for decades before finally being issued in 2018. Prince has said, "It's one of my favorite songs two sing because the melody is so heartbreaking."[29] He credits her use of the dulcimer, her style and technique for giving the recording "such a haunting feel that it would make even the hardest thug shed tears." In all of his renditions, Prince opts to begin the song at the second verse: "I am a lonely painter, I live in a box of paints." In a way, that deliberate choice seems appropriate for Prince. Perhaps he connected with that image of the "lonely painter" but didn't have a use for what preceded it. In 2002, after his conversion to the Jehovah's Witnesses, Prince consistently changed Joni's "I'm frightened by the devil" to "I *used to be* frightened by the devil," making it consistent with his own beliefs. He also omits the song's third verse: "I met a woman . . . she knew your devils and your deeds." It's a case of Prince knowing exactly *what* he wants to say and exactly *the way* he wants to say it, and making sure the words are a reflection of that.[30]

In the opening verse of Joni's "A Case of You," the singer tells her beloved, whom she has just accused of being "constantly in the darkness,": "If you want me I'll be in the bar." Hence, the idea of drinking "a case of you" as opposed to a case of some other beverage. The lyrics are picturesque and emotionally open: "You're in my blood like holy wine, so bitter and so sweet." The narrative is descriptive: "On the back of a cartoon coaster, in the blue TV screen light/I drew a map of Canada, Oh, Canada! with your face sketched on it twice." The expression "cartoon coaster" is puzzling at first. Then you realize that a drink coaster might typically be made out of cardboard, that the French word for "cardboard" is "carton," and then you guess that maybe she is using a mix of English and French as is often done in parts of Joni's native Canada, singing "carton" like "cartoon." Whatever is going on here, you get the impression that the singer is attempting to describe a scenario and not finding the exact words. Joni claims she can handle her lover's deficiency, but she betrays a vulnerability—*I may still be on my feet, but I'm feeling a bit tipsy*. And there's the double entendre of the title: a "case" of you, like it's a medical condition. All of this draws you in and invites you to appreciate the song *on its own terms* or not at all. It is surely one of the most quirkily intimate songs in hers or anyone's catalog. Back when Prince first covered it in 1983, "A Case of You" was a deep cut from *Blue*. In the years since it has come to be regarded as a key song in Joni Mitchell's canon.

LOST IN TRANSLATION: HOW YOU SAY?

In "I Wonder U," a song from his 1986 album *Parade*, Prince does something akin to what Joni does in "A Case of You." Something uniquely intimate is expressed in misspeaking the precise words. Prince "exquisitely captures that notion of 'lost in translation' superbly," says Simon Williams.[31] Although "I Wonder U" was recorded in Los Angeles, "the European vibe is clearly apparent."[32] And lest anyone consider it an interlude or mere segue to the better-known songs on *Parade*, the singular genius of "I Wonder U" comes out in *the way* the words are rendered in this brief number (it runs only a minute and 40 seconds), however quirky or misspoken:

> The pause between "I" and "how you say" indicates the foreignness of the language or, perhaps, an internal dialogue—a person searching for the right word or words. And then there is the kicker "I wonder you." Wonder—noun, a reaction to something that is beautiful. A word that indicates thought, consideration, preoccupation. A simply genius, foreign conceptualisation of the word love. Easy to understand how a non-native speaker may mistake this word for the one they wanted. Beyond that, it is also a word often used synonymously with adoration or awe. Here, the singer is conveying a sense of complete devotion to his beloved. The phrasing of each of the lines indicates this struggle to translate a compelling feeling; love, dreams, a constancy of desire and need. "Though, you are far, I wonder you, you're on the mind." It's beautiful the way the struggle is summed up in a misspoken colloquialism that reinforces the fixed presence of the object in the thoughts of the singer.[33]

In its full brilliance and odd charm, "I Wonder U" could speak for all of *Parade*. Like Joni Mitchell's *Hejira* a decade earlier, Prince's album exudes the air of its geography; *Hejira* is a travelogue, *Parade* is a blend of continental sophistication—the accompanying film was shot in Nice, France—and earthy funk. Prince's soundtrack album to *Under the Cherry Moon* was more warmly received by European audiences than by those in his native America, where it was a platinum hit[34] but was still considered a "difficult" record. Much of its appeal got lost in translation back in 1986. In the time since, its estimation has grown, and *Parade* is considered a benchmark album in Prince's catalog.

EPILOGUE: NO REGRETS, COYOTE

"I've been traveling so long, how'm I ever going to know my home," Joni Mitchell asks in "Black Crow," from her album *Hejira*. Another song on the same album, "Coyote," deals with romance between two people who, despite the physical chemistry, are worlds apart: "We just come from such different sets of circumstances." She is the road warrior-musician; he is a local rancher. She imagines him starting work just as she is getting home from an all-nighter in the studio. To Joni, the artist/musician is a different breed with a unique perspective. On *Hejira*, she expresses that perspective with eloquence and verve. A one-night stand may not be ideal, but there are no regrets in the end.

> I'm porous with travel fever. But you know I'm so glad to be on my own.
> —Joni Mitchell, from "Hejira"

The roving desire to create, to paint, to write, to play, to sing; in a manner of speaking, to recount the experience of moving clouds: *this* is the ethos of the artist. You live differently and you love differently. In a wry, self-mocking way Prince sings in "Guitar" (2007) about romance being interrupted by the urge to record music: "I got that call, so I jumped in my car/I love u baby, but not like I love my guitar." He has also talked about the blessing and curse of always hearing in his head. "When you're called, you're called," Prince told Charles Johnson, aka The Electrifying Mojo in 1986. "I walk around and go to the bathroom and try to brush my teeth and all of the sudden the toothbrush starts vibrating!" he says, suggesting that the creative muse can inspire even in the most mundane setting.[35]

You dream differently too. In another song on *Hejira*, Joni says she had a dream of flying, but like the aviator of the song's title, "Amelia," her's was "just a false alarm." In his own flying-in-a-dream song from 2010, Prince elaborates on a similar idea, albeit with a different result. Able to pilot the flight with his thoughts, he achieves oneness with everyone and everything and the result is universal music in perfect harmony: "Every living soul sang the most beautiful melody ever sung" ("Future Soul Song").

> We got high on travel, and we got drunk on alcohol. And on love the
> strongest poison and medicine of them all.
> —Joni Mitchell (from "A Strange Boy")

> Yellow sunrise over their bodies in bed, two people in love with noth-
> ing but the road ahead.
> —Prince (from "Rock and Roll Love Affair")

Hejira, which means "exodus" or "migration," is Arabic in origin and typi-cally refers to the flight of the prophet Muhammad from Mecca to Medina in 622, an event that marks the start of the Muslim era. It is related to the word for making a pilgrimage, *hajj*. Thus, *Hejira* has the connotation of not just travel but religious obligation. It is a fitting title for an album of road songs, particularly for Joni Mitchell, who approaches art and expression with something akin to religious devotion. Ultimately, that approach is what her most accomplished musical disciple, Prince Rogers Nelson, learned well and displayed in his own body of work. "Rock and Roll Love Affair," released in 2012,[36] would easily fit on an album of road songs, a la *Hejira*, had Prince released one of his own. Like the mismatched lovers in "Coyote," the pair in Prince's song are subject to the pitfalls of romance on the road: "She believed in fairy tales and princes, he believed in the sounds coming from his stereo. He believed in rock and roll." The road warrior-musician is like a pilgrim; or as Joni sings in "Coyote," "a prisoner of the white lines on the freeway"; one who is perpetually on the move, an acute observer and charter of change; one who shares the experience with others by creating art that is both sonically rich and visually vibrant.

Notes

1. https://www.facebook.com/jonimitchell/.

2. "The Color Indigo: The Color of Intuition, Perception and the Higher Mind," Empowered by Color, accessed January 3, 2023, https://www.empower-yourself-with-color-psychology.com/color-indigo.html.

3. Additionally, the covers of *Clouds, Wild Things Run Fast, Dog Eat Dog, Turbulent Indigo, Taming the Tiger, Both Sides Now, Travelogue, The Beginning of Survival* and *Dreamland* are all self-portraits.

4. Fr. Marc Boulos says that in the Bible, there is hope in the destruction of what human beings construct because we are ultimately only interested in the things that God constructs. https://ephesusschool.org/hope-in-destruction/.

5. "Prince's Debut TV Interview from 1985." MTV, April 21, 2016, https://www.mtv.com/video-clips/ev9cwl/mtv-news-prince-s-debut-tv-interview-from-1985.

6. Jon Bream, *Prince: Inside the Purple Reign* (New York: Macmillan, 1984), 19.

7. Bream, *Prince*, 21.

8. Bream, *Prince*, 25.

9. Bream, *Prince*, 25.

10. Bream, *Prince*, 17.

11. Lindsay Zoladz, "Remarkable Records of Joni Mitchell's Changes," *New York Times*, October 30, 2020, https://www.nytimes.com/2020/10/29/arts/music/joni-mitchell-archives-early-years.html.

12. Steve Marsh, "The Press," *MPLS St. Paul Magazine*, December 2016, 86.

13. "[RETRO REVIEW] Around the World in a Daze: Rolling Stone Album Review of Prince's Around the World in a Day Album by Jon Pareles June 6, 1985 @furthermucker @gonzomike @zaheerali @questlove," Soulhead, July 23, 2014, https://www.soulhead.com/2014/07/23/retro-review-around-world-daze-rolling-stone-album-review-princes-around-world-day-album-jon-pareles-june-6-1985/.

14. Anthony DeCurtis, "Free at Last," *Rolling Stone*, November 28, 1996.

15. Mark Savage, "Prince's Sign o' the Times: An Oral History," BBC News, September 24, 2020, https://www.bbc.com/news/entertainment-arts-54203180.

16. Neal Karlen, "Prince Talks: The Silence Is Broken," *Rolling Stone*, September 12, 1985, https://www.rollingstone.com/music/music-news/prince-talks-the-silence-is-broken-58812/.

17. Karlen, "Prince Talks."

18. Karlen, "Prince Talks."

19. The pair would use the phrase "White Flags of Winter Chimneys" from *Hejira*'s title track for the title of their 2009 album.

20. Robert L. Doerschuk, "The Sound of Emancipation," Musician (April 1997), https://sites.google.com/site/themusicinterviewarchive/prince/prince-1997-musician-magazine-interview.

21. Doerschuk, "The Sound of Emancipation."

22. Doerschuk, "The Sound of Emancipation."

23. In 1997, Joni and her daughter were reunited.

24. "Chelsea Morning" is the second song on Joni's album *Clouds* (1969).

25. The reign of the two Princes was interrupted by Michael Bolton's cover of Percy Sledge's "When a Man Loves a Woman."

26. David Wild, "A Conversation with Joni Mitchell," *Rolling Stone*, May 30, 1991, https://www.rollingstone.com/music/music-news/a-conversation-with-joni-mitchell-172726/.

27. Miles of Aisles includes a song called "Love or Money." Prince would release his own song with the same title in 1986.

28. Listen at approximately the 3:00 mark.

29. *Joni Mitchell: Songs Chosen by Her Friends & Fellow Musicians*. Hear Music, 2005.

30. He also altered the lyric "when you know you're a wizard at three" to "a *genius* at three" from "Twisted" in 2002, presumably out of similar religious objections.

31. Simon Williams, "I Wonder U," Simon Williams Blog, April 16, 2016, https://simonc williamsblog.wordpress.com/2016/04/16/i-wonder-u/?fbclid=IwAR08hpYmIjcT3YI7KQM VkSTl32Ybw3YIek-xeMYEijAK_cIM0cx_3JTuXY4.

32. Wiliams, "I Wonder U."

33. Williams, "I Wonder U."

34. It reached #3 in the US behind Whitney Houston and Patti LaBelle; and "Kiss" was a #1 single on three *Billboard* charts.

35. Mcmorris55, "Electrifying Mojo Prince Interview," YouTube, April 21, 2009, https://www.youtube.com/watch?v=NJZCoxZ5COY.

36. A different version appeared on his final album, *Hitnrun Phase Two* in 2015.

Chapter 5

BEFORE THE REVOLUTION

A Conversation with Gayle Chapman

JUDSON L. JEFFRIES

In late January 1980, Prince, accompanied by five bandmates, made his television debut on *American Bandstand*. A staple of American culture, having aired for more than thirty years by the time Prince appeared on the program, was a highly sought-after opportunity by many musical artists who endeavored to appeal to a young audience. Prince's appearance was sandwiched between two fairly noteworthy events: President Jimmy Carter's announcement that the US would not participate in the 1980 summer Olympic games and the international debut of the Rubik's Cube, a mind-bending and frustrating piece of square shaped plastic, that for reasons unknown to this writer, gained a large following.

Prince's band consisted of six members. Among them stood the lone woman behind what appeared to be multiple keyboards. The incredibly talented and sumptuously beautiful Gayle Chapman stood out in grand fashion. However, in the eyes of my peers, they were given short shrift in terms of Gayle's on-air camera time. Sometime in 2017, after the publication of the special issue of the *Journal of African American Studies* devoted solely to Prince's work and legacy, this writer had the pleasure of making Gayle's acquaintance. The years have been kind to Gayle, as the only thing that seems to have changed much since 1980 is the color of her hair. Had someone the imagination and foresight to posterize Gayle as was the case with sex symbols Farah Fawcett and Bo Derek, such a venture would have likely proved quite lucrative. Despite her movie star looks, the twentysomething Chapman was, unfortunately, positioned on the far right of the television screen and outside of the frame for much of the telecast.

What appears below is material extrapolated from a year-long conversation that began and occurred off and on since the spring of 2020.

Judson L. Jeffries: Gayle, did you realize that for a period of time you were a heartthrob among a certain cohort of young men?

Gayle Chapman: Really, no, I didn't realize that.

JLJ: Oh yeah; I don't remember boys my age talking much about white female musical artists around that time. You were among a small group of white women artists that caught the attention of those in my age cohort and probably older. They were Teena Marie, whom I didn't realize wasn't Black until much later, and Deborah Harry of Blondie.

GC: Wow, I would have never known that, I wasn't nearly as visible as those other women.

JLJ: No, you weren't, but what happened after that *American Bandstand* episode is guys started to wonder who you were and started asking around. Guys started doing their own research, whatever that consisted of, since Google wasn't around. Still guys were able to look you up and find out little tidbits about you, probably from magazines and whatnot.

GC: Ok, that's really interesting, I had no idea. Were you one of those guys?

JLJ: Yeah, I was one of those guys!

But let's move on. I understand that you're in process of writing your memoirs, how far along are you?

GC: I'm in the preliminary stages, but I'm having fun recalling people, places, and events that I hadn't thought about for some time.

JLJ: Speaking of your memoirs, what was your reaction when you found out you were going to be on *American Bandstand*?

GC: Oh yeah, of course, I was excited.

JLJ: Were you super excited? I mean this is *American Bandstand*.

GC: I don't know if I was super excited, but I was excited . . . I grew up watching it as a kid.

JLJ: What about your parents and other relatives? What did they have to say when they heard you were going to be on the show?

GC: I don't remember anyone make a big deal out of it.

JLJ: That's really hard to believe. This is Dick Clark's *American Bandstand*; how could they not realize that this was a big deal? I mean it's not *Soul Train*, but still.

GC: Yeah, I don't remember anyone in my family making a big deal about it.

JLJ: Ok, so tell me about the *American Bandstand* experience; were you guys lip synching?

GC: Yes, we were lip synching.

JLJ: What was the deal with Prince that day?

GC: What do you mean?

JLJ: I mean, what was the deal with his behavior? Why was he trying hard to be eccentric?

GC: I don't know, maybe he thought that people would find that intriguing. What I remember is that Prince told us we were not to smile or speak. Other than saying our names I don't think we said anything.

JLJ: The one thing I do remember is Prince seeming to take exception to Dick Clark saying, "This is not the kind of music that comes out of Minneapolis."

GC: Yeah, Prince didn't like that, he was a bit put off by that.

JLJ: Ok, anyway, tell me something about your upbringing. Where did you grow up?

GC: I grew up in Duluth, Minnesota.

JLJ: Where is Duluth?

GC: Minnesota.

JLJ: I know that, what part of Minnesota?

GC: [Laughter] Oh, the northeastern part of the state.

JLJ: What did your household look like?

GC: I grew up with both parents and my siblings in a three-story house with a basement.

JLJ: How many siblings do you have?

GC: I have a brother and a sister.

JLJ: What else?

GC: We were churchgoing people, my dad was a deacon in the Presbyterian church three doors down from our house. We always went to the church nearest where we lived. I would get invited to play at other religious institutions with friends to play guitar and sing, and each of us would get paid fifty dollars per service.

JLJ: Fifty bucks was a lot of money back then.

GC: Yes, it was for a young teenager.

JLJ: What did your father and mother do for a living?

GC: My father was a general agent for Northwestern Mutual Life Insurance. My mother was a homemaker.

JLJ: Tell me something interesting about your mother?

GC: Like what?

JLJ: Like, anything?

GC: Ok, well, she was a concert cellist, she loved the arts, the opera, the ballet. Her influence on my life is profound.

JLJ: Wow, now that's interesting!

GC: She was an interesting person, for sure.

JLJ: Ok, what were you like as a young person?

GC: How young?

JLJ: I'm talking about high school.

GC: I didn't like high school.

JLJ: I didn't ask if you liked it, I asked what were you like?

GC: Well, I'm telling you that I didn't like it! Plus, I was an introvert, then and now.

JLJ: Why were you an introvert?

GC: I don't know, I just was. I think most people are a bit introverted until they gain life experience and grow into their level of performance and gain confidence. For instance, other than playing music at a church as a young person, I was never introduced to other professions by my parents, other than what they did . . . which was insurance and homemaking. So, like most people, I didn't start to really grow until I went to college and work outside the home.

JLJ: For those who might be familiar with Duluth, tell me what high school you attended?

GC: Duluth East High School.

JLJ: What instruments do you play besides keyboard?

GC: I play guitar and the piano.

JLJ: Man, oh man, I thought I did my homework on you, I didn't know you played the piano.

GC: Oh, I loved playing the piano when I was growing up, but I spent most of my time playing the guitar . . . I spent five hours a day practicing the guitar.

JLJ: Did you play any other instruments?

GC: I tried the banjo . . . didn't like it.

JLJ: When did you realize you were musically inclined?

GC: Well, my mother says that I was writing my own little ditties at 2 years of age.

JLJ: Who were some of your favorite artists?

GC: Earth, Wind & Fire, Frank Zappa, Marvin Gaye and the Isley Brothers, Ronnie Laws, Joni Mitchell, Bonnie Raitt, George Duke and George Benson.

JLJ: Who were some of the artists that influenced you?

GC: Joni Mitchell and George Benson are two I can think of right off the top of my head.

JLJ: Tell me something that is very interesting of which relatively few people are aware?

GC: Ok, I got straight As in chorus in high school.

JLJ: I said something interesting.

GC: That is interesting.

JLJ: Maybe to you.

GC: Ok, I was the youngest person to sing in the opera chorus for *Lucia Di Lammermoor* as well as *Carmen* with the New York Metropolitan Opera when they came through Duluth, Minnesota. I was fourteen and fifteen, as they came two years in a row.

JLJ: Wow, that's very interesting, very interesting indeed.

GC: Told you.

JLJ: Let's transition to Prince.

GC: Ok.

JLJ: How did you hook up with him?

GC: Chazz Smith, whom I knew, introduced me to him.

JLJ: Chazz is his cousin, right?

GC: Yes, Chazz is Prince's cousin.

JLJ: Did you audition for Prince?

GC: Yes, I did.

JLJ: Did things go well?

GC: Well, I ended up playing with him, so yes, I would say everything went well.

JLJ: Ok, I don't wanna get too deep into this, otherwise it might take away from your book, but what was the name of the band back then.

GC: I don't think we had a name because I don't think we were officially a band.

JLJ: What do you mean by that?

GC: What do you mean, what do I mean by that?

JLJ: What do you mean you weren't officially a band? Do you mean, you weren't officially a band like some say that the Monkees weren't officially a band? Why were you not a band?

GC: Well, I'll just speak for myself. I thought of myself as one of Prince's employees. When someone is interviewing and auditioning musicians, there is a vetting process, whether it's intentional or not. You have to be a team player and be willing to follow the leader. If you can't, you don't last long in high ego environments.

JLJ: Oh, I see.

GC: Do you?

JLJ: Did the others share that same viewpoint?

GC: I think a few of them did. We never considered ourselves as equal partners, that was never a consideration.

JLJ: Do you have a title in mind for your book yet?

GC: Yes, I'm thinking of calling it *My Respectful Memories of Prince*.

JLJ: That's lame.

GC: [Laughter] I like it.

JLJ: Like I said, it's lame.

GC: Do you have any experience in this area?

JLJ: Actually, I do. I've written eight books, all of which have catchy and appropriate titles.

GC: Well, then come up with a title for my book.

JLJ: I just might do that.

GC: Let me know when you do. Thanks much!

Chapter 6

FROM THE EARLY DAYS OF ROCK AND ROLL TO THE MINNEAPOLIS SOUND AND BEYOND

Pepé Willie Talks about His Life in the Business

TONY KIENE

(This is part two of a two-part interview.)

Tony Kiene: So after all that, you lose your record deal. I can't imagine the letdown.

Pepé Willie: I didn't want to see or hear from anybody. I didn't even want to leave my place. Turned the shades down. It was devastating. I know that Prince felt bad for me. At the same time, he was being courted by some of the major labels out in Hollywood. So as bad as I felt for myself, I couldn't help but be happy for him.

TK: What brought you out of your funk?

PW: I got a call from a friend, Tony Sylvester, Panama Tony they called him. Also known as Champagne Tony, an original member of the Main Ingredient, along with Donald McPherson, Luther Simmons, and later Cuba Gooding Sr. Tony was going to produce an album for the Imperials and needed some material. So he asks me if I knew any musicians that he could use. I said, "Do I ever. I've got two of the baddest cats you'll ever find."

I asked Prince and André [Cymone] if they wanted to go to New York with me. They said yeah and off we went. Prince and André put up, all expenses paid, at the New York Hilton. I stayed with Ike at his place in Harlem. Prince shouldn't have been there because I'm pretty sure by now he'd signed with Warner Bros. But any chance he got to play he was going to do it. You couldn't tell Prince no. He lived music, every day, even back then.

TK: What did Tony think of Prince and André?

PW: Oh, oh, oh. Let me tell you. He said, "Pepé. You were right. These guys are great." We were in the Sound Palace in Manhattan. André had this song he was working on, "Thrill You or Kill You." I think Prince was in the early stages of composing "I Feel for You." And I wrote "If You Feel Like Dancin'" while we were there. There was a lot of other stuff we did as well. But at the end of the day, for some reason, the sessions didn't really work out. So Prince, André, and I retrieved all the music. Kept it for ourselves. Some of the songs would later make up much of the 94 East Album, *Minneapolis Genius*, which featured Prince on every song and André on all but one.

Then, there was this song that I had written with Ike and Tony. It was for the Imperials, which they recorded and eventually released. Are you ready for this? It was called "Fast Freddie the Roller Disco King." Skating rinks were a big thing at that time. Anyway, we recorded all the music and we scrapped the vocals. It became "One Man Jam," which was an appropriate title because Prince played just about everything on it. Dré played bass and I added some percussion, but that's it.

TK: Wasn't there some controversy over the ownership of that song?

PW: Was there ever. Tony and Ike got into this dispute over how much each of us contributed and what portion of the songwriting credits we all should get. I decided I'm not going to fight over percentages. So I just took my name off it altogether and let them split the rights to it fifty-fifty. I don't know if they ever would have stopped arguing about it otherwise.

TK: April 1978. Prince releases his debut album *For You*. What were you doing at this time?

PW: Everything I could to help him. I didn't have a deal anymore; he did. So I decided to dedicate all my time toward whatever Prince needed. I started to work closely with Owen, who became Prince's first manager. Sometime after the album came out, Owen, his wife, and myself jumped in his Honda Accord and headed to Chicago. We visited a lot of record shops on the South Side, hung posters, did some additional promotional things. Some people thought Prince was going to be there too. "No," we told them, "We are just here to promote the album, pass out some Prince book covers to the kids." You know, things like that.

As soon as we get back to Minneapolis, Prince asks me how it went. I said it was great and all, and I let him know that the radio stations were playing his record all the time. Then I said, "You know what you should do, Prince. Call some of these stations and thank them for playing your music. Then, whenever you do a show there, maybe you can do a voice over for them or shout out their call letters from the stage, something."

TK: Prince's response to that?

PW: He looks at me as only he could and asks, "Do you think it's a hit?" My mind starts spinning, and I go, "What? What are you talking about?" He says, "The album. Do you think it's a hit?" I'm like sure, of course it's a hit. Prince says, "Then I don't need to call them."

TK: Well, we know Prince never lacked confidence.

PW: For sure. Still, there were some bumps back in those early days.

TK: Such as?

PW: Well, for example, sometime later I took him on this promotional thing in Charlotte. We visited one of the radio stations, and he did an in-store signing at the Soul Shack. Tomi Jenkins from Cameo was also there to promote their album. But Tomi, bless his heart, had ten, maybe twenty people at most in his line. Prince had hundreds, maybe thousands. They lined up out the door and around the block—all teenage girls or women in their twenties.

Eventually, things started to get a little wild. Security seemed kind of lax, so I whispered to Prince that maybe we should think about calling it a day. I've seen what can happen in these situations. But he was so intent on signing every single autograph. From the very beginning, he would do whatever he could for his fans.

I understood, but then I said, "Next time I tap you on the shoulder, that means we're outta here." He nodded. The scene became even crazier, so I tapped him, he jumped up, and we were through the rear door and into the car. Back at the hotel, his mood turned solemn. "Pepé. I'm starting to feel like a piece of meat," he told me. I wasn't sure what to say at first, but I let him know this likely wouldn't be the last time something like this happened.

TK: *For You* has been out a couple months, now Prince has to put a band together.

PW: Automatically, André was in. There was no question there. He and Prince were basically brothers, after all. Bobby's in next, who gets Matt [Fink] an audition. It was Prince's cousin Chazz who brought Gayle Chapman into the mix. And then Dez Dickerson, who'd already started to make a name for himself around town, rounded things out. That was Prince's first band after he was signed to—Warner Bros.

TK: How do those early rehearsals go?

PW: Well, at first. They set up at Del's Tire Mart on the West Bank, but someone robbed the place and made off with a lot of the gear, which had to be replaced. I told Prince and André, "You guys are going to rehearse at my house. No one's coming up in there to do nothing."

TK: So it was settled?

PW: Pretty much. The band spent the better part of the next six months in my basement studio: twelve hours a day, nearly every day. From 10 a.m. to 10 p.m. Then, we had to kick them out. They may have never left if we hadn't.

TK: What were those days like?

PW: So much fun. At least for Kristie, Marcy, and me. Prince worked those guys hard. And there were times they'd all get a little frustrated. I always made it a point to remind them that they had the opportunity of a lifetime. Prince was signed, they weren't. They were there to support him and Prince's success would ultimately result in their own.

TK: Do you think they believed that at the time?

PW: Yes, I do. It was always obvious that André and Dez would eventually go off to do their own thing. They were natural front men themselves. There was a small period of time that summer when Prince was out in Los Angeles tending to something. So during the break, I took Dez to New York so he could work on some of his own stuff.

Although I don't know how, Prince found out while he was still out west. He's not happy and calls me in New York. I think he said, "What are you doing with Dez? He's my guitarist." My response was I'm doing the same thing for him that I did for you and André when I took you out to New York. I was just helping him out. Prince still didn't like it, but hey, he got over it.

TK: While they were in your house all that time, did you continue to talk to Prince and the band about the business side of things?

PW: Absolutely, as much as I could. Prince was so far ahead of the game for someone his age. He'd thought a lot about publishing already. And, one day I said, "You know. It's time to create your own publishing company." So we requested the necessary paperwork from BMI [Broadcast Music, Inc.], filled out the forms, and mailed them back. A few weeks later, Prince's first publishing company, ECNIRP Music, was officially incorporated.

Another week or two goes by when Prince receives a letter, along with those same forms from his attorneys in LA. It comes with a bill for $900. That's what they were going to charge him to set up his publishing. Since I was responsible for all his mail, I was the first to see it. I go down to the basement, show this to him, and say, "This is the type of thing you have to watch out for. Your people are trying to get $900 out of you for something you've already taken care of for the price of a stamp." Which back then was what, maybe eleven, twelve cents?

TK: Wow! What a lesson that was. What do you think that meant to him?

PW: I always believed that Prince trusted me. Still, in that moment, I think it made him feel safe, protected. I hope so, anyway. And maybe, just maybe, he thought to himself, "Yeah. Pepé knows what he's talking about."

TK: Rehearsals can't go on forever. How do Prince's first professional gigs come about?

PW: It was getting close to the end of the year, 1978. Prince comes to me and says, "We're ready. I want to do a show." I agreed with him. The band was ready. Owen agreed. So we were like, "Okay. Let's do it." We settled on The Capri Theater on West Broadway. Kristie, Marcy, and I took care of everything locally. All the promotion. Renting the proper lighting. Whatever was needed.

Kristie designed and printed all the tickets. Now, originally there were supposed to be three shows. Friday, Saturday, and Sunday night in early January. Owen had made arrangements with Warner Bros. to bring in all their top brass. The idea being to make one of the gigs a sort of a showcase for the label. People like Russ Thyret, Barry Gross. Mo Ostin [president of Warner Bros.] might have even been there too.

TK: For that showcase, legendary local deejay, the late Kyle Ray, gives the introduction by declaring, "Ladies and gentleman . . . The Power. The Glory. The Minneapolis Story. Prince!" But that night didn't quite go as planned, did it?

PW: I thought it was good. The girls did too. So did Chazz. Jon Bream gave it a good review in the paper. But Warner Bros. didn't think Prince was ready to tour. There were some technical issues that didn't help that night. But still, anybody who was there had to know—it's just a matter of time. Prince was too talented to keep down much longer.

TK: How did Prince take it?

PW: Hard. He wanted to get right to work on the next album. But there were some other issues then too. He and Owen had a falling out. I agreed to become Prince's interim manager, but I told him from go, this was only temporary. I was not a manager and didn't want to become one. Prince needed a professional.

So I took him to Miami, where I was able to get him signed with Don Taylor, Bob Marley's longtime manager. That didn't last long and I never found out why. Tony Winfrey and Perry Jones stepped in from Warner Bros., for a while at least. Then eventually, Prince ended up with (Bob) Cavallo, (Joe) Ruffalo, and (Steve) Fargnoli. That was his classic management team through the next decade or so. I felt he was in pretty good hands by this time.

TK: Is that when you stepped away a little bit?

PW: Sounds about right. When *Dirty Mind* came out, that's when I made the decision to leave the Prince camp, so to speak. I didn't really like what he was doing on that record. The language caught me off guard, the overt sexual themes. That wasn't all. Like I said, he was in good hands, he was starting to establish himself. And, I still had my own thing to get back to.

TK: Did you continue to spend time with him then?

PW: Yes. Even though Shauntel and I weren't together, to me, Prince was family. Nothing was ever going to change that. In all those years, I never took a dime from him. No matter what, I was always going to be there to support him. Whatever he needed, he just had to ask.

TK: So what was your relationship like now?

PW: We still hung out whenever we could. Talked on the phone a lot. I used to call him on the road. He'd use the name Groucho (as in Groucho Marx) when he checked into hotels. The name he later used was Peter Brave-strong, but back in the early days it was Groucho.

I went to a lot of the parties he'd give. Birthday parties, regular parties, rehearsals, all kinds of stuff. We went all out for that one. He invited the three of us to the filming of the "1999" video. That was downtown at the Minneapolis Armory. We always went to see him play at First Avenue. There were so many great times.

TK: Since you mentioned 1999, allow me this segue. As we sit here talking, we're what, a week and a day from the super deluxe reissue of 1999. All told, there will be sixty-five songs on there, all of which were written by Prince, save one. That one song is yours. So, what would you like to say about that?

PW: That's takes me back. It had to be spring, summer of 1982, I think. The weather was decent—it had to be around that time. I was driving with Morris in his Mustang. The one Prince bought him actually. It was a big year for Morris. The Time's second record was about to come out. So was the Vanity 6 debut.

I don't remember exactly what Morris and I were up to. We were parked on the street downtown, near Kim Upsher's apartment. Kim was one of Prince's first real girlfriends. She was one of the First Avenue waitresses in *Purple Rain*, along with Jill Jones. So we're just sitting there on the street, when we notice Prince walking toward the car.

TK: Was that a surprise? For him to just be walking around downtown?

PW: Yeah, kind of, I suppose. He wasn't quite that big yet, even at home. But, sure. That seemed a bit unusual. Maybe he was there to see Kim. Not sure. But he approaches the driver side window and hands Morris this cassette. Morris pops it in the deck. I didn't recognize it at first. But then Morris goes, "Pepé. That's your song, that's your song." It was "If You See Me," from the Cookhouse Five. Prince was calling it "Do Yourself a Favor," though.

He reworked it, sped up the tempo, added this humorous little monologue at the end. I guess you'd call it a monologue. I don't know. Either way, it was funny as hell. It was clear he had a good time doing it. Anyway, he's still standing there and says, "Pepé. I'm going to put this on one of my albums."

So I'm like, "Yeah, man. That's great. Thanks a lot." We talked a bit more, and then he was gone. Off to wherever.

The amazing part of it all, to me at any rate, is that he must have done it all from memory. He didn't have access to the master tape, much less a copy of it. The song had never been released anywhere. It had been six years or more since we first recorded it. Unbelievable. The other thing was, the irony behind it, and I don't think I ever told him this, but the song was about his cousin Shauntel. It was a breakup song. Maybe he always suspected as much, I don't really know.

TK: Let's jump ahead a year or so. There's talk around town that Prince is doing a movie.

PW: I heard some rumblings and wondered: What was this all about? Then, out of the blue, Prince calls me up: "Pepé. I'm doing a movie and I got this part for you." He went on and said he wanted me to play the owner of this club, which of course is First Avenue. I was excited, you know, I was all in for this. But then a few weeks went by, then months, and I hadn't heard anything more from him.

Should I call him? Am I waiting for him to call me? Is there a script? What'd I miss? Then that fall, 1983, there were announcements on TV, radio about auditions for the film. I figured I knew my way around a movie set, so I went down and auditioned. I was cast as a Day Player just like I had been back on the Sonny Carson film.

TK: What did Prince say when he saw you?

PW: "Hi." Not much more. He never brought up the part again, which of course, went to Billy Sparks. I assumed he changed his mind. I was cool with it. I was just happy to be there.

TK: Were you part of a lot of scenes?

PW: Just a few. There was one scene that I filmed with Morris where we are sitting down in a club and we're watching this guy juggle knives up on stage. He keeps dropping them, so we're supposed to laugh at him. The director had heard Morris and I laughing together just around the set and that together, our laughs were hilarious. So that's how that came about.

TK: Obviously, that scene didn't make the cut.

PW: No. The only time I'm on screen is just for a split second. I'm one of the guys . . . after Prince does "Purple Rain" and runs back to his dressing room, I'm one of the people he passes in hallway. Last one, I'm pretty sure.

TK: Still, the experience must have been something.

PW: Absolutely. Since I already knew the Revolution, the Time, Dez and his band, the Modernaires, I hung out with those guys. When the other extras were eating boxed lunches, I went to eat with the Revolution. Mark, Matt, Bobby, Lisa and Wendy. Much better food.

TK: Was it apparent during filming that Prince and Morris were at odds with one another?

PW: There was some tension there, for sure. But I didn't really know anything about it. But as the film wraps, Prince and Morris get into this big argument. Prince says to Morris, something to the effect of, "You owe me." And Morris is like: "I owe you? I owe you? If anybody owes anybody, you owe Pepé."

My first thought is: "Okay, don't go bringing my name into this." I didn't know what it was about. After that, Morris left. I always thought he'd come back, but he never did. The Time was supposed to go out with Prince again on the *Purple Rain Tour*. But no. Morris was done.

TK: When did you next hear from him?

PW: The next time I talked to Morris was right before the movie came out. He called me from Los Angeles and tells me, "Pepé. Prince is trying to destroy me." I didn't know what he was talking about. But he was distraught. I flew to LA the next day. I had to help him. But I also wanted to figure out what was going on with him and Prince. Try and find a way to mend their relationship. It wasn't right, whatever it was. But, I couldn't make that happen.

Morris didn't even have a ticket to the *Purple Rain* premiere. This was going to be his coming out party, and he wasn't even invited. So I get out there and first thing we do is go see Mo Ostin at Warner Bros. He gives us three tickets to the premiere, one for Morris, one for his mom, and one for me. Mo even gave Morris and I money to buy some clothes.

TK: Yeah. I remember when Morris is interviewed on the red carpet, or purple carpet as it were, the two of you both had on white suits. Maybe yours was a little more cream colored.

PW: Yep. Courtesy of Mo Ostin.

TK: Clearly, Prince saw you that night.

PW: Yes. He never said anything, but he was definitely shocked to see us there.

TK: After the premiere party in Hollywood, what was next?

PW: I went to work helping Morris set up his team. Management, attorneys, accounts, PR, the whole thing. There had been requests to interview Morris about his part in the movie, but those inquiries went through Prince's people. Apparently, all the people looking to get to Morris were told he wasn't available.

I called a friend of mine, Dixie Whatley, at *Entertainment Tonight* and asked if she would like to talk to Morris. That was one of his first appearances.

Sandy Gallin, an all-time legend in the industry, was Morris's manager now. Sandy booked him all over the country. I must have accompanied Morris on eighty interviews that summer. *Rolling Stone, People Magazine*, David Letterman, Merv Griffin, CBS *Nightwatch*, and so on and so on.

TK: By 1985, Morris is on a solo deal with Warner Bros. He's becoming a star. Prince is the biggest star on the planet at this point. What were you up to that year?

PW: I was contemplating selling the rights to all the songs I'd recorded with Prince to Prince. It was thirteen or fourteen tracks from the 1970s I believe. But a friend of mine, Jeffrey Pink, who owned Hot Pink Records, suggested I put some of them out myself.

Sounded like a good idea, but I wanted Prince to know about it. He was so huge, so busy, it hard to reach him. So he called his manager at Warner Bros., Bob Cavallo. I explained what I was doing, that I wanted to get word to Prince. Bob said, "I don't think Prince would want to know about it." I couldn't understand why he said that, what he meant by it. But, oh well.

Of course, we paid Prince for all his contributions to the album. The checks were cashed. So, I figured we were good and didn't think too much more about it.

TK: When you're remastering those tracks, putting that first 94 East record together (*Minneapolis Genius: The Historic 1977 Recordings*), you receive another interesting call from another old friend. A friend who'd also left the Time in pursuit of a solo career.

PW: We were in New York, Tony Sylvester and I, putting the finishing touches on the album, when Jesse Johnson calls me up. I'm thinking how does he even know where I am. Regardless, he asks me if he could record "Do Yourself A Favor." I guess he heard Prince's version and really liked it. I thought about it for a second and decided yeah. "Go ahead and do it. Prince is never going release it." So Jesse put it on his *Shockadelica* album.

TK: Eventually, Prince hears about all of this. How does he take it?

PW: I didn't see Prince again until sometime around late 1985, early 1986. He'd been in France shooting another movie. So, I'm at First Avenue one night with some friends and Prince is there. He comes over to me, and I could tell he was pretty salty already. The first thing he wanted to know was why I didn't tell him about what I was doing with my album.

I let him know I called Bob, and that Bob told me you wouldn't want to know about it. So I said to him, "That's not on me. That's on your people. I tried to tell you." Then he quickly turned the subject to Jesse. Wanted to know why I gave Jesse permission to do the song. He says, "I was going to put that out." I soon came to regret my response. But at the moment I thought it was pretty funny. I asked him, "When were you planning to put it out? 1999?" Everybody around started to laugh. That made him madder and he walked off.

TK: What were you thinking after that?

PW: What have I done? In the dozen years or so since I started working with him, that was the first real serious argument I ever had with Prince. Our first real blow up. It was pretty upsetting. The next day my lawyer calls me from New York and says, "I heard you got into a fight with Prince at some nightclub." How in the world could he possibly know that? It wasn't even 24 hours ago. He said, "Word travels fast."

TK: When did you next see Prince?

PW: It was at Bobby Z's house. Bobby was having a party and I assumed Prince would be there at some point. He walks in later. I'm a little nervous, but I make my way over to him and ask, "Are we good?" He looks at me and smiles and says, "Yeah, Pepé. We're good." So we shook hands, hugged, talked for a few minutes. Then he went one way, I went the other.

TK: After that, did you see him, talk to him much more?

PW: Less and less. He built Paisley Park. And I'd go out there from time to time for different things. Saw him perform out there at parties and whatnot. But not much.

TK: On October 1, 1988, you were inducted into the Minnesota Black Music Hall of Fame. At the time there's only a few others in there. Prince, obviously. The Time. Jimmy and Terry, Flyte Tyme Productions. That next night when Prince takes the stage at Madison Square Garden on his *Lovesexy* tour—does that seem like kismet to you? You're having this big moment in Minneapolis and Prince is back on your old stomping grounds in New York City.

PW: I suppose, now. To tell you the truth, I had no idea where he was that night. I was hoping he would be there. Prince got something almost every year from the Minnesota Black Music Awards. But he usually didn't show up. He'd send Sheila (E.) or someone else in his place.

TK: There was another big moment for you in 1988. Your daughter Danielle was born.

PW: My biggest achievement ever. Life changing.

TK: With fatherhood, how did you balance work?

PW: Like any parent, I imagine. Had to pay the bills. Gotta take care of the family. PMI's been going strong now since 1976. We've worked with a lot of talented people over the years, mostly artists from around here. One of the things I've always done with PMI is to teach young artists the business side of things. That's actually the company motto: "The music may be different, but the business is the same." We (PMI) even created a couple of publications over the years (*The Music Outlet, Common Sense Music*) just to help reinforce how important that is, to know how to navigate this industry.

TK: You were around when this whole thing was getting started, the beginnings of the Minneapolis Sound. Who are some of the artists you've worked with more recently?

PW: There's Micailah Lockhart, Monaye Love, Eric Waltower. All really gifted. One of the artists I'm proudest of is Marshall Charloff. Marshall came to me as a gospel artist, but he's so much more than that. Multi-instrumentalist, amazing songwriter, could always do a near perfect imitation of Prince. In fact, Marshall and Matt Fink . . . Dr. Fink from the Revolution, formed The Purple Xperience, one of many Prince tribute bands out there. But they were one of the first, and to my mind the absolute best.

It's funny, Prince really gave Matt a hard time about being in a tribute band: "with a guy that dresses up like me." And once the Revolution started back up, Matt had to leave. Then, you know, after Prince passed, there were all these symphonies, orchestras, here in the States and around the world that would do these Prince tribute concerts. A lot of them brought Marshall in to sing at these shows.

TK: What are some of the other things you've done?

PW: I produced some tracks for Anthony Gourdine, this is back in the early nineties. And it was right around that time Little Anthony and the Imperials decided to reunite. It was just like the old days. I spent some time on the road with them. Brought back a lot of great memories. And it created some new ones as well.

TK: Didn't your uncle Clarence tell you that in 2004, when Prince went into the Rock and Roll Hall of Fame, Little Anthony and the Imperials were the first act on the ballot that didn't make the cut that year? Could you, Pepé Willie, have imagined that? Prince and the Imperials inducted into the Hall of Fame the same year.

PW: No. No. That would have been mind-blowing, at least to me.

TK: Little Anthony and the Imperials are eventually inducted into the Rock Hall in 2009.

PW: One of the happiest nights of my life. I loved sharing that night with them in Cleveland. They were so excited. It was long overdue, but they made it. My uncle Clarence, all those guys, guys that I came up with in this business, were now Rock and Roll Hall of Famers.

Then, later that same year, the Imperials performed at the Rock and Roll Hall of Fame 25th Anniversary Concert. This was at Madison Square Garden. I was able to catch up with folks I had known back at the Brooklyn Fox. Stevie

Wonder, Smokey Robinson. Stevie seemed to remember everything about those days back in Brooklyn. Smokey, uh, not so much.

TK: What has 94 East been up to all these years?

PW: Continued on with our music. I've never stopped writing songs. We put out a two-disc set *Symbolic Beginnings*, which included "The Cookhouse 5." The first time those songs were ever released. The original recording of "If You See Me" was released as a single and included on a compilation called *Purple Snow: Forecasting the Minneapolis Sound*. That was put out by this label in Chicago, the Numero Group.

It had a lot of songs from seventies, stuff that came out of here. Stuff that had never been heard before. Songs by André [Cymone], Alexander O'Neal, Flyte Tyme, Sue Ann Carwell, the Girls. There was Pierre's band the Lewis Connection, and Mind & Matter, which featured a young Jimmy Jam. 94 East also put out an album that included ten brand-new songs, plus new remixes of "10:15" and "Fortune Teller." This was the first time those two songs had ever been available. In recent years, we've released a hand full of singles to radio. Starfleet Music, WKKC, stations like that.

TK: The band started performing live too.

PW: Yeah, for the first time really. That's something we never got around to after our deal with Polydor was canceled. It was all about Prince back then.

TK: What were some of the gigs you did?

PW: One of the first shows we did—there used to be this annual thing in Minneapolis called the Prince Family Reunion. Of course, Prince wasn't part of it. It was just a bunch of veterans of the Minneapolis Sound that would get together and play for hours. Sort of like an all-star concert. 94 East played one of those shows.

That was a big night. The show went about five, six hours long. It was the first time Mazarati had played together in twenty years. The Family also reunited. This is shortly before they reformed as Deluxe. Dez was there. Prince's sister Tyka sang. So many others that night; Bobby Z, Dr. Fink, Michael Bland, Stokley Williams, Margie Cox. I don't remember everybody.

Around that time, Rick French, who's a trustee with the Rock and Roll Hall of Fame, invited us to perform at a benefit concert for the Hall. We were on the bill with the Imperials, Deniece Williams, the Chantels, Patty Smyth, the Atlanta Rhythm Section, a few others.

TK: In 2011, there was a benefit concert sponsored by the Minneapolis Urban League, right there in the heart of North Minneapolis, at the intersection of Plymouth and Penn Avenues. Tell us a little about that.

PW: Arms Around the Northside is what it was called. That spring a tornado that went through the neighborhood did a lot of damage. A lot of people needed help. I invited Marshall Thompson of the Chi-Lites to perform. He had written and recorded a track for President Obama's reelection campaign. He sang that. 94 East opened that show, and then we helped back up André [Cymone], who was playing his first show in Minneapolis in I don't know how long—twenty-five, twenty-six years?

That was also Bobby Z's first public performance since his heart attack. Bobby sat in on drums with André, as did Chazz. Malo Adams, a real talented cat who fronted Tribe of Millions. Malo was mentored by both André and Prince. He was on guitar that night. Matt [Fink] was there too. That was cool, with Dré, Bobby, and Matt you had three guys from Prince's original band. That also brought back memories.

TK: In this particular incarnation of 94 East, it's just you, Kristie, and Marcy. Who did you get to play behind you on some of these shows?

PW: Matt [Fink] played keyboards with us some of the time. Marshall [Charloff] on guitar, who I talked about before. Homer O'Dell from Mint Condition played guitar with us at some point. Jim Behringer did too. Jerry Hubbard Jr. played bass with us before. Jerry was with the Time for *Purple Rain* and then Jesse Johnson's Revue. Let me see, who else? Russ King on keyboards. Mario Dawson on drums. Mario's also played with Alexander O'Neal, Jellybean Johnson, St. Paul Peterson, fDeluxe.

TK: Just a bit earlier, you mentioned the record you released with "10:15" and "Fortune Teller," Prince called you about that, didn't he?

PW: Here's what happened. I'm at home one day when the phone rings. I answer, "Hello. Who's this?" The voice on the other end says, "This is Prince." I couldn't believe it so I asked again and he said, "It's Prince." Real monotone, you know, that's often how he spoke.

Still, I didn't believe it was him. This is gotta be a friend of mine playing a joke on me. So, I tried to get him to talk more and soon realized that it really was him. Now I am excited, it had been a few years since we talked. But, I'm also thinking "Why are you calling me?"

TK: Why was he?

PW: He wasn't a symbol anymore. He was Prince again and in the process of trademarking his name. So we talked about the record 94 East was doing, which listed him, you know, 94 East featuring Prince, on the cover. He didn't want anyone using his name. I understood that.

We talked a bit about the past and all we'd done together. I mentioned that Charley Groove Records in the UK, who released *Symbolic Beginnings*, sub-licensed those songs all over the world. There were records out there in Europe, Japan, elsewhere, with my music and Prince's photo on the cover. Neither one of us were getting paid. I apologized to him for that. Then I asked him about "Do Yourself A Favor," which had been on the bootleg circuit for years by that time. I just wanted to know "How did that get out?"

TK: What was his answer?

PW: He said, "Pepé. Somebody stole it from my house." Just the way he said it, said those words, that was the Prince I knew. His voice was relaxed; he'd let his guard down. He was himself all of a sudden. Not this mystery man, but the kid from over North. We talked some more and agreed in principle that 94 East could use his name on our album. His attorneys would contact mine to work out all of the details.

Then I said, "Hey man, let's get together for lunch. Go and shoot some hoops, just like the old days." This is what he says to me. He goes "I don't talk to people." In my mind I'm going like "You don't talk to people? What the f#@k does that mean?" And also, the way he said it. Just like that, Prince changed back to that guy I didn't know. That was weird.

TK: Did you ever see or speak with him again?

PW: One time. In Las Vegas. This is when he was doing his residency out there, *3121*, at the Rio. I don't remember if this was before or after his Super Bowl performance. The weather is always pretty nice there, so I don't have a frame of reference for what month it was.

TK: Was that why you were there, to see Prince?

PW: No. I was there to spend time with my nephew Keith Middleton. They call him the "Wild Child." Keith was one of the stars of *Stomp* at the Orpheum Theatre, Off Broadway. After ten years or so they moved the production to Planet Hollywood in Las Vegas.

TK: You have some pretty famous great-nephews as well?

PW: Keith's sons. Qaasim is the oldest. He got his start really young in the Naked Brothers Band on Nickelodeon. He was a finalist on *American Idol*. He's done some television, film. Things like *The Music in Me*, *The Get Down*, *Steps*, and most recently *When They See Us*.

Qaasim's younger brother Khalil's been on some of those same projects. He was just in the cast of *City on a Hill* and has a film coming out in 2020, *16 Bars*. Funny thing, when Qaasim and Khalil were younger, they were actually babysat by Jill Jones, who lived across the street from them in Brooklyn. Then there's the youngest, Makai, he's not in the business, yet.

TK: And what about their mother, Toni Seawright?

PW: She was the first ever Black Miss Mississippi, then a runner-up in the 1988 Miss America pageant. She sang background for Teena Marie, Freddie Jackson, several others. She's appeared on Broadway a number of times, including in a revival of *The Wiz* with Stephanie Mills.

TK: Talented family, indeed.

PW: No kidding.

TK: Sorry, I didn't mean to veer off track. Back to Vegas—how did you run into Prince?

PW: I'd been attending the rehearsals for *Stomp*. But this particular day I decided to do something else. I was eating lunch on the strip, not far from the Rio, where Prince was. It was mid-afternoon and I thought, maybe he's doing a soundcheck. I go over and find the artist entrance. The door is locked, but I hear the music coming from inside, I know its Prince.

Chazz was supposed to have come with me on this trip but couldn't make it. I call him, but he doesn't answer, so I put the phone up to the door hoping he might be able to hear it on his voicemail. Then I talked into the phone and I'm like "Hey Chazz, that's your cousin."

TK: So how did you get in?

PW: There's supposed to be an attendant there, guarding the place. I wasn't sure where he'd gone, but then he comes running fumbling for his keys. He must have thought I was someone who had access, so I went with that. He apologized for not being there and opened the door.

TK: What did you see?

PW: I'm walking down this back hallway and then, all of a sudden, I'm looking at the stage from behind, kind of off to the side. There's Prince, with his back to me. I definitely don't want to interrupt so I make my way out into the back of the club there. Take a seat and start watching Prince and his band rehearse.

TK: Must have taken you back to the old days?

PW: No doubt about it. I'm just hanging out in the back corner, then there's a break. Prince sees I'm out there. Not sure if he knows it's me yet. And he starts to walk out into the main room, but on the other side of the club. Goes all the way to the back, turns, and now he's coming towards me. He gets right up on me and I say, "Hey Prince. How you doing?"

Without stopping, he says, "Hi," and keeps walking back to toward the front of the room. Just "Hi." That was it. Mind you, he's been playing his guitar this whole time. Just messin' around on it, but still playing. And I'm asking myself, "What kind of s#@t is this?" He went back up on stage and just disappeared behind the curtain.

TK: That's it?

PW: That's it. That's when security came out and told me that I had to leave the premises. That was the last time I ever saw or spoke to Prince.

TK: A little more than nine years later Prince is riding high on his critically acclaimed *Piano and A Microphone Tour*. It was sort of a hit and run deal, like he used to do. Announce a date, show up, play, do it all over again.

Then that first Thursday in April . . . April 7, 2016, Prince cancels a couple of concerts in Atlanta. Were you worried when you heard that?

PW: I always worried about him. And it was odd for him to miss a show for any reason. But they said he had the flu. So that's as much as I thought about it. The next week, after he made up those gigs and his plane had to land in Illinois on the way home. That was scary.

I think I talked to Matt, maybe Bobby that week. Everyone thought the same thing, he's just sick, he has the flu. Of course, he had the party at Paisley Park that weekend. Then he's hanging out at Electric Fetus, riding his bike around. Seemed like no big deal.

TK: Thursday morning, April 21st, what's the first thing you remember about that day?

PW: I was sitting on the sofa at home, don't know that I was doing much of anything. The phone rings. It was my daughter Danielle. First thing out of her mouth, "Dad. Did Prince die?" What is she talking about? I say, "No, he's just got the flu." Then she says that a friend of hers who works at Paisley Park told her Prince was dead. Kristie overhears us talking and gets online. Then I can hear her in the other room, saying, "It's a hoax. It's a hoax."

As soon as I hang up the phone with Danielle, it rings again. This time it's Owen [Husney], who lives in Los Angeles now. "Did you hear about Prince," he asks me. Again, I was like "He's just sick, right?" Owen says, "No," and tells me to turn on the television. They were reporting that a body has been found at Paisley Park. I knew it couldn't be him. But then it was. I was literally in shock, I couldn't move. Kristie started to cry. Then Marcy called, she was crying. I began crying. I just could not believe that he was gone.

TK: I'm sure your phone kept ringing all day.

PW: Family, friends, others who were part of this whole thing; this thing that Prince had created. Media requests started to come in from places like *Rolling Stone, Billboard*, the BBC, *The Guardian*, local outlets.

I'd do these interviews and each time I would tell myself, "Keep it together Pep. Don't cry now." And each time I break down, without fail. A few days after he passed, I'm driving down the freeway and I see one of these electronic billboards and it's got a photo of him and it reads, "Prince: 1958–2016." I had to pullover on the side of the road. I start sobbing again and at the top of my lungs I screamed his name, "Priiiiiiince."

TK: Part of me wants to say, "I can't imagine what you were going through." And most certainly, I cannot. I didn't know Prince. You knew Prince for forty-five, forty-six years, you were family. Nonetheless, I get it. I still cry over Prince. To this day I still cry.

PW: Me too. I just finished golfing one day. This was in Florida, maybe a year later. I get in the car and Prince comes on the radio. I started to cry like a baby. It was too overwhelming. I had to turn the radio off.

You think about all these legends that died so young. Jimi, Janis, Jim Morrison, Elvis. Then there's Prince. You just thought he'd be around forever. Me and Chazz used to laugh and try to imagine Prince at sixty, singing "Soft and Wet," or whatever. He wasn't supposed to die. Not like he did, not when he did.

TK: We're three and a half years on. What do you personally take from his death today?

PW: I've been around awhile now, but Prince dying totally changed my life.

TK: What do you mean exactly?

PW: I tell Kristie and Marcy all the time that if Prince taught us anything it's that life is too short. I've tried to find a way to push aside everything negative in my life. I just want to be happy. I want to make sure that the people around me, the people I love, are happy. Because life is just too short not to be.

TK: Looking back on it all. The time you spent with him. The things that you saw him accomplish. What does Prince mean to you?

PW: What Prince meant to me, and still means to me for that matter, is the same thing he means to all his fans, to the people that love him. Let me give you an example. I had a friend who was trying to get Prince tickets. He wasn't a huge fan, yet, but he really wanted to go to this concert. He went online to buy the tickets and kept getting kicked out the system. The demand just was so high.

He calls me and says, "I can't get through. It just won't let me in." I pleaded with him to keep trying, because he won't regret it. He finally gets into the system, gets the tickets. After the show he calls me up and says, "Pepé. I can't thank you enough. The was the greatest thing I've seen in my entire life."

TK: There's Prince, racking up fans to the very end.

PW: That's the perfect way to say it. Anyone who ever saw Prince live was changed by the experience. The music, his performance. There was no one like him. Prince was the ultimate showstopper. That's why the world turned purple when he died. All those landmarks, the Eifel Tower, Empire State Building.

TK: Any final thoughts you'd like to share with us?

PW: Man, I tell you. I feel so blessed, so happy to have had the opportunity to help raise Prince in this industry. To have been there by his side in those early days. The industry has always been notoriously harsh on those that actually make the music, especially Black artists. To have witnessed everything that Prince achieved. And to imagine the things that he still might have accomplished, if he was still here. Astounding.

I miss him so much, love him so much. He was like my little brother, you know? In my mind, Prince was bigger than Elvis. I remember, this is just after Prince died, Stevie Wonder said something to the effect of "If Michael Jackson was the King of Pop, Prince was the Emperor." What more can be said about him. That pretty much says it all.

Section II

MUSICOLOGY AND INSTRUMENTAL EROTICISM

Chapter 7

"THE WAYS HE COULD LIVE DIFFERENT LIVES"

Performative Multiplicity, Identity Play, and Studio Autonomy in Prince's 1980s Recordings

WILL FULTON

Entertainment manager Owen Husney's first reaction to hearing Prince's demo tape in 1978 exemplifies how Prince's early recordings were judged as if they were performed by a group of musicians:

> I just thought, this group is phenomenal. The guitar player was great, the drummer was right on—the drummer was working with the bass player to create an incredible rhythm section, there was keyboards on top, and the vocals were over-the-top great . . . and I said, "Who's the group?"[1]

As Husney soon found out, however, there was only one multi-tracked musician on the demo that was playing and singing all of the parts: Prince. Over the course of his career, building on techniques pioneered by Stevie Wonder and others, Prince produced well over one thousand recordings (including unreleased material) as a technological one-man band.[2] On his 1978 debut album, Prince performed all of the instruments and voices and was touted by Warner Bros. Records as "the new Stevie Wonder," a reference to Wonder's ability to create the sound of a full band by performing all the instruments and vocals.[3] Prince continued recording in this manner in and beyond the 1980s, releasing several albums bearing the succinct credit "Produced, Arranged, Composed and Performed by Prince," and even had a home studio specifically designed so that he could record himself without the assistance of an engineer.[4]

In doing so, he consolidated creative control, artistic credit, and financial compensation for his music as a solo enterprise. Prince's career as a recording artist, which is marked by both a solo recording process and a struggle for ownership and control over his master recordings, exemplifies the politics of musical autonomy in popular music. If there is a "me/we" dichotomy in Black popular music as described by Philip Bailey and Public Enemy, in which the "we" (communal ethos and collective energy of bands like Earth, Wind & Fire) shifted toward "me" (individual producer/entrepreneurs in the 1980s[5]), Prince would largely represent the individual operative whose primary "modus operandi" is solo recording, employing (but not empowering) others only as needed.[6] In seeking to free his own music from record label control, Prince often replicated corporate power structures in his working relationships with employees in the 1980s, including contributing musicians and engineers.

The rise of late twentieth-century neoliberal culture shaped such popular music practice. As Dale Chapman states, "the individual human subject (as conceived by neoliberal thought) is understood as an 'enterprise of one,' empowered to maximize their position within the economy through deft negotiation of risk and reward. The idealized subject of neoliberalism is a kind of multitasking virtuoso, whose acquisition of multiple skill sets enables her to remain an agent, rather than object, of volatile market conditions."[7] This chapter addresses how Prince, using multitrack recording and pitch shifting, can aurally evoke characters (drummers, bass players, guitarists; male, female, and androgynous; Black, white, brown, and undefined; human, deity, and other) in seeming interaction: an "enterprise of one" representing all actors in an aural play.

Prince created a remarkable amount of music independently of other musicians. However, in his early years, he has also been accused of incorporating ideas from other musicians for which he retained credit and copyright, and therefore financial compensation. His quest for creative autonomy was shaped by his struggle for independence from record label control (as Stevie Wonder had experienced) while allowing him authority in the creative process and all royalties as sole producer, musician, and songwriter. Although his formative recordings made in the late 1970s stress a replication of the collective aesthetic of R&B and funk groups, in later recordings, Prince explored the ambiguities about who or what prospective listeners were hearing. As digital drum machines became common in popular music in the 1980s, Prince combined layered vocals, electric guitars, synthesizers, and MIDI sequencing to create electronic pop recordings that transformed R&B into a pop style that reflected both the genre liminality of 1980s new wave and techniques drawn from the collectivity and interaction of funk and R&B.[8]

Expanding on the interplay between performative characters pioneered by Wonder and others, as well as employing pitch-shifting techniques to evoke different characters, Prince's recordings feature a range of voiced personas, including Camille, Spooky Electric, and God, as well as characters developed for protégés (such as Morris Day and Vanity) to perform on Prince-produced songs. Identity play is exhibited in Prince's work in myriad ways, from his use of multiple pseudonyms (such as Alexander Nevermind and Jamie Starr) to his recorded alter egos, notably the helium-voiced, androgynous Camille. Keyboardist Lisa Coleman, who worked with Prince in the early-to-mid-1980s, argues that these characters were significant for him personally:

He couldn't squeeze it all into just Prince. . . . He needed other outlets. If he could have been Vanity 6 he would have done it; if he could have been The Time he would have done it. These were the ways he could live different lives.[9]

This chapter examines the development of Prince's music-making process and considers how technological autonomy led to the creation of performative characters and alter egos (what Coleman calls his "different lives") in seeming interaction. Prince used recording techniques such as pitch-shifting vocals to explore identity play while challenging identity and genre taxonomy. An analysis of recordings on which Prince performed nearly every instrumental and vocal part, "Let's Work" (recorded 1981), "If I Was Your Girlfriend," "Bob George," and "Adore" (all recorded 1986), along with a study of their production histories, will show how Prince developed an industry based on solo recording by transforming the collective practices of R&B, while challenging racial, gender, and genre norms in a segregated music industry.

EARLY YEARS AND RECORDING PRACTICE

Prince began his career performing in R&B bands, although, in his case, largely as an amateur. The son of a jazz pianist, Prince started recording multiple instrumental parts for songs at recording studios as a teenage musician in Minneapolis. The Central High School newspaper interviewed him in 1976, marveling that the largely autodidactic Prince already "played several instruments, such as guitar, bass, all keyboards, and drums."[10] His first band, Phoenix, formed in 1972, performed a range of material, including

Grover Washington and Carole King songs, and Prince "tried to imitate the Jackson 5," performing "I Want You Back."[11]

Prince began experimenting with overdubbing techniques even before he had the opportunity to hone his craft in professional recording studios. He "used cassette tape recorders to overdub separate performances onto dual tapes. He kept playing tapes back and taping more sounds on the other deck, teaching himself how to arrange and produce."[12] He recorded with his group Champagne at Moon Sound, an eight-track recording studio run by Chris Moon.

When the group broke up, Prince began recording parts for Moon at Moon Sound in 1976. Moon was looking for someone who could write and record music for his lyrics and found eighteen-year-old Prince's abilities to play multiple instruments to be both astounding and economical, noting: "I don't want to pay for a bass player."[13] Prince "added a bass line, drums, electric guitar, and cascading backup vocals. Awestruck, [Moon] handed Prince a key to the place and handwritten instructions on how to work the equipment."[14] Moon Sound provided eighteen-year-old Prince with unlimited access to studio equipment and a rare opportunity for autodidactic study of record production.

Prince would "stay the weekend, sleep on the studio floor" at Moon Sound, and recalled that he often worked around the clock by himself, learning to engineer his own sessions: "Anyone that was around then knew what was happening. I was working. While they were sleeping, I was jamming. When they woke up, I had another groove."[15] Whereas studios normally charge an expensive hourly rate, Prince had unreserved access to Moon's equipment. He learned early on the value of producing recordings by himself, which would greatly shape his intensive work ethic. During the late 1970s, amid the immense popularity of discotheques, when the market was increasingly driven by records rather than live performance, Prince found that he could produce a track in the studio by himself or with the assistance of an engineer and leave with a marketable product. This was evident to those who worked with him. Peter Doell, an engineer who worked on *1999* (Warner, 1982), marveled at Prince's recording technique:

> I remember days when Prince would come into the studio at, like, nine AM, kick you out of the room for about twenty minutes, then write a song. Then he'd come back, and you'd better have the drums tuned and ready, because he's going to play the daylights out of those drums. . . . Then he'd go in and do the bass, keyboards, and by one o'clock you're mixing it, and by four o'clock you run off and have it mastered. . . . He was an unbelievable cottage industry.[16]

During 1977, Prince recorded demos extensively at Moon Sound. After shopping demos around to various labels, Prince signed with Warner Bros. in 1978. Although Warner executives intended to market Prince within the genre matrix of R&B/funk/soul that was increasingly described in the industry charts and record label divisions as "Black Music" (a segregating practice that would generally limit marketing budgets and commercial expectations), Prince sought to reject being pigeonholed as such. He refused Warner's idea that Earth, Wind & Fire's bassist Verdine White produce his debut album and insisted on stipulations in his contract that assured he alone would have creative control and the right to produce his own music. This was remarkable for a completely untested producer, and Prince remains one of the youngest recording artists to be offered complete creative control in a recording contract.[17]

His first album, *For You* (1978), introduced the credit "Produced, Arranged, Composed and Performed by Prince." The opening track of the album, the *a cappella* "For You," contains forty-six tracks of Prince's layered vocals singing in harmony. Following this opening, the listener is treated to a series of songs in which Prince serves as his own band, multi-tracking the guitar, bass, drum, and keyboard parts. Prince maintained that these recordings benefited from a unanimity of performance: "Because I do all the instruments, I'm injecting the joy I feel into all those 'players.' The same exuberant soul speaks through all the instruments."[18]

When his first single, "Soft and Wet," became a R&B hit, Prince traveled on a promotional tour to meet fans, signing autographs at record stores but not performing. He had not yet performed any of the album's songs in concert. At this point, Prince's music existed only in the recording studio. This is not unheard of in popular music. Recording artists (generally singers) who did not perform live instruments themselves—often described as "track acts" because they would perform live along with the prerecorded track—were often marketed.[19] But Prince's circumstances were different, as he was the singing "act," as well as the producer and the band.

In the following year, Warner released his second album, *Prince* (Warner, 1979). His first promotional video, for the single "I Wanna Be Your Lover," featured intercut images of Prince playing all of the instrumental parts. However, while Prince's technique of solo recording had a considerable impact on his style and remained an important part of his critical reception, the visual promotion of his technological one-man band was short-lived.[20] To facilitate live performance, Prince put together a touring band in late 1978 that soon became central to his visual marketing, and in 1982 was christened "the Revolution."

Following his eponymous second album in 1979, Prince built two home studios and began a period of intense productivity and experimentation. He had a sixteen-track home studio installed in a rented house in Wayzata, Minnesota (a studio credited on albums as "Somewhere in Uptown"), where he recorded the album *Dirty Mind* (Warner Brothers, 1980) in May and June of 1980. Prince then moved to a house in Chanhassen, Minnesota, in April 1981, where recording engineer Don Batts installed a sixteen-track studio (credited on albums as "Uptown" and later upgraded to twenty-four tracks) and had the space wired in such a way that Prince could engineer his own performances. He lived in this house until 1985 and there produced hundreds of recordings, including most of *Controversy* (Warner Bros., 1981), *1999* (1982), albums for protégés (the Time, Vanity 6, and Apollonia 6), as well as songs that would appear on *Sign o' the Times* (Warner, 1986) and other projects.

The recording sessions at these home studios were largely engineered by Prince (credited under the pseudonym "Jamie Starr"). Batts set up Prince's "Uptown" home studios to serve Prince's way of operating: "I 'automated' Prince's home studio so it would function without me. It was all preset so it didn't have to be changed for a session."[21] By setting up the wiring and microphones to Prince's specifications, Batts made it possible for Prince to record without an engineer.

While additional recording and mixing for these albums occurred at Hollywood Sound Recorders and Sunset Sound by a number of engineers, these two "Uptown" home studios (and the privacy of self-engineering) provided Prince with a locus for artistic control, experimentation, and the means of record production outside of the label system. Prince claims he found his creative voice during this period:

> It was a revelation recording *Dirty Mind*. . . . I realized that I could just write what was on my mind. . . . [T]he other albums stuck to the more basic formula that I'd learned through playing Top 40 material in old bands.[22]

This "revelation" came about outside the studio system funded by budgets controlled by Warner. It was fostered by Prince's style of private recording and freedom from label control over recording sessions. The idea was to reduce the creative input of any additional persons to a minimum. Keyboardist Lisa Coleman, who had recently joined Prince's touring band in 1980 and was living at the house, recalls witnessing Prince's self-engineering process during this period:

You know, he'd start with the drums but he'd already have the song in his head. And he'd like go and press "Record" on the machine and then run over to the drums and you'd kinda hear like him jumpin' over things and trippin' over wires, sit down on the drums, and then count himself off, tick, tick, tick. And then he'd play and he'd have . . . lyrics written down on a piece of notebook paper and so he'd try to sing it in his head, and sometimes you'd hear him like kinda grunting and singing a little bit of the song on the drum track.[23]

Providing valuable insight into Prince's process, Coleman goes on to describe how Prince created a lively instrumental track by evoking a competitive atmosphere between his "players":

And then he'd imagine in his head like: he told me this, like you have to kick the bass player's ass. Like when you're playing the drums, kick the other guy's ass, like put things in there that's gonna make the other guy—which was all him, you know—[he'd] do something unexpected or like, try to keep up, you know. So it was so cool 'cause then he'd go do the drum track . . . and then he'd go and get the bass and play the bass and then that weird drum lick would come up and then he'd go, "Oh," you know, like the bass player, and then try to keep and then try to kick the guitar player's ass, etcetera, etcetera.[24]

This re-creation of the competitive and interactive forces of multiple musicians playing together is exemplified by the Prince recording "Let's Work" (Warner, 1981).

"Let's Work"

Recorded in mid-1981 at the Kiowa Trail Home Studio (credited as "Uptown") with Prince engineering (under the name Jamie Starr) and at Hollywood Sound, "Let's Work" features Prince performing drums, electric bass, electric guitar, Oberheim OB-X synthesizer, handclaps, lead and several backing vocals. Although recording studios are traditionally divided into a discrete control room where the engineer runs the mixing board and signal processors and live room(s) where musicians record instruments and vocals, Prince records mostly from the control room with the exception of live drums. Recording engineer Ross Pallone, who engineered sessions for *Controversy* at Hollywood Sound, remembers:

After he did the drum tracks for each song, he'd track everything else in the control room. [To record guitars], I'd set him up with a remote control for the multitrack machine. . . . Once he was happy with the sound, he'd excuse me from the studio. . . . [H]e would do all his own punching. . . . I was amazed at watching him play guitar then reach over the locator and punch himself in, and continue to play. For bass, we used to record direct, and he played a Fender bass and Fender Stratocaster guitar.[25]

Even when working in large studios and employing engineers, Prince preferred to complete most of the recording work in privacy. Pallone recalls that this extended to vocals ("he wanted to do it in the control room and he wanted to do it alone"), the final mix ("I would leave, and he would finish it up"), and social life while in the studio ("He rarely had anyone come to the studio, he was pretty much a loner").[26] If Prince was having fun, he was entertaining himself with music in a largely solitary space. This recording atmosphere of near-solitude is surprising for the robust party groove of "Let's Work."

In keeping with Prince's practice, the drums were recorded first, then the bass, guitars, synthesizers, and vocals. The track begins with a count-off, with Prince's vocal captured on the drum microphones yelling "1-2-3," followed by a riotous chorus of layered vocals ("Let's Work!") over a hard-edged, two-measure B-Dorian funk groove that alternates between i7 and IV, the harmony throughout. Boisterous crowd vocals and exuberant instrumental performances evoke the character of a large R&B band. Layered, slightly heterophonic handclaps are present throughout and contribute significantly to the recording's energy. At measure nine (0:16 on the album recording), the guitar and Oberheim synthesizer rest, and the song's primary bass line and drums introduce the verse groove (see Example 1).

The syncopated bass line features slap bass techniques largely developed by Larry Graham (of Sly and the Family Stone and Graham Central Station) and played slightly behind the beat. A fan of Graham, Prince collaborated with him on several occasions; he once complained that André Cymone, his touring bassist in the early 1980s, "always played on top of the beat" while Prince was "trying to get him to sound like Larry Graham" and play behind the beat.[27] In "Let's Work," Prince accents the upbeats in his bass performance. To the extent that Prince was imitating Graham's bass playing on this or another track, it is one of several ways in which Prince's multilayered solo band performances evoke the sounds and moods of multiple performers in interaction. Coleman's description of Prince's drummer playing "that weird

Example 1. Prince, "Let's Work," introduction excerpt (begins at 0:16). Transcribed by author from the *Controversy* album (Warner, 1981).

drum lick" to challenge his bass performance is exhibited at measure sixteen when Prince plays two syncopated hi-hat pops (popping the hi-hat open quickly) on four-e and four-a, a drum fill he uses repeatedly in the recording.[28]

Preceding this measure sixteen drum fill and building anticipation for the return of the Oberheim chords in measure seventeen, Prince creates two other events that help propel the groove forward. In measure fifteen, he adds a loud hall reverb effect to the beat-four snare (the last event to take place in the actual chronology of the recording, as it occurred during the mix), opening the reverb effect after the snare is played such that it is heard more on four-and. He then interrupts the ongoing bass line with a hard-snapped D on two-and of measure sixteen, clearly remembering that he had ended the measure with a drum fill while recording the bass. These three syncopated events (reverberated snare, bass snap, hi-hat fill) are marked as *x*, *y*, and *z* in Example 1. Occurring in half-measure intervals, they work in tandem to keep the groove exciting as it transitions to the next section.

From this instrumental groove, "Let's Work" additively builds in instrumental and vocal layers to the first chorus, starting at 1:03. During the chorus, Prince continues to develop the rhythmic tension as the obstinately on-beat synthesizer alternating tonic octaves contrast with the syncopated bass line and vocals, as well as a triplet hi-hat "pop" drum fill (as discussed above) audible at 1:12. The harmony synthesizer alternates between harmonizing the chorus vocals and a *sforzando*-like swell that contributes to the rhythmic push-and-pull between on-beat and syncopated rhythmic events. Following a snare roll, an eight-bar vocal break ensues in which the instruments "work" the groove beginning at 1:21 (see Example 2).

The bass becomes more active, and a new, harmonized lead Oberheim synthesizer riff is introduced in m. forty-one playing in rapid, staccato sixteenth notes, with two layered tracks performed in parallel sixths, starting on one-e (indicated in Example 2 as Oberheim Lead 1&2). Prince's bass guitar introduces a new syncopated pattern in mm. forty-one to forty-three, slapping D on three-and and the popping A-B (alternated as A-D in m. forty-two) on four-e and four-and. These syncopated bass accents, percussive strikes on the guitar strings, and a guttural vocalization (like a whispered scream) in m. forty-four and the rhythmic pitch bending of the Oberheim Lead (in mm. forty-three and forty-seven) contribute to the rhythmic and timbral vibrance of the eight-measure vocal break.

Throughout the recording, Prince adds and subtracts layers to the rhythm section; the bass and drums play throughout. In the final chorus, Prince interweaves the two primary vocal hooks—the introduction's shouted "Let's Work" and the chorus vocal—with a new vocal adlib so that the three different vocal groups interject phrases in tandem: "Let's work!"; "nothing can stop us now"; "nothing gonna stop us" (this exchange begins at 3:39). With these layered vocal and instrumental parts interjecting in rhythmic dialogues, Prince creates a lively party atmosphere for "Let's Work," replicating the energy of a funky R&B band's performance by creating a competitive environment for his "players" and exploiting elements of rhythmic tension throughout.

Examples 2A and B. Prince "Let's Work" vocal break (begins at 1:21). Transcribed by author from the *Controversy* album (Warner, 1981).

Examples 2C and D. Prince "Let's Work" vocal break (begins at 1:21). Transcribed by author from the *Controversy* album (Warner, 1981).

THE REVOLUTION YEARS

In the years following *Controversy*, Prince would increasingly create music using the Linn LM-1 drum machine and synthesizers. While this transition is in keeping with a general shift in the post-disco 1980s production aesthetics of popular music, the LM-1 offered something Prince personally desired: an efficient method to record songs faster. Prince began incorporating his Revolution band members on recordings more frequently for his following album *1999* (Warner, 1982), and significantly on the three subsequent albums marketed as "Prince and the Revolution": *Purple Rain* (Warner, 1984), *Around the World in a Day* (Paisley Park/Warner, 1985), and *Parade* (Paisley Park/Warner, 1986). Keyboardist Lisa Coleman and guitarist Wendy Melvoin increasingly contributed to compositions.

However, collaboration during the Revolution years was limited. While music videos promoting these albums usually presented Prince and the Revolution performing together, often the song recordings were actually made by Prince alone; this is exemplified by the "When Doves Cry" recording and video (Warner, 1984). Revolution keyboardist Matt Fink recalls that the "Revolution" albums were still "90% Prince" and that while a few songs came about in collective jam sessions during rehearsals, mostly "he would just go in and do them, and then present them to us on a tape when it was finished, and I'd say 80% of the time, that's how it was done. Whereafter he'd hand us a cassette of the mixed song, say 'Okay, go learn this and we'll start rehearsing it.'"[29]

This level of distance was similar in Prince's studio work, as he found the "most comfortable method of collaborating" to be sending "tapes back and forth."[30] Coleman recalls: "Prince would send us masters and we would work on them and send them back. They were skeletons. The melody and lyrics, maybe a piano part."[31] Rather than interactive collaboration in the studio, Prince preferred the technologically mediated collaboration of others adding parts when he was not present. He would then blend the contributed parts into the final mix, incorporating only the tracks he liked. In 1986, Prince disbanded the Revolution and returned to his style of solo recording for the remainder of the 1980s. Following the disbanding of the Revolution, Coleman and Melvoin felt Prince owed them publishing royalties on tracks to which they contributed.[32]

In addition to producing his own records, Prince sought other outlets for his music long before starting Paisley Park Records in 1985. Beginning with the Time in 1981, Prince developed and produced records through a production deal with Warner. Rather than allowing singers to craft their own personas on recordings, however, Wendy Melvoin describes: "Prince [recorded] a guideline for vocals. . . . He did that every time. You had to copy every lick, every breath, every sigh, no question, especially with his ghost bands. They had to follow everything he did, precisely."[33] Several of Prince's "guideline" vocal demos can be heard on the posthumous demo collection, Prince, *Originals* (Warner, 2019).

This collection includes Prince's vocal demo for the Time's "Jungle Love," and his affected performance of the character then enacted by Time singer Morris Day, which Melvoin recalls, originated "in a pimp persona Prince used to mess around with, for which he put on an old man's 'hustler' voice."[34] Coleman states that Prince would often speak in comic voices and create characters, confirming that Day's persona evolved from a comic character Prince developed: "He'd do all these different voices and stuff and, you know, he's really funny. He had all kinds of crazy voices. Like the Time records. If you listen to the Time—that's just him just messin' around."[35] Similar vocal personas were developed for Vanity (b Denise Matthews), Apollonia (b Patricia Kotero), St. Paul (b Paul Peterson), among others.

IDENTITY PLAY AND PERFORMED CHARACTERS IN THE LATTER 1980s

His fascination with creating recorded personas led to a period of increased identity play, as Prince crafted a series of solo-produced recordings in which he performed characters with the aid of vocal affect and electronic modulation, such as the Camille persona, which he introduced in 1986. The androgynous, helium-voiced Camille, likely named after the "nickname of the nineteenth-century French hermaphrodite Herculine Barbin," came about as a product of experiments with tape speed variation: slowing the tape down, recording the vocal, then resetting the tape speed such that the vocal pitch is higher.[36] This technique had been used earlier on Wonder's "Maybe Your Baby" and Sly Stone's "If You Want Me To Stay" (notably two songs Prince performed in concerts and likely influenced him) and first employed by Prince for "Erotic City" (Warner, 1984). Prince's use of vocal pitch shifting was most extensive in 1986, a year several Camille tracks were recorded. Brian Rossiter posits that Prince's Camille character employs pitch-shifting effects to "problemat[ize] the concept of his identity," "continuously calling into question his gender, sexuality, and racial heritage."[37]

Camille was Prince's most prominent voice-manipulated character, and the one most conspicuously credited; vocals on four tracks on *Sign o' the*

Times (1987) are attributed on album liner notes as "Lead Vocal by Camille." In 1986, Prince considered releasing an album under the pseudonym Camille that featured a collection of his helium-voiced tracks. Further, Prince considered writing a movie in which he and Camille would pursue the same woman, and according to recording engineer Susan Rogers, "was thinking of battling with himself. He had this whole idea that Camille would be his competition" in the marketplace.[38] Prince, whose creative impulses seem to be fueled by competition and, as Coleman describes, spent his career recording himself playing the roles of competing "players" in his one-man band, was now creating other imagined recording artists to compete with that he would perform himself.

Susan Rogers recorded most of the Camille tracks. During and after the Revolution years, Prince worked extensively with Rogers, who was hired as a technician in 1983 and engineered recordings for Prince until leaving his company in 1988.[39] Rogers assisted with the design of the recording facilities at Prince's ten-million-dollar Paisley Park recording complex in Chanhassen, Minnesota (built in 1985). She also started the Vault, an actual bank vault that was held in the basement of Paisley Park and is said to contain thousands of master recordings, a significant number of which remain unreleased commercially, including several "Camille" recordings.

In my email exchange with Rogers, she explained the technical process for creating the Camille voice:

> We worked at 30 ips [tape speed]. Anything recorded at 15 ips would be an octave higher when played back at 30. We didn't always slow the machine down a full octave. Using varispeed, most brands of tape machines can be changed +6 semitones. We chose the speed to find the timbre change we were looking for.[40]

Prince employed voice manipulation to create multiple pitched voices on "If I Was Your Girlfriend," a track recorded in November 1986 at Sunset Sound.

"If I Was Your Girlfriend"

Originally considered for inclusion on the shelved 1986 album *Camille*, "Girlfriend" was released as the second single from *Sign o' the Times* (1987), credited on the album as having "Lead Vocal by Camille." Based on my own pitch-shifting attempts with "Girlfriend," which is in B-flat minor, I posit that they used the VSO (variable speed oscillator) to slow the tape down approximately -3 semitones to record Prince's lead Camille vocal (sung at G minor), while the low-pitched basso backing vocals were recorded at approximately +3 semitones (sung at D-flat minor). The instrumentation for "Girlfriend" (with all parts played by Prince) includes Linn LM-1 drum machine, bass guitar, and Fairlight CMI sampler. Foley sound effects play an important role in the track's opening collage, which was added later. Rogers describes Prince's solo recording practice for vocals:

> We'd get the track halfway or three-quarters of the way there and then set him up with a microphone in the control room. He'd have certain tracks on the multi-track that he would use, and he'd do the vocal completely alone. I think that was the only way he could really get the performance.[41]

In the case of "Girlfriend," this solo recording practice led to a distorted vocal track. Rogers had made a mistake, and "the pre amp gain was accidentally set 10 dB [decibels] too hot for the vocal channel," but since she wasn't there to monitor the recording, she didn't know until it was finished.[42] Ultimately, Prince liked the timbre of the distorted vocal and chose not to re-record it, likely because it further estranged "Girlfriend" from the normative.

Due to the gender play of the lyrics and the use of the Camille voice for "Girlfriend," it was one of the most transgressive singles in mainstream popular music at the time of its release, and disorienting in terms of the protagonist's gender and sexuality. bell hooks notes that her "college undergraduates [puzzled] over 'If I Was Your Girlfriend,' trying to work out whether Prince is a man or a woman."[43] Meanwhile, the unusual timbres and sound events of "Girlfriend" create a dream-like space for the listener.

The track begins with a collage of four Foley sound effects sampled and triggered by Prince from the Fairlight CMI keyboard (an orchestra tuning up; a department store hawker saying, "look at our bargains over here, ladies!"; a church organ playing Mendelssohn's "Wedding March" melody; a crescendoing female vocal). Rogers recalls that she "purchased a lot of sound effects CDs that I kept in my gig bag for Prince," and that they "used them frequently."[44] These juxtaposed samples evoke a dreamscape, while introducing a female vocal sample that would play a central role in the recording's climactic ending.

The opening melodic phrase operates like a horn section (in live performance it was often played by trumpet and saxophone), but is a processed sample performed on the Fairlight CMI with a slow attack that sounds almost backward, creating what Griffin Woodworth calls a "subtle dynamic between identification and estrangement."[45] The instrumentation also features synthesized strings, a two-measure Linn LM-1 ostinato (with a synthetic beat-four clap that echoes on the quarter note), a two-measure filtered loop, and a one-measure funk bass part similar to Larry Graham's bass line from Sly and the Family Stone's "Thank You (Falletinme Be Mice Elf Agin)" (Epic, 1969).

The climactic section of "Girlfriend" occurs during the vamp and rap. Sections of intimate conversation—where one "raps" to their prospective mate—are common in R&B, and featured prominently in the recordings of Isaac Hayes ("Ike's Rap," Enterprise, 1971), Barry White ("I'm Never Gonna Give Ya Up," 20th Century, 1973), the Floaters ("Float On," ABC, 1977), and others. Prince employed intimate raps with the audience during narrative sections of his live shows, as well as in sex-themed ballad recordings like "Do Me, Baby" (Warner, 1981) and "International Lover" (Warner, 1982). As is the case with "Girlfriend," these previous ballads end with simulated sexual climaxes. Although the seduction monologue of "Girlfriend" varies from traditional R&B practice, Prince (performing as Camille) is busy seducing the listeners in this section, while speaking with a disarming intimacy rare in popular music.

This section begins at 3:41, as a syncopated synthesizer overdub plays a four-bar phrase (the drum machine ostinato continues throughout; the bass continues through all but the final eight measures). The higher-pitched lead vocal is accompanied by lower pitched backing vocals, here repeating the chorus "If I was your girlfriend" dispassionately, almost mechanically. With growing urgency, Camille speaks intimately, offering to undress, dance a ballet naked, give a bath, provide an orgasm, insisting that only if "I was your girlfriend" the intended listener would trust Camille with everything; Camille seeks the private rapport of intimate friends.

At 3:55, a new instrument sounds, one previously audible in the song's introduction: a looped "stock vocal sample" (by Rogers's recollection), female with strong vibrato, singing "oooh," played on the Fairlight CMI sampler keyboard.[46] It enters with a descending F/B-flat/D-natural, an arpeggiated B-flat major 6th chord, dissonantly looping on D-natural for two measures before slowly bending upward (like a glissando). As the vocal sample was performed with a strong vibrato, the vibrato rate decreases when the sample is played on the low D-natural to a slow warble, then increases with the pitch, creating a dizzying effect. As Camille becomes increasingly insistent, speaking more rapidly, the pitch starts to increase, ultimately ascending nearly four octaves chromatically at the rate of approximately a quarter note per pitch starting at 4:30.

The chorus vocals double in rate, occurring in every bar as if in a mechanical loop. As the pitch rate increases, so does the vibrato rate, while Camille's voice raises to almost a shout. The tension becomes almost hysterical, as the pitch rate rises in sixteenth-note durations before a fortississimo high C (a sexual climax) at 4:39. Camille promises (after sex) to "hold you long and together we'll stare into silence." The vocal sample, bass, and synthesizer tracks are abruptly silenced, and the drum machine, filtered loop, and Camille continue for eight measures (4:40–5:01). Camille supposes that they will "try to imagine what silence looks like," speaking (presumably post-coitus) in halting, hushed tones before the track abruptly ends with the words "we'll try" occurring in unison with a double snare hit.

With the closing section of "If I was your Girlfriend," Prince creates a strange, dream-like environment, with chorus vocals sounding abnormally low (detached, as if mechanical), a lead voice sounding abnormally high, and a female vocal sample that is controlled to a hysterical high pitch before going silent, followed by a meditative soliloquy on silence. The vocal sample is clearly symbolic of a woman in this scene. Thus, Prince, as producer and performer, controls the scene and manipulates the female machine-vocal to reach a performative climax, while retaining total control over all of the performed characters.

But although "Girlfriend" is credited to Camille and performed with voice modulation, it is still in a sense a Prince love ballad (he performed it live without voice modulation or apparent persona), though in the recording it is a modulated Prince in a liminal space, where identity is fluid as he imagines himself as her "girlfriend." Rogers, who engineered "Girlfriend," recalls that when she heard the lyrics, she was moved: "I encouraged him to release it as a single. I'd never heard a man say that before, [it was] wonderful, a good thing to say, a good thing to put out there."[47] "Girlfriend" was ultimately released as a single in 1987, perhaps in part due to Rogers's suggestion. Warner executives protested the choice. It was met only with limited commercial success, yet remains a favorite of Prince fans.

"Bob George"

"If I Was Your Girlfriend" was recorded during the same month that Prince used voice manipulation to record high and low vocals for "Bob George," a track that is very different in mood, yet is also staged as a spoken conversation between performative characters. "Bob George" would later be included on the infamous Black Album in 1987. Rogers recalls that "Bob George" and other Black Album tracks "were odds and ends, things we would do on a day off. When he was making an album, sometimes he wanted to break away and do something just to get it out of his system."[48]

"Bob George" was recorded was among three tracks that were mastered and pressed on vinyl acetate, intended for DJ play at Sheila E.'s birthday party on December 11, 1986. Rogers recalls that Prince "wanted to record some mindless party songs for her ... [but they] were never intended for an album."[49] The misogynistic, violent lyrics should not be regarded as representative of Prince's style—he convinced Warner to cancel the *Black Album*'s release in 1987, deeming it as "evil" (the album later saw a limited released in 1994 to fulfill a contractual obligation with the label).[50] However, "Bob George" remains a favorite of Prince fans, and is an important example of his studio work during this period. Using voice manipulation, Prince creates a dystopian interpretive framework in which he performs multiple characters in interaction, while sardonically commenting on racial taxonomy.

"Bob George" features two pitched voices: A low-pitched bass lead voice, evoking an African American gangster caricature, and a high-pitched, comic, presumably white police officer (sounding an octave higher). The association of bass voices and African American masculinity, exemplified by 1970s figures such as Richard Roundtree's Shaft, Barry White, and Isaac Hayes, was comically addressed by Eddie Murphy in the 1984 film *Beverly Hills Cop*. In a confrontation with a nasal high-voiced, African American cop, Murphy's character Axel Foley advises the officer to speak in a "more natural" manner, ie., to not speak like an uptight white person, but with bass voice and Black dialect.[51] In "Bob George," Prince creates an interpretive framework based on these taxonomic categories, pitting the lead gangster character's basso against a police officer's nasal, higher-pitched voice.

While the high-pitched (officer) vocals were created through tape speed variation, the basso lead voice was created using the recently released Publison Infernal Machine, a sound modulation device that Susan Rogers was experimenting with at Sunset Sound studios while waiting for Prince to arrive (on the day he would write and record the song). Rogers recalls: "I figured he would like the pitch change and he did."[52] The Publison allowed for real-time pitch shifting, and was set so that Prince's vocal would sound one octave lower than voiced. The modulation also gave the vocal track a harsh timbre (the sound of two dissonant pitched vocals), which likely inspired Prince to create the deranged protagonist of "Bob George."

The title of the song refers to two names discussed in discrete sections. In the first half, Prince's gangster character is complaining about his girlfriend dating "Bob" (named for Prince's then co-manager Bob Cavallo), the manager of "Prince, that skinny motherfucker with the high voice?!" By naming himself disparagingly in the lyrics, Prince creates further distance from the character he is portraying. The aural mask provided by the pitch shifter allows for identity play but also a moment of career-related vengeance. After the scene culminates in a violent confrontation with the police, Prince (performing in voice-manipulated character) calls "Mr. George"—a character inspired by *Billboard* critic Nelson George—and threatens him.

The sardonic titling of the *Black Album*, and the context in which Prince recorded "Bob George" arose from the racialized climate and critical reception of 1980s pop. This climate is exemplified by the awarding of "Favorite Black Album" to Prince and the Revolution at the 1985 American Music Awards. At the ceremony, Madonna and Huey Lewis present the winner of the "Favorite Black Album" award for *Purple Rain* (an album that blended rock, pop, and R&B) to Prince and his band the Revolution (ironically, a predominantly white, Jewish band). Though Prince had sought to be marketed as a mainstream pop star that transcended the industry's Black Music categorization, his phenomenal successful *Purple Rain* was still being regarded within the American Music Awards as a "Black Album." On the other hand, during this same period, Prince also felt he was being chastised by R&B music critics such as Nelson George, who reprimanded Prince (as well as Michael Jackson) in *Billboard* magazine and in other writings for purposely distancing himself from Black culture in order to court the mainstream audience.[53]

As mid-1980s hip-hop presented masculine images of African American men (exemplified by LL Cool J and Run DMC), Prince's and Michael Jackson's arguably transracial and androgynous performances were increasingly criticized. In this context, "Bob George" and the *Black Album* can be seen as cathartic for an African American performer caught between marginalization due to his race (as shown by the reception of *Purple Rain* at the American Music Awards) and disparagement from Black critics for attempting to transcend pigeonholing of his music and preconceptions about Black masculinity. The voice manipulation allows for a type of aural mask behind which Prince can take aim at his critics while lampooning stereotypical taxonomies of African American males. "Bob George" provided an opportunity to address his critics, hardcore rap, and the culture of popular music in general behind the veil of voice manipulation, on what was created initially as a private recording for a DJ party.

The form of "Bob George" is twelve-bar blues (in B) and features a sparse Linn LM-1 drum machine track, synthesizer bass, additional synthesizer pads (Fairlight CMI), lead electric guitar, and Foley sound effects (sirens, gunshots, screams, and telephone ringing) sampled and triggered on the CMI keyboard. These sampled and manipulated Foley sound effects, as they were similarly used in "If I Was Your Girlfriend," serve to support the aural scene created between Prince's voiced characters in "Bob George." Prince's vocal

Example 3. Prince, "Bob George" verse section (begins at 1:25). Transcribed by author from the *Black Album* (Warner, 1994).

merges blues performance and syncopated rap rhythms, creating a sardonic connection between genres. This is evident in the verse section beginning at 1:25 in the recording.

With subtle pitch referencing and dynamics, Prince's vocal employs the narrative arch of the twelve-bar blues (as one would in an expressive instrumental solo). This is evident in measure forty-five, in which he increases tension and pitch on the line "skinny motherfucker with the high voice" to accompany the shift from I to IV, as well as in measures forty-eight and forty-nine, on the line "Yesterday's fool?" and "kill you now?" as the harmony moves from I to V. Prince then accentuates the blues connection by introducing his character's "gun" (an electric guitar), and alternating between percussive vocal rants, blues riffs, and Foley gunshot sound effects (triggered from the Fairlight CMI synthesizer), before the first scene culminates in a confrontation with the police.

This is followed by another dialogue of performative characters, where the basso character confronts an aural stand-in for Nelson George. In a phone conversation with "Mr. George," the character threatens the critic. Beginning at 3:30, Prince enacts an aural interaction with the police, then a telephone confrontation with "Mr. George":

> GANGSTER: Is Mr. George home? (sound effects—chatter)
> Hello, Mr. George? (sound effects—chatter)
> This is your conscience, motherfucker (sound effects—chatter)
> . . . I'll kick your ass, twice!

Employing two different voice manipulation techniques (Publison real-time pitch shifting for the low "gangster" voice; VSO tape speed variation for the high "officer" voice) and a series of sound effects (sampled and triggered on the Fairlight CMI synthesizer), Prince creates an aural play that parodies racial signifiers in which he performs all characters. In the confrontation with (his critic) Mr. George, Prince retains complete control of the conversation, reducing the critic's responses to babble. As a pop performer, Prince can't confront a *Billboard* magazine critic or publicly parody the racialized climate of American pop without threatening his commercial standing in the marketplace. But the aural mask of voice manipulation allows a space for performative anonymity, wish fulfillment, and the escape from commercial expectations of a mainstream recording artist.

"Adore"

During the same month as he recorded "Girlfriend" and "Bob George," Prince evoked the roles of interacting vocalists toward a very different end for "Adore," a tender homage to R&B balladry and the tradition of soul vocal group performance. "Adore," the last track on the *Sign o' the Times* album, was inspired by two recently released R&B albums: Patti LaBelle's *Winner in You* (MCA, 1986) and Luther Vandross's *Give Me the Reason* (Epic, 1986). Unlike the largely solo performances of LaBelle and Vandross, however, "Adore" features prominent backing vocals (performed by Prince) that interact playfully with his lead vocal. In the tradition of R&B vocal groups, such as the O'Jays and the Stylistics, Prince creates a call and response relationship between his lead and backing vocalists throughout the recording.

"Adore" was recorded by Rogers at Sunset Sound in November 1986. In contrast to the largely electronic timbres of Prince recordings during this period, the track blends analog and digital instrumentation, with Prince on

LM-1 drum machine, bass, Hammond B3 organ, Wurlitzer electric piano, synthesizer, and vocals, as well as Eric Leeds on saxophone and Atlanta Bliss on trumpet. According to Rogers, the saxophone and trumpet parts were most likely recorded after the vocals, as "vocals were recorded about halfway through the arrangement process" on ballads while "horns and additional sweetening were selected to compliment the vocals."[54] Given the practice described by Rogers, Prince programmed and recorded his drum machine part, and then recorded his bass, Wurlitzer, and Hammond B3 parts, at which point she would have set up the vocal microphone and left the room. Chorus vocals were often recorded and mixed first, allowing Prince to feed off their energy while recording the lead vocal, while Leeds and Bliss were clearly reacting to the vocals on their sax and trumpet adlibs.

On the album, "Adore" is introduced with a segue from the live performance of "It's Gonna Be a Beautiful Night" (the album's only live track and the only track to feature the recently disbanded Revolution), such that the crowd noise carries over into the song's intro. While this crowd noise was added later during album sequencing, it creates the mood of an exuberant live performance of a R&B group. Prince creates a referential nod to the tradition of live R&B performances and the conventions of soul vocal groups (notably, in 1996, he would record covers of Stylistics and Delfonics songs).

The opening chorus of "Adore" (beginning at 0:32) features lead and chorus vocals harmonizing, evoking the sound of R&B group performance. Prince, by this point had ten years of experience in recording layered vocal harmonies and clearly chose to vary the timbres of the different voices for "Adore," creating the sound of a performing group. The first responsorial phrase occurs at 0:53 when the lead vocal passionately answers the group vocalists' line, "your beauty I'd still see." This type of call and response is indicative of the dialogic relationship between parts that build throughout the recording and is particularly evident in the second verse and bridge, which starts at 2:17.

Prince employs a variety of vocal arrangement techniques in this section, including imitation, harmonized emphasis of specific phrases, and anticipating and reacting responses to the lyrics of the lead vocal. At 2:22, the "sound" of the angels' tears is evoked by the backing vocals (a descending 4th vocalized as "Ohh-ahh") in anticipation of the lyric. Then, a solo baritone backing vocal emphatically states "I ain't cheatin' on you, baby" (at 2:38) again anticipating the lead vocal.

As shown in Figure 4, Prince's sense of humor is exhibited in an exchange beginning in measure forty-seven. The dutiful backing vocals, having supported the previous lyric "you can burn up my clothes," begin to echo the

Example 4. "Adore" verse section (begins at 2:48). Transcribed by author from the *Sign o' the Times* album (Warner, 1987).

following line "[you can] smash up my ride," but stop after "smash up" when the lead vocal comically interrupts, interjecting "well, maybe not the ride!" This comic exchange is further exhibited in measures fifty to fifty-one. After the group vocals emphatically repeat the line "I'm a man of exquisite tastes," when the lead vocal describes his fineries ("hundred-percent Italian silk, imported Egyptian lace") Prince's "backup vocalists" intimate that they are impressed, responding with "Ohh!" (see Example 4).

These exchanges between vocal parts evoke a group dynamic in action, and a humorous take on the interplay between R&B group vocalists. Prince is creating vocal characters in "Adore" that appear to be aware of each other in the performance, reacting to each other's phrases, and even interrupting one lyric mid-phrase. He may have planned portions of these interactions, but it is likely that others came about while he was tracking his vocals in solitude in the control room at Sunset Sound studios, punching in phrases on different tracks to compliment others. With "Adore," Prince consciously references the tradition of R&B vocal groups. It is a love song but also metageneric: a solo-produced R&B performance that is about—and self-consciously indexes—the tradition of group R&B vocal performance.

CONCLUSION

Prince's 1980s music is populated by performative characters: competing instrumentalists, crooning group vocalists, alter egos, pseudonyms, and ghost bands. As Prince performed many of these characters, he created interpretive frameworks evoking bands, scenes, and caricatures that played on tropes in African American cultural production. In most cases where he employed collaborators during this period, their agency was limited.

Perhaps more than any other artist, Prince professionalized the solo per-formance-producer in popular music. In the late 1970s and early 1980s, by creating a "cottage industry" for self-produced song production that retained the vibrancy of the R&B collective, as well as downsizing input from engineers and technicians, he struggled to come as close to a solo performance and production as possible. Although, as shown in his work with Susan Rogers, as well as Lisa Coleman and Wendy Melvoin, even his "Produced, Arranged, Composed, and Performed by Prince" productions benefited from the labors of engineers and musicians in several ways.

Further, to a listener of Prince's recordings discussed above, he was never performing "alone." As characters like Camille, the gangster of "Bob George," seemingly competing instrumentalists in "Let's Work," vocal sound effects in "If I Was Your Girlfriend," and responding backup vocals in "Adore" inhabit and enliven his recordings, they create the effect of collective performances with interacting voices. Meanwhile, voice manipulation and character play allows Prince an opportunity to craft presentations of identity that both subvert and comment on race and gender norms and stereotypes, while Prince remains a largely solo auteur in control of all these characters.

That he would go on to fight for complete control of his catalog from Warner Music in later years is a clear extension of his fight for autonomy and creative control. Prince continued to record as well as perform at Paisley Park (a facility he owned) until his sudden passing in 2016. Following a 2014 contract renegotiation with Warner, he retained rights to nearly all of his master recordings, centralizing control over his career in a way most recording artists could not conceive of.

Prince changed style and process considerably after the 1980s. By 1991 he was recording with a new band (the New Power Generation) that produced several albums using a somewhat collective performance process in the studio. During this period, he sought to distance himself from his 1980s production aesthetics that had since become so popular, and stated in a 1991 interview: "Everyone else went out and got drum machines and computers, so I threw mine away."[55] Although he would return several times in his later career both to solo recording and technological MIDI-based producing, he rarely returned to the type of identity play shown in the Camille recordings or in "Bob George." However, the voice manipulation techniques and gender identity play he employed on these recordings would prove an inspiration to a range of early twenty-first-century artist-producers, as evident in Beyoncé's "I Been On" (Columbia, 2013) and Erykah Badu's "Dial'Afreaq" (Motown, 2015).

During the 1970s and 1980s, as the recording studio and the live concert increasingly represented distinct sites of music making, the studio became a locus for introspection and experimentation. Using multitrack recording and pitch shifting, Prince aurally evoked characters, bands, and vocalists interacting while negotiating a marketplace in which taxonomies of racial and sexual identity—and specific expectations for African American performers in the marketplace—exist in a dynamic relationship with post-soul individualism. These recordings represent the negotiation of that dynamic within the creative cocoon of the recording studio, where technology is employed both as an agent of transformation and as self-empowerment by a musician seeking increased control over his music. Recording technology and voice modulation provided a space in which identity and representation were fluid and allowed for a new world of experimentation for both the performer and listener. As Lisa Coleman states, these personas and alter egos recording provided Prince with "ways he could live different lives."

Notes

1. Tom O'Dell (dir.), *Prince, The Glory Years* (London: Prism Films, 2007).

2. It would be difficult to ascertain a precise number of recorded songs because only a portion of his vast recordings has been made commercially available. However, a number of these commercially unreleased recordings have appeared on various bootleg albums and are well known to Prince enthusiasts.

3. Dave Hill, *Prince: A Pop Life* (New York: Harmony Books, 1989), 6.

4. See "Kiowa Trail Home Studio," *Prince Vault*, 2016, accessed January 8, 2023, http://www.princevault.com/index.php?title=Kiowa_Trail_Home_Studio. It would be difficult to ascertain a precise number. See "Kiowa Trail Home Studio."

5. Earth, Wind & Fire's Philip Bailey states: "We came up in an environment where it was a little more community-minded.... I don't think [Earth, Wind & Fire] would fly so much today because it's just become a me/mine society." Robert Walser, "Groove as Niche: Earth,

Wind & Fire," in *This Is Pop: In Search of the Elusive at Experience Music Project*, ed. Eric Weisbard (Cambridge, MA: Harvard University Press, 2004), 275. Public Enemy's founding producer Hank Shocklee argues that this shift has had a negative impact on both the music and the industry: "I think one of the reasons the record business is hurting today is because they've lost the interaction between people, because everyone has adopted the 'Prince-Kashif-Teddy Riley-ism.' The lone musician—he's the band. There's nothing wrong with that [but] you're making people vibrate to your own frequency. When you listen to the Jimi Hendrix record or the Doors or your Sly and the Family Stone, Kool and the Gang or Earth, Wind & Fire—you're feeling the energy of them cats connecting." Philip Stevenson, "Hank Shocklee," *Tape-Op* 51 (January/February 2006), https://tapeop.com/interviews/51/hank-shocklee/.

6. Griffin Woodworth, "'Just Another One of God's Gifts': Prince, African American Masculinity, and the Sonic Legacy of the Eighties," PhD diss., UCLA, 2008, 41.

7. Dale Chapman, "The 'One-Man Band' and Entrepreneurial Selfhood in Neoliberal Culture," *Popular Music* 32, no. 3 (October 2013), 452.

8. See Theo Cateforis, *Are We Not New Wave? Modern Pop at the Turn of the 1980s* (Ann Arbor: University of Michigan Press, 2011).

9. Liz Jones, *Slave to the Rhythm* (London: Time Warner Books1998), 79.

10. Lisa Crawford, "Nelson Finds It 'Hard to Become Known,'" *Central High School Newspaper*, February 16, 1976, https://princetext.tripod.com/i_hs.html.

11. Charles Smith quoted in Ronin Ro, *Prince: Inside the Music and the Masks* (New York: St. Martin's Press, 2011), 9.

12. Ro, *Prince*, 12.

13. Ro, *Prince*, 14.

14. Ro, *Prince*, 14.

15. Jason Draper, *Prince: Chaos, Disorder, and Revolution* (New York: Backbeat, 2011), 14.

16. Doell quoted in Draper, *Prince*, 37.

17. See Ro, *Prince: Inside the Music and the Masks*.

18. Prince quoted in Jon Pareles, "A Re-Inventor of His World and Himself," *New York Times*, November 17, 1996.

19. See Chuck Taylor, "Summit Gets Down To Business Of Dance Music," *Billboard*, August 3, 1986, 3.

20. Prince, his management, and Warner Brothers, likely soon realized that showing how Prince made the music did little to promote the 'show'—the visual, touring act related to the album. Evidence supports this view, as a second video for "I Wanna Be Your Lover" was filmed that showed his touring band miming the instrumental parts. Further, although Prince continued to record largely as a solo producer on his following three albums (and many subsequent recordings), "I Wanna Be Your Lover" is the *only* promotional video that foregrounds Prince as multi-instrumentalist. Subsequent videos feature his band miming Prince's parts on the instruments, as evident in videos for "Automatic" (Warner Brothers, 1982) and "When Doves Cry" (Warner Brother, 1984). In addition, his band is featured photographically on every album cover or insert with the exception of *Controversy* (Warner, 1982) during this period, even though the credits often read "Produced, Arranged, Composed and Performed by Prince." Thus, the image of a band continued to play a significant role

in the marketing of Prince (suggesting that his music is made by a group of musicians), even as his musical style was continually impacted by the use of solo multitrack recording.

21. Jake Brown, *Prince 'In the Studio' 1975–1995* (Phoenix: Colossus Books, 2010), 47.

22. Brown, *Prince 'In the Studio'*, 74.

23. Eric Deggans, "Biggest Regret in 2008: Not Publishing this Wendy and Lisa Interview," *Tampa Bay* Times, December 30, 2008.

24. Deggans, "Biggest Regret."

25. Brown, *Prince*, 87–89.

26. Brown, *Prince*, 90–93.

27. Draper, *Prince*, 29.

28. Deggans, "Biggest Regret."

29. Brown, *Prince*, 104.

30. Draper, *Prince*, 69.

31. Jones, *Prince*, 103.

32. See Deggans, "Biggest Regret."

33. Melvoin quoted in Jones, *Prince*, 79.

34. Draper, *Prince*, 28. This voice is evident in Prince's unpublished demo for the Time's "Chocolate" (demoed 1982, released 1989), as well as the studio jam "Cloreen Bacon Skin," recorded 1982, track 8 on *Crystal Ball*, NPG Records, compact disc.

35. Deggans, "Biggest Regret."

36. Draper, *Prince*, 82.

37. Brian Rossiter, "'Ain't That a Bitch?': Prince, Camille, and the Challenge to 'Authentic' Black Masculinity," *Art of Recording Practice Conference Abstracts*, 2010, http://www.artofrecord production.com/aorpjoom/arp-conferences/arp-2010/22-arp-2010/34-arp-2010-abstracts.

38. Rogers quoted in Ro, *Prince*, 157.

39. Rogers engineered tracks for *Purple Rain* (Warner, 1984), *Around the World in a Day* (Paisley Park/Warner, 1985), *Parade* (Paisley Park/Warner, 1986), *Sign o' the Times* (Paisley Park/Warner, 1987), and the *Black Album* (recorded 1987; released Warner, 1994), as well as Prince productions for other artists, and various other unreleased albums and songs.

40. Susan Rogers, email message to author, January 9, 2016.

41. Brown, *Prince*, 175.

42. Brown, *Prince*, 177.

43. Jones, *Slave to the Rhythm*, 18–19.

44. Jones, *Slave*.

45. Woodworth, "'Just Another One of God's Gifts,'" 85.

46. Rogers, email to author, January 9, 2016.

47. Jones, *Slave to the Rhythm*, 141.

48. Rogers quoted in Draper, *Prince*, 94.

49. Rogers quoted in Brown, *Prince*, 194.

50. Prince quoted in Jones, *Slave to the Rhythm*, 148.

51. Murphy (as Detective Axel Foley) in *Beverly Hills Cop* (Paramount Pictures, 1984).

52. Rogers, email response, January 9, 2016.

53. It should be stated that George largely praised Prince in *Billboard* during the mid-1980s, although he was occasionally critical of Prince's crossover self-marketing, as evident in this

1985 column: "For every act that successfully uses AC ballads to cross over or new wavey rock'n'roll, there are so many others who miss, not just with pop radio or MTV, but with their core black audience. . . . It is worth noting that for all his rock'n'roll posturing it was Prince's funk, both on his 'A' sides ('When Doves Cry') and 'B' ('Erotic City,' '17 Days'), that made for his best singles" (George 1985, BM1–12). George's most strident critique of Prince's crossover (again coupled with praise) came after "Bob George," in his R&B monograph *The Death of Rhythm and Blues*. Nelson George, *The Death of Rhythm and Blues* (New York: E. P. Dutton, 1988).

54. Rogers, email response, January 9, 2016.

55. Scott Poulson-Bryant, "Fresh Prince," *Spin* (September 1991), 40.

Chapter 8

EROTIC CITIES

Instrumental Anthropomorphism in Prince's Compositions

BRIAN JUDE DE LIMA

INTRODUCTION

The tragic death of Prince Rogers Nelson in 2016 has prompted many to reflect on and examine the work and legacy of this twentieth-century Mozart in ways previously unexplored. As a man who was constantly honing his craft as an instrumentalist, songwriter, composer and producer, Prince was innovative in so many areas that his influence in music and entertainment has been far-reaching. For example, the early works of Prince Rogers Nelson played an influential role in the proliferation of computer-based synth-pop acts such as Ready for the World, Zapp and Roger, Depeche Mode, and the Pet Shop Boys, all of whom successfully incorporated this style into their own sound.[1]

While Prince has made unique contributions to the world of music, much has been made over the years of his use of sexually charged lyrics and his erotic stage histrionics. Despite people's preoccupation with this particular aspect of Prince's persona, surprisingly few scholars have taken it upon themselves to delve into these matters in any new and creative ways. To be sure, Prince's compositions, such as "Head" (1980), "Let's Pretend We're Married" (1982), "Erotic City" (1984), "Darling Nicki" (1984), "Computer Blue" (1984) and "Purple Rain" (1984), all contain sexually charged semiotic gestures. Furthermore, Prince's use of sexual metaphors—which embody what I consider as synthetic human ejaculation, is evident within many of his earlier compositions between the years of 1980 to 1984. For example, in his composition "Dirty Mind" (1980), Prince uses a chromatically rising melodic line between scale-steps five and eight towards the end of several sections.

This melodic gesture seems to emulate the male phallus going through the various stages of an erection.[2]

Prince's use of perverse dialogue and androgynous clothing could also be viewed as a juxtaposition of binaries. That is, his music is rife with sexual innuendo and eroticism. Conversely, within these very same sexually charged frameworks, Prince also teases toward an opposing binary—that is, his reconciliation for praising of a higher power within sexually charged themes. For example, Prince's live performances negotiated onstage sexual iconography that included the wearing of lingerie to the throbbing bass and synth stabs played by the provocatively dressed women in his band. To further justify this position, consider the sexual innuendo from his composition "1999," "I have a 'Lion' in my pocket, and baby he's ready to roar." In contrast, at the beginning of the composition, Prince, along with band members Lisa Coleman and Dez Dickerson, take turns singing the lyrics with Dickerson referencing the "second coming" of Jesus Christ from the Book of Revelation, stating, "but when I woke up this mornin', could've sworn it was judgment day."

Another example of this combination of both perversion and praise is evident in the composition "Let's go Crazy" (1984). In this composition, taken from the album *Purple Rain* (1984), Prince begins the song by preaching like a church minister, accompanied by a church organ, "Dearly beloved, we are gathered here today to get through this thing called life . . ." Toward the end of the song, the band begins to play an ostinato variation on a I-V cadence, and the song intensity increases as Prince states the lyrics, "he's coming . . . he's coming . . . coming." I am suggesting that Prince is really referring to human ejaculation here, and "he's coming" is a play on words. When Prince states the word "coming" for the final time, the band drops out, and he begins to solo with a frenzied vivacity with his guitar and improvisation acting as the role of the "dominant," and his listeners, the roles of the "submissive," all building toward the climax. Finally, the band rejoins in with equal intensity and Prince and band members loosely quote the ending of Bill Haley's "Rock Around the Clock" without resolving to the tonic; instead, they resolve to a deceptive cadential b7 chord. In deconstructing this (song's) climax, I am proposing that Prince's improvisation was transcended into a metaphor— his guitar serving as his phallus, and the notes he played were his ejaculate.

Some of Prince's topics are so varied that they may seem somewhat disjointed to the listener, ranging from controversial themes that relate to world issues such as in the songs "1999," (1982) or "Sign o' the Times" (1987), to sexual, misogynistic ditties, as in his composition "Let's Pretend We're Married" (1982)—once again, all while giving praise to a higher power. The connection between these contrasting themes is that Prince has managed to expose mankind's megalomaniac appetite for power, sex and immortality while also elucidating its vulnerability as a subservient to an unknown higher power. Even Prince's former stylist, Michaela Angela Davis, once said, "Every song was either a prayer or foreplay."[3]

If one was to analyze some of Prince's earlier songs that ranged from 1980–1984, the controversial lyrics seem to take precedence over the music at times. For example, in the song, "Let's Pretend We're Married," Prince states, "I want to fuck you so bad it hurts, it hurts, it hurts . . ." Conversely, the final lyrics toward the end of this composition has Prince once again embracing his religious beliefs by stating, "I'm in love with God because he is the only way 'cuz you and I know we gotta die someday . . ."

Of course, sexually charged lyrics are an obvious attribute of Prince's sound, but what about the instrumental music that supports his lyrics? Previous literature or studies have failed to recognize the anthropomorphic nature of his musical arrangements. By this, I am proposing that Prince's musical arrangements are acting as surrogate human genitalia during coitus, reminiscent of all aspects of Dr. William Masters and Virginia Johnson's four stages of "sexual response cycle"—excitement, plateau, orgasm, and resolution.[4] Dr. Masters and his assistant Virginia Johnson were pioneers in the field of human sexual response for the diagnosis and treatment of sexual disorders and dysfunctions from 1957 until the 1990s.[5] Thus, like Masters and Johnson's "sexual response cycle," Prince's instrumental parts have been crafted to emulate the stimulation, throbbing, pulsating, and wet actions of human sexual intercourse.

Moving forward, this essay seeks to explore Prince Rogers Nelson's journey of "ejaculation," one that he channeled into many of his earlier musical works, while also negotiating this instrumental anthropomorphic sexuality to his audience.

LITERATURE REVIEW:
EXPANSION OF SCHOLARSHIP AND COMMON THEMES

There is a small body of literature written about Prince's use of sexuality and androgyny within pop culture. In his 2008 article entitled "Prince as a Queer Poststructuralist," musicologist Robert Walser does an outstanding job of positioning Prince as an artist that defies societal compartmentalization and taxonomy. Walser makes the argument for society's inability to stabilize a classification for Prince as being a misogynistic patriarch (akin to the way his father was portrayed in the 1984 movie *Purple Rain*), or a master of reconciling feminine signs and symbols. For example, and androgynous dress code aside, Prince sometimes favored the use of his falsetto voice that could be interpreted as a feminine alter ego (after all, he did have an alter, "Camille," under which ego he anonymously recorded). To further explicate this point, take note of his 1986 composition "Kiss." The entire composition (with the exception of some vocal fills) is sung in a feminine falsetto voice and can be related to philosopher Gilles Deleuze and psychotherapist Felix Guattri's work entitled *Anti-Oedipus: Capitalism and Schizophrenia* (2009) containing their theory of "body without organs."

According to Deleuze and Guattri, and by way of Walser, the body without organs is:

> The experience of schizophrenics who come to understand their bodies as undifferentiated masses, unarticulated by the social apparatus of differentiation. Thus, the body without organs is the body that resists hegemonic coding, the body that is detached and able to be transformed.[6]

This quote from Walser is reminiscent of French philosopher Jacques Derrida's thinking on abolishing written and spoken taxonomies about objects, attitudes, music, dogmas, or even people, as they are, in essence, undefinable.[7] In this light, binaries are not thought of in terms of hierarchies but rather become complimentary to one another.[8] For example, although Prince was born as a male, as a performer, he reconciled the masculine with the feminine—in his onstage dress attire, different singing registers, and content of lyrics that ranged from misogyny—the sexual interlude in "Let's Pretend We're Married," to the endearing thematic material of "Nothing Compares to You" (1985). Thus, from this vantage, Prince becomes a master of transformations, refusing to be classified as (n)either the masculine or feminine archetype. Philosopher Nancy J. Holland also attests to this point in her article, contextualizing Prince's composition "When Doves Cry" (1984) as an "attempt to elicit and represent what might be characterized as female desire outside of the male-dominated sexual economy."[9] In this light, much of his music disrupts tired imperatives about active masculinity versus passive femininity;[10] after all, he did claim, "I'm not a woman, I'm not a man, I'm something that you'll never understand,"[11] and then continued to evade contextualization of his identity by legally changing his name to a *symbol*—a combination of the male and female gender signs that ultimately retains the morphology of its female sign.[12]

Although there is no published literature that examines the exploitation of instrumental anthropomorphism in Prince's music such as this study,

Professor Annie K. Potts of the University of Canterbury cites African American multi-instrumentalist Questlove and his take on Prince's songs stating:

> Prince's music possesses a Shakespearean narrative arc, involving ris-
> ing action, comic relief, climax and denouement. If this is the case,
> it is a feminist Shakespearean narrative arc, more often subverting
> the expected masculinist climax in favour of (or in the service of) a
> woman's sexual power and "satisfaction."[13]

I draw attention to the fact that Questlove and my discourse are intertwined
yet exclusive. Where Questlove illuminates the Shakespearean arc as a common narrative within Prince's music, I propose a more sexually charged
theme analogous to the Masters and Johnson's sexual response cycle. Where
our discourse intersects is that we both agree that the climax of Prince's songs
is fueled by a masculine persona.

METHODOLOGY

Several of Prince's songs have been examined for their sexual overtones in
anthropomorphism denoted by his instrumental arrangements. By using a
post-structuralist lens, an attempt has been made to look for the architectonic
structure of Prince's perverse musical cannon (pre *Sign o' the Times*). Also, by
using a post-structuralist lens, I suggest that the anthropomorphism which
exists within Prince's musical arrangements is overlooked and perhaps not
even noticed by most listeners, but it plays a vital role in his controversial
and unconventional music.

In all, six songs from the period of 1980–1984 have been examined for
their instrumental anthropomorphic content: "Erotic City," "Let's Pretend
We're Married," "Darling Nikki," "Purple Rain," "Computer Blue," and "Head."
The reason the researcher solely focused on these six compositions is because
they offer their audience a glimpse into the diachronic evolution of Prince as
a master of ecstatic climaxes—verbal, and what has not been examined thus
far in the literature—the instrumental. By examining these six songs, I am
offering the reader a lens into how Prince draws his listeners into worlds that
reconcile both the religious transcendence of gospel, with that of orgasmic
overtones—leaving behind the limitations of spoken discourse.

ANTHROPOMORPHISM IN MUSICAL ARRANGEMENTS

Anthropomorphism in music is more prevalent than one might think. Some of the earliest recordings by jazz artists involved the artists making animal-like sounds or sounds mimicking human speech on their instruments. For example, in the composition "Livery Stable Blues" (1917) by the Original Dixieland Jass Band, the band members start to emulate animals. We can also hear anthropomorphism in the music of Bubber Miley and Charles Irvis, who gained notoriety in Duke Ellington's band for making growling sounds on their horn that emulated the human voice. Another example is Brazilian master percussionist Paulinho Da Costa, who made his drums sound like a human voice having a conversation with guitarist and band leader Bola Sete.[14]

Conversely, musicians have also used musical instruments in denoting artificial intelligence, such as machinery and robotics, as a compliance for anthropomorphism. For example, in the composition "The Robots" (1978) by the German electronic band Kraftwerk, the human voice is processed through an electronic vocoder to give the listener not just an impression of advancement in human technology, but rather an advancement in human evolution—man makes machine—machine tries to takeover man, such as in Jim Chriton's 1973 epic, *Westworld*. That is, the robotic sound of the voice is manipulated to show an advancement in the human body—the machine being more efficient than man himself. Kraftwerk also cleverly uses anthropomorphism and onomatopoeia in the composition "Boing Boom Chuck" (1987). In this composition, I am asserting that the words "boing boom chuck" act as a drum set; there are two hits on a bass drum ("boing boom") followed by a snare drum ("chuck"). Once again, listeners are subjected to an advancement in technology by way of artificial intelligence versus conventional antediluvian paradigms of music construction.

Another example of anthropomorphism in music comes way of "Lil' Louis" and his version of "French Kiss" (1989). This composition is a strong example of instrumental arrangements that have adopted human characteristics and in this case, even emulate Masters's four stages of psychological arousal.[15]

Louis's use of the sequencer is pivotal in that it is sped up slowly and mapped against the moaning sounds of a woman having an orgasm. As the sequencer speeds up, the woman's moaning becomes more intense—giving listeners the sense that her orgasm is reaching a climax. When the climax has finally approached, the sequencer begins to play a melodic line that ascends and then descends, taking on the impression of a penis aggressively thrusting in and out of the vagina.

British electronic band *Depeche Mode* juxtaposes sounds of human deep-breathing with artificial breathing sounds from a synthesizer in their composition "I Want You Now" (1987). Eventually, the samples of human breathing fade out, and the artificial breathing remains imprinted in the listener as if it was a real human breathing.

In the composition "Golliwog's Cakewalk" (1908), Claude Debussy also uses anthropomorphism by first taking the theme of Rich Wagner's "Tristan and Isolde" and displacing its melodies to sound like human laughter. Debussy uses a form of sarcastic mimicry in measures 63 through 67 by invoking what may be interpreted as laughter with grace notes displacing the original Wagner "Tristan Chord"—in essence, poking fun at Wagner's highbrow musical aristocracy.

According to author Elizabeth de Martelly, Debussy purposely brought Wagner's composition into a world where binaries are juxtaposed.[16] For example, de Martelly purports that in measure 63–67 of "Golliwog's Cake-walk," Debussy uses a parodied quotation from Richard Wagner's composition "Tristan and Isolde"; it is anthropomorphic in that it signifies that Golliwog's body is woven into this music.[17]

De Martelly also makes the argument that Debussy was, in essence, bringing Wagner's world of highbrow composition down to a world associated with that of the "lowbrow."[18] de Martelly further purports:

> Where Wagner's opera is harmonically complex and "refined," the syncopated cakewalk represents a lowbrow, "wild," and "animalistic" musical idiom. Here, Debussy frames Wagner and the cakewalk as "humorously" incompatible, from disparate worlds incapable of communicating with one another. Indeed, this tension also evokes extra-musical associations as a confrontation between Golliwog as Africanized "primitive" and Wagner as the epitomized figure of high Western culture.[19]

SEXUAL ANTHROPOMORPHISM IN PRINCE'S MUSIC

Although Prince was a prolific composer who contributed to teasing sexual innuendo to the forefront of soul music,[20] I believe there are deeper and more subtle reasons why his music has made a lasting sexual impression on his listeners. It could be argued that Prince's music has an anthropomorphic sexual quality that is quite subtle—the sexual nature does not solely lie within his lyrics but is also disguised within the instrumental arrangements themselves. First, if one were to look at a Prince performance (pre-*Sign o' the Times*), the possibility of various sexual influences come to mind, such as gyrating men with guitars making orgasmic faces while singing blues lyrics (think Chuck Berry and Muddy Waters). Also, one could just as easily draw similarities to Jimi Hendrix stroking his guitar and holding lighter fluid between his legs—squirting it all over the guitar before he sets it on fire. Similarly to Hendrix, Berry, and Waters, author Dodai Stewart states that Prince's sexual obsession with his guitar was a metaphor for his phallus:

> He stroked his long purple instrument like he was rubbing his cock, the guitar solo transformed into masturbatory act, his head thrown back, eyes closed, mouth open, each note building on the next into an explosion of indecent abandon.[21]

Prince has used his guitar as a symbol of a phallus on the verge of ejaculation; indeed, at the end of the movie and song *Purple Rain*, his guitar ejaculates onto the crowd.[22] After viewing this, I have examined several of Prince's compositions, and I believe that Prince's success is partly attributed to the layering of a dualism that consists of: a) his sexual lyrics/onstage antics, denoting themes ranging from misogyny, dominance, and perverseness; and b) the instrumental arrangements that denote the human body's actions during intercourse (akin to Masters and Johnson's research on the stages of psychological arousal).

FINDINGS

When listening to the composition "Erotic City," individuals may be drawn into its reoccurring ostinato bass line and drum pattern, but this is only an obvious, outer-layered aesthetic. Prince begins moaning at the introduction of the song and builds for twenty seconds thereafter. As Prince begins to moan more intensely, the instruments become denser in the mix, adding to the sexual intensity of his moans. When Prince finally begins with the opening lyric: "all of my purple life . . ." he is singing in the bass register. The significance of this point is that "Erotic City" also has an interesting element that could be viewed as an alter ego of Prince. By this, I maintain that some of his lyrics are also sung in unison by a computer-generated, giggly voice in the soprano register—giving the listener a "naughty versus nice" juxtaposition of binary oppositions.

The lewd lyrics alone do not carry this song into the realm of the erotic; the brilliance here is that Prince has blended the sexual lyrics with the modulation effect of the synth brass. Specifically, the synth brass portrays the lyrics "we can fuck until the dawn." Furthermore, the layered electronic drums coming in and out throughout the song sound like they are processed by a phaser special effect—giving it a high amplitude and low decay reminiscent of a man or woman thrusting their hips up and down during intercourse. Toward the end of the song, laser shots from the keyboard ring out, representing a climactic ejaculation.

"Let's Pretend We're Married" is one of the more sexually charged compositions by Prince. Toward the end of the composition, Prince's singing cuts out, and the listener is left with only a pulsating synth bass that is throbbing like a phallus under the stress of arousal—sexual messages that cause the blood vessels and spongy chambers of the penis to dilate. As the listener is subjected to the throbbing bass, the piano begins to add layers of broken atonal chord clusters that sound somewhat mysterious. The throbbing bass continues throughout this section with only the drum machine as an accompaniment. The perverse dialogue below is illuminated by the instrumental arrangement that has become a metaphor for Prince's lewd intentions for "Marsha." For example, Prince states to Marsha, "Look here Marsha, I'm not sayin' this just to be nasty, but I want to fuck the taste out of your mouth; can you relate?"

In relation to this section's anthropomorphism, I am insinuating that the synthesizer is playing chords that are pitch bent with a glissando effect—sounding as if they could be Prince's own tongue sliding over Marsha's body. Prince then makes the following claim to Marsha: "I want to, I want to, I want to, I want to, I want to, I want to, I want to fuck you." As Prince makes this claim, the delay effect on his voice is sped up to sound like a multitude of Prince personalities sexually overpowering Marsha with misogynistic intentions (giving the listener a glimpse into the world of one of his many alter egos).

If we examine the graph taken from Masters and Johnson's female sexual response cycle,[23] it is possible to draw a correlation between the separate instrumental part's amplitude, attack, and decay that embody Prince's perverse song structures. For example, if one were to plot the sexual intensity of this composition as per individual instrument, the throbbing synth bass line would be denoted by the letter 'B'—note the oscillating wave that is a metaphor for the throbbing bass line. Next, the atonal piano melodies that randomly wash over Prince's perverse lyrics would be the letter 'A' as it randomly appears and then disappears. Finally, Prince's perverse speech would be recognized as the letter 'C' in that it slowly builds and immediately drops off (and then eventually restarts).

By having Prince's voice and musical instruments follow the same trajectory as Masters and Johnson's female sexual response cycle, Prince has successfully reconciled what seems to be a representation of female sexual gratification outside of the archetypal misogynistic male- enforced sexual economy.[24] In this sense, and by way of Masters and Johnson's sexual response cycle, Prince's sexual liberation of the female orgasm places him as an early genre-defying pioneer.

A possible reason why Masters and Johnson's female sexual response cycle is adaptive to Prince's compositions is because Prince himself has been somewhat incognito about his sexual identity. For example, in his 1979 composition "I Want to Be Your Lover," Prince states, "I wanna be your mother and your sister too." Five years later, in his 1984 composition "I would die 4 U," Prince would up the ante of disguise, promulgating, "I'm not a woman . . . I'm not a man . . . I'm something you'll never understand." To help bring clarity to Prince's discursive dialogue, author Dodai Stewart raises an excellent point that regardless of how one feels about astrology, it is important to remember that Prince was, and identified as, a Gemini. The zodiac sign of the twins. Duality was in his DNA and was reflected in his music and persona.[25] To further Stewart's point, in his 1981 composition "Controversy," Prince states, "I just can't believe all the things people say . . . controversy. Am I Black or white, am I straight . . . or gay?" Prince's obsession with duality in his sexual orientation is also apparent in his 1988 composition "Lovesexy," stating, "You got me dripping . . . dripping all over the floor, the floor . . . if I come back as a woman, I want a body like yours." I am further claiming that this sexual "duality" has been exemplified within Prince's musical output. That is, Prince's stage presence can first be viewed as described in the 1981 *New York Times* article which referred to his "androgyny," "fluid body movements," and "flamboyantly minimal stage costume" when describing his aesthetic during an onstage performance.[26] "He wore heels. His hair was long. He wore makeup. His obsession with women and their bodies overflowed into a desire to be inside their skin."[27] Next, I am suggesting once again that his instrumental arrangements have acted as surrogate agents to his sexual appetite. Stewart suggests that "through music, fashion, dance, and lyrics, Prince presented sex as a complicated, multifaceted, amorphous, often religious experience that could be negotiation."[28] It is further suggested that this negotiation was realized only when his instrumental arrangements peppered his lewd lyrics.

"Darling Nikki" is possibly one of the strongest examples of how sexual anthropomorphism is displayed by the instrumental parts in Prince's compositions. Lyrics aside, the musical arrangement alone is reminiscent of being a primordial "cock tease," and a "luridly captivating tale of a sexual tryst."[29]

For starters, "Darling Nikki" was already classified as a dangerous and vexing monument in the eyes of some politically powerful women in the United States. For example, Tipper Gore, then wife of US senator and future vice president Al Gore, famously decided to lead a campaign against all explicit lyrics in music after buying her preteen daughter the soundtrack to Prince's 1984 movie *Purple Rain*.[30] Gore was shocked after her daughter pointed out the lyrics that make reference to "masturbating with a magazine," and thus "rounded up a bunch of her Washington housewife friends, most of whom happened to be married to influential members of the US Senate, and founded the PMRC."[31] The Parents Music Resource Center was founded on the ideals of shielding the vulnerable public from the lewdness and delinquency of what Gore termed in her 1987 book, *Raising PG Kids in an X-Rated Society*, "porn rock."[32] To examine what might have made Gore feel offended or somehow "violated," the focus here is on how the instrumental arrangement behind "Darling Nikki" is almost as powerful, if not as powerful, as the polemic lyrics themselves.

For example, as Prince begins singing, the instruments take a back seat to his provocative lyrics and only sparingly support. Once Prince has completed singing each vocal stanza, an onslaught orgy of instruments becomes a *tour de force* for the ears. The electronic bass drum is now emulating a double bass drum in sixteenth notes. This quadrupled figure might be akin to the speed of Darling Niki's vibrator—the "many devices that money could buy."

After Prince sings his last stanza, the vibrator effect created by the double bass drum is now intensified by the synthesizer playing oscillating major thirteen chords a minor third apart. This keyboard oscillation continues at a high intensity to the end of the song, all while Prince's is screaming in ecstasy. In this sense, the keyboards have also become a different intensity setting on the metaphorical vibrator used by "Darling Nikki."

When the song is completed, the song is played backward lasting just over a minute. The vocals, unreversed are Prince singing, "Hello, how are you? Fine fine 'cause I know that the Lord is coming soon . . . coming, coming soon."[33] The word "coming" can be interpreted as being polysemous. It can be viewed as referring to the "second coming of Christ," but likely, given Prince's palate for lyrical perversion, it is referring to ejaculation.

"Purple Rain" may seem like an endearing ballad, and on one level it is, but I believe there lies a deeper meaning to what Prince is referring to as "Purple Rain." From *Songfacts 2016*, an anonymous blogger stated:

Closely watch the end of the movie *Purple Rain*, you have seen him masturbate his guitar as if it was his penis and a neon purple ejaculate spews from the head of his guitar. Listen to the lyrics again and catch the inside joke. Purple Rain is a shower of semen which fluoresces purple under black light.[34]

This anonymous assessment is on par with what I am suggesting. For example, as the song draws to a close, Prince begins his instrumental solo that is a play on the song's theme. What is important to note is that after Prince and the band perform a plagal cadence (IV–I), Prince's guitar solo escalates into a frenzy of major ninths. This interval creates a new climax as this melodic note within his solo has not resolved to a tonic chord tone. When Prince finally plays the major third of the tonic, this resolution is met with the piano part playing a major pentatonic scale up and down the octave several times, akin to rain droplets—denoting what I believe to be a metaphor for Prince's semen ejaculating on his audience.

Similarly, *Esquire* columnist David Holmes also recounts a live show in which Prince used his guitar as phallus and ejaculated at the end of the song's climax. Holmes states:

In 1985, there was a 20-minute live Prince video that MTV showed pretty much every hour on the hour. It was a medley of "Baby I'm A Star" and "I Would Die 4 U" that ended with a very long, never-boring guitar solo, at the end of which Prince's guitar literally ejaculated. The neck shot white foam all over the crowd, and the crowd *roared*. Men and women, straight and gay, atheist and devout, parents and children—they left that show with Prince's guitar jizz all over their faces, clothes and hair, and they *loved it*.[35]

In the composition "Computer Blue," the song begins with band members Wendy and Lisa hinting at some sexual play with each other. The supporting musical arrangement also adds to the sexual soirée on various levels. To begin, the keyboards and guitar are playing a somewhat Middle Eastern sounding riff of a minor second followed by a perfect fourth. This ostinato pattern is the backdrop for Prince's guitar making squealing noises somewhat reminiscent of the misogynistic cat calls men might make as women pass by. The original video, taken from the movie *Purple Rain*, depicts more of a sadomasochistic theme at play. For example, Prince's whole body is oiled, and he is wearing a blindfold that is barely transparent. Prince, is gyrating his hips in a stiff fashion and the synth brass line that has a slow attack, is echoing the movement of his hips. The "master and servant" scenario becomes realized as band member Wendy drops to her knees and starts to mimic the act of fellatio on Prince. This act of fellatio performed by Wendy on Prince is possibly one of the strongest examples of anthropomorphism, as the notes spewed from Prince's guitar once again become an allegory for his ejaculate.

Conversely, this lewd scene from *Purple Rain* also serves for a different possible scenario. What I am now proclaiming is that Prince is reconciling with his faith in God by acting as a priest—the members of his band are acting as the holy congregation—and the lyrics and music are the Gospel. Thus, when band member Wendy drops to her knees in what seems to be an act of fellatio, I am now suggesting that she is receiving the "body and blood" of Prince as a Christ figure.

As well in the composition "Head," when Prince starts to sing the chorus "Head till you get enough . . . head till your love is red . . . head love you 'til you're dead," the keyboards begin to play a synth brass sound that starts small and gradually swells giving the listener the imagery of a person receiving oral sex—the mouth moving up and down the shaft of a penis. At the climax of this composition, there is a synth solo that is performed using a bubbly synth sound akin to the semen within a man's penis that is about to ejaculate. Furthermore, the heavy use of the pitch bender on the synth solo is also allegorical of what one may consider to be a male penis being stroked back and forth.

DISCUSSION

The six Prince compositions presented lead listeners into a world where the titillating backdrop of instrumental arrangements also parallels (and at times, eclipses) the sexually suggestive lyrics. Prince has successfully taken his audience to all destinations erotic while whetting their appetites for the next course.

The similarities between both his lyrics and the musical arrangements, when analyzed using Masters and Johnson's "Sexual Response Cycle," demonstrate that his instrumental anthropomorphism did not take a backseat to the lewd lyrics, but rather gave the listener a "double penetration" of the senses—lyrics and instrumental arrangements.

If one considers Derrida's analysis of privileged binaries in literature and art (man/woman, night/day, good/evil), eventually, according to Derrida, the binaries will become so extreme that they end up crossing into each other and roles become reversed and/or synthesized.[36] Thus, original hierarchies become the underprivileged, and the underprivileged become the privileged. In this manner, the lyrics, which can be viewed as having a dominant role as the primary source of titillation, can now be viewed as submissive or at least equal to the musical arrangement. Consequently, by viewing Prince's music as an equal synthesis of binaries (or at times, the privileged binary)—lyrics and instrumental anthropomorphism, the public may finally begin to realize the *tour de force* he has left behind. To only consider his lewd lyrics as the driving force behind his sexually crafted themes becomes a fallacy of false representation and of an outer-layered aesthetic—missing the substratum that lies beneath—the "devil in the details"—his anthropomorphic musical arrangements.

Make no mistake, what has transpired from these early years of musical genius is no easy feat by any artist. By this, I mean that Prince has managed to stretch and push the limits of sexuality within the six proposed themes while also arousing his public into consensual submission. In this manner, Prince has taken upon the role of "master," with the public as his "submissive." Therefore, by teasing at themes of androgyny, master and servant, or saint versus sinner, Prince tackles what may be controversial subjects, but are in all actuality, exactly what he had been hinting at in 1987—"Sign o' the Times." By exposing human sexuality against a backdrop of dualistic themes, man dominates woman ("Let's Pretend We're Married"), or woman dominates man ("Kiss"), Prince has managed to successfully reconcile both binaries into a synthesis that has no description, giving rise to the later part of his career's undefinable name of *Symbol*.

CONCLUSION

Within the compositions that have been examined in this article, between the years of 1980–1984, Prince has successfully juxtaposed a tripartite orgy that embraces funk, faith, and filth whilst also juxtaposing himself as a Christ figure to the masses—his listeners and "congregation."

Although Prince has been a controversial topic for nearly forty years (with critics and others having tried to sum up his music as perverse—the result of a combination of lewd lyrics along with sexual onstage antics), I have conversely presented an alternative lens that may explain why many may find his music to be so appealing. By examining the use of anthropomorphism (the ascription of human characteristics to what is not human), this researcher has evinced how certain instruments in Prince's musical arrangements helped to enhance the perverse lyrics he sang and added to his onstage sexual prances. Thus, when one experiences Prince's bold musical perversion, they may not be aware that they are dealing with the "experience" itself as being a gestalt. That is, Prince's lewd lyrics and perverse onstage antics are all contributing aggregates forming a unified form of sexual onslaught. More importantly, and not as obvious to many, the sexual nature of anthropomorphism within his musical arrangements became the fuel that enabled his lyrics and onstage antics to reverberate an auditory representation of sexual onomatopoeia.

Perhaps now, fans will finally hear and view Prince's songs in a new light—recognizing that his early works are perverse, instrumentally arranged masterpieces that ooze sexual innuendos and eroticism. To this end, Prince Rogers Nelson's lewd onstage antics and song lyrics were not the only factors that contributed to his sexually charged compositions; rather, the musical arrangements of his earlier compositions embodied and reflected the stages of the human sexual response cycle.

In the wake of his passing, it is the memory of his music and onstage theatrics that will have canonized him as a marriage of "saint and the sinner." While we will never again get to see or hear Prince create, arrange, and play music in the future, the oeuvre of music that he has left behind will forever be indelibly etched in our memories and available for newer artists to draw on.

Notes

1. Elias Leight, and Maura Johnston, "18 Awesome Prince Rip-Offs: A Handful of Artists That Made Their Songs a Little More Purple," *Rolling Stone*, April 21, 2020, https://www.rollingstone.com/music/music-lists/prince-songs-rip-offs-71562/.

2. James Perone, *The Words and Music of Prince* (Westport, CT: Praeger, 2007); Matt Thomas, "The Words and Music of Prince," *Popular Music and Society* 33, no. 1 (2010): 124–26, http://dx.doi.org/10.1080/03007760902786082.

3. Charlotte Wareing, "Prince's Sexually Charged and Most Explicit Song Lyrics." *Mirror*, (April 22, 2016): http://www.mirror.co.uk/3am/celebrity-news/princes-sexually-charged-most-explicit-7810310.

4. William Masters and Virginia E. Johnson, *Human Sexual Response* (Bronx: Ishi Press, 1966).

5. Suzann Gage and Sylvia Morales, Katharina Allers, and Federation of feminist women's health centers, *A New View of a Woman's Body: A Fully Illustrated Guide* (Los Angeles: Feminist Health Press, 1991), 46.

6. Robert Walser, "Prince as Queer Poststructuralist," *Popular Music and Society* 18, no. 2 (1994): 79–89, https://doi:10.1080/03007769408591556.

7. Mahdi Shafieyan, "Binary Oppositions and Binary Pairs." *2nd International Conference on Humanities, Historical and Social Sciences* 17 (2011): 195–99.

8. Jacques Derrida, *Of Grammatology*, trans. Gayatri Chakravorty Spivak, 40th anniversary ed. (Baltimore: Johns Hopkins University Press, 2016).

9. Nancy J. Holland, "Purple Passion: Images of Female Desire in 'When Doves Cry,'" *Cultural Critique*, no. 10 (Autumn1988): 89–98, https://doi:10.2307/1354108.

10. Annie K Potts, "The Intersectional Influences of Prince: A Human-Animal Tribute," *Animal Studies Journal* 5, no. 1 (2016): 152–86, https://ro.uow.edu.au/cgi/viewcontent.cgi?article=1216&context=asj.

11. Prince, "Purple Rain," side 2, track 4, Warner Bros., 1984.

12. Robert Walser, "Prince as Queer Poststructuralist," *Popular Music and Society* 18, no. 2 (1994): 79–89, https://doi:10.1080/03007769408591556.

13. Annie K. Potts, "The Intersectional Influences of Prince: A Human-Animal Tribute," *Animal Studies Journal* 5, no. 1 (2016): 156.

14. Bola Sete, *Bola Sete at the Monterey Jazz Festival*, Audio CD (Verve Records, 2000).

15. Masters, 1966.

16. Elizabeth de Martelly, "Signification, Objectification, and the Mimetic Uncanny in Claude Debussy's 'Golliwog's Cakewalk,'" *Current* Musicology, no. 90 (Fall 2010): 8. https://academiccommons.columbia.edu/download/fedora_content/download/ac:184585/CONTENT/current.musicology.90.demartelly.7-34.pdf.

17. De Martelly, "Signification."

18. De Martelly, "Signification."

19. De Martelly, "Signification."

20. Don Kaplan, "Prince Was a One-Man Sexual Revolution," *New York Daily News*, April 21, 2016, http://www.nydailynews.com/entertainment/music/prince-one-man-sexual-revolution-article-1.2610247.

21. Dodai Stewart, "On Prince, Blackness, and Sexualit," *Splinter*, April 22, 2016, https://splinternews.com/on-prince-blackness-and-sexuality-1793856349.

22. Andrew Friedman, "Prince Was the Baddest Motherfucker on the Planet." *FACT Magazine: Music News, New Music*, accessed January 11, 2023, http://www.factmag.com/2016/04/22/prince-tribute-baddest-mf-on-earth/.

23. Masters, 1966.

24. Nancy J. Holland, "Purple Passion: Images of Female Desire in 'When Doves Cry,'" *Cultural Critique*, no. 10 (Autumn 1988): 89–98. doi:10.2307/1354108.

25. Stewart, 2016.

26. Robert Palmer, "The Pop Life; IS PRINCE LEADING MUSIC TO A TRUE BIRACISM?" *New York Times*, December 2, 1988, http://www.nytimes.com/1981/12/02/arts/the-pop-life-is-prince-leading-music-to-a-true-biracism.html.

27. Stewart, 2016.

28. Stewart, 2016.

29. "'Controversy': Remembering Prince's 'Darling Nikki' and The PMRC," Smells Like Infinite Sadness, last modified April 23, 2016, http://smellslikeinfinitesadness.com/controversy-remembering-princes-darling-nikki-and-the-pmrc/.

30. Toby Salkc, "How Prince's Lyrics Led to the Parental Advisory Label." *New York Daily News*, April 21, 2016, http://www.nydailynews.com/entertainment/music/prince-lyrics-led-parental-advisory-label-article-1.2610382.

31. Salkc, "How Prince's Lyrics."

32. Salkc, "How Prince's Lyrics."

33. William Poundstone, *Big Secrets: The Uncensored Truth About All Sorts of Stuff* . . . (HarperCollins, 2011) Kindle. {There are no page numbers in a Kindle edition.}

34. "Purple Rain by Prince," Songfacts, accessed January 11, 2023, http://www.songfacts .com/detail.php?id=2012.

35. David Holmes, "What Prince Taught Me about Love. And Sex. And Time," *Esquire*, April 21, 2016, http://www.esquire.com/entertainment/music/a44221/prince-a-remembrance -dave-holmes/.

36. Lucie Guillemette, "Jacques Derrida: Deconstruction and Différance / Signo—Applied Semiotics Theories," Signo, accessed January 12, 2023, http://www.signosemio.com/derrida/ deconstruction-and-differance.asp.

Chapter 9

SIGN O' THE TIMES IN D(CONSTRUCTION) MINOR

Variations on an S Theme

SABATINO DIBERNARDO

PRELUDE: O YEAH[1]

Prince Rogers Nelson, the musical superstar known better simply as
Prince, died April 21. He was 57.[2]

After the passing of Prince on April 21, 2016, this variation on an S theme could
only be written in "the saddest of all keys"[3] and with a minor deconstructive
transposition. This lyrico-philosophical tribute to Prince is inspired by the
most intriguing iteration of signifiers along a semiotic chain of substitution-
ary marks that became a *sign* o' the times, a *symbol,* and a *name* for the icon
(formerly known as) S. Such was his fame and such was the phonic necessity regarding this unpronounceable glyph that even this mark under the
undecidable sign of a questioning mark or a question mark of undecidability
required and received its own supplemental[4] name: "Love Symbol #2."[5] Under
this and previous sign(ature)s, a provocative, controversial, and brilliant
artist-musician made us listen, feel, and think playfully about serious matters
and seriously about playful matters. Thus, without recourse to an essentialist
meaning behind or underneath Prince's performative speech act,[6] this enco-
mium is composed parasitically—both lyrically and philosophically—as a
(post)structural inhabitation of a song and a sign—"Sign o' the Times"—in
the *form* of a song and a philosophical *style* about a sign that marked both a
time (indeed, times) and an album that would come (retroactively) to bear
traces of a name. This new "name," an imagistic "neologism" inaugurated by
Prince's performative gesture, would come to *engender* the time of a question

for fans, reporters, and lawyers alike regarding this singularly creative symbol fashioned by the artist formerly known by more than one signifier, mark, and name.

Although this nominal renunciation/renaming has often been reduced simply to a marketing or legal stunt by some eccentric musician who, perhaps, took himself way too seriously, this act of attempted self-erasure had the momentous effect of decomposing the "self"-identity of a composer by a non-musical composition that "deconstructed" this constructed subject-identity as a legal fiction that could be controlled, maintained, trademarked, and owned by a record label. Indeed, through this act, listed by *Rolling Stone* magazine as among the twenty-five boldest career moves in music history,[7] Prince would abandon his elite status as a first-name-only celebrity in favor of an unpronounceable symbol that would serve as the signifying mark of a subject that could only be named somewhat "improperly" *ex post facto* by what he had ceased to be: S ("The Artist Formerly Known as Prince").[8] Thus, and with only a polite nod to the critics, we, too, will take this symbolic and nominal act seriously but with a seriousness befitting the aesthetic seriousness of a song about a sign that was, like his music, as creative as it was subversive and emblematic of the double-entendre-driven, binary-subverting, and homophonic-loving sensibilities of the life and music of the seminal artist formerly known as Prince (Rogers Nelson) . . . The Artist Formerly Known As Prince . . . the artist formerly known as S.[9]

Time

At a certain moment in time, Prince (Rogers Nelson) ceased to be
properly named (and controlled)
by a "proper" name by way of an "improper" speech act.

time

An unpronounceable and undecidable
Sign o' the Time that became a Time o' his Sign

S

The first step I have taken towards the ultimate goal of emancipation from the chains that bind me to Warner Bros. was to change my name from Prince to [S]. Prince is the name that my Mother gave me at birth. Warner Bros. to the name, trademarked it, and used it as the main marketing tool to promote all of the music that I wrote. The company owns the name Prince and all related music marketed under Prince. I became merely a pawn used to produce more money for Warner Bros. . . . I was born Prince and did not want to adopt another conventional name. The only acceptable replacement for my name, and my identity, was a symbol with no pronunciation, that is a representation of me and what my music is about. This symbol is present in my work over the years; it is a concept that has evolved from my frustration; it is who I am. It is my name.[10]

("I hereby rename myself" S)

This "name," like the "name" of God revealed to Moses through a divine speech act (I Am Who I Am), cannot be uttered or spoken—only its supplement. "It" wavers undecidably between an implicit and/or explicit (speech) act of performativity; uncertain, undecidable, and (almost) unprecedented . . .

In this single gesture, the multitalented musical performer performed an inaudible speech act that sought to problematize the legal copyright[11] to the musical production and performance of labor by the trademarked signatory "Prince." Indeed, *this* name and the production of musical labor performed under *this* name had been tied to a "force of law"[12] requiring him to abide by the arbitrary but, nevertheless, legally binding effects of decisions made by a record label regarding the release of music composed under *this* name. In a similarly provocative fashion, S would utilize his body as a canvas for "Controversy"[13] of the non-sexualized sort by inscribing a mark (viz., "Slave") across his cheek that would inaugurate a public questioning of musical pro-prietorship instigated by debates with his record label leading to the questioning of the property of and proprietary rights to a signifier, a mark, a label, and a name.[14] As a sign of "enslavement," this ironic double coding would highlight both the legal and existential issues that precipitated the advent of the glyph as Prince was "enslaved" by two labels that worked metonymically in tandem (viz., i.e., "namely") "his" record *label* (viz., Warner Bros.) and "his" nominal *label* (viz., Prince). At stake was a certain logocentric swirl of metaphysical questions regarding the "proper"—as in names, sign(ature)s, and ownership with legal, monetary, and existential implications. This problem of the "proper" led Prince to try and sever himself *per se* (in himself) from himself (without thereby destroying the artist-*subject* Prince) and his record label . . . (S O' the Times Mess with your mind) . . . even if only to *mess with their minds* a little bit. Ironically, the very construction of this musical subject "Prince" had necessarily (i.e., structurally) subjected him to a subjugation by the record company's legal authority over their *own* act of creative identity construction and monetary investment/purchase: the artist-subject-commodity "Prince." Consequently, as he had done previously in songs and movies, Prince had to create another character, subject position, and image/icon/symbol to distance himself from himself.[15]

Times
At a certain moment in time, Prince (Rogers Nelson) ceased to be
properly named (and controlled)
by a "proper" name by way of an "improper" speech act.
times
An unpronounceable and undecidable
Sign o' the Time that became a Time o' his Sign
S

"My Name is Prince,"[16] the first song on the S album released in 1992, would foreshadow and prefigure the self-referential renaming in Prince's press release the following year. Consequently, only after the fact and by way of a retroactive communicative necessity would it become the eponymous *Love Symbol Album* (i.e., the phonic supplement required to "name" the unpronounceable glyph/album).[17] On this album, the glyph was displayed in all its asymmetric beauty[18] and introduced to the world a symbol after which (both chronologically and metonymically) a famous artist would die nominally and resurrect (himself) nominally under this uncertain sign and undecidable mark. As Prince noted in the press release, this "replacement" (i.e., substitution/supplement) and "representation" for his name, his identity, and his music—"a symbol without pronunciation"—had been "present in [his] work over the years." Thus, it is no hermeneutical stretch to read the layers of irony and intertextuality set into play by a generative act of "naming" an album symbolically with an eye/I toward what was to come and concomitantly subverting it with the opening song about an explicit self-referential affirmation. This song, with its title/chorus suspended undecidably between a constative, and a performative speech act, takes back what it affirms (latterly) under the mark of a glyph on the cover and, what was then yet to come, a performative speech act appropriating that symbol and renaming/reaffirming his new/old name (viz., "My Name is S"). This brilliantly paradoxical inclusion of both "names" would mark the "complex irony"[19] of their co-existence as acts of (re)naming himself that would efface the distinction between self and artist, producer and product, music and musician, symbol, and name.[20]

"Sign o' the Times," also on the S album, would add yet another layer of irony to this intriguing play of intertextuality regarding "signs" and "times," naming and renaming, all of which Prince explains in a prophetic tone: "the sign o' the time will mess with your mind." Now, whether this "mind-messing" is of the diagnostic/apocalyptic sort signified by the song lyrics or of the foreshadowing symbolic sort that graces the album cover—and the subsequent self-referential signification of both his own *signi*ficance in the opening song and the *signi*fying agency of renaming himself yet to come—remains undecidable. Nevertheless, it will have come to be read after the fact as naming himself twice over and folded back on itself/himself: his name is Prince/S and he/it is a sign o' the time.

This subversive strategy intervened at the weakest point of seeming stability; namely, Prince himself (as a noumenal in-himself) or essential self and identity. However, this seemingly stable "self" and "identity," and the fragility of these ostensibly self-evident concepts, would be put into question by this questioning "sign," which thereby revealed the highly constructed and mythologized "self" and "identity" of both Prince's self-identity *and* the metaphysical underpinnings of proper names[21] as a metaphysical desire for a stable, proper, natural essence with an unassailable center or sole/soul identity. The irony doubles over in its attempted effacing of this stable self-identity by reconstructing an identity that could not in any "proper" way identify him that, then, garnered Prince/S even more publicity, exposure, and self-identity under a new mark that simultaneously marked an undecidable name. Even if signifiers are contingently arbitrary and without essence, they still have powerful effects.

Some say a Man ain't happy unless a Man truly dies
Oh why?
Time
At a certain moment in time, Prince (Rogers Nelson) ceased to be
properly named (and controlled)
by a "proper" name by way of an "improper" speech act.
time
An unpronounceable and undecidable
Sign o' the Time that became a Time o' his Sign
S

The problem of Prince's proper name, however, begins long before this renaming. It begins with the birth and naming of Prince Rogers Nelson, where the name hovers between a proper name and a royal title; that is, the inability to maintain a strictly maintained border or compartmentalization between the binary opposites proper/improper without appeal to some correspondence notion of language and naming,[22] a phantasm that tries to keep names and titles in their "proper" places. This post-structuralist problem of the hierarchical binary opposition "proper/improper" in its semiotic context is exemplified throughout Prince's musico-lyrical-performative "deconstruction"[23] of the privilege typically accorded to one over the other (such as music/noise, decent/obscene, sacred/profane, religious/secular, male/female, sexism/feminism)[24] by undermining and effacing them without erasing them. When this problem of the proper was applied to the legal rights and ownership of musicians to their musical production of labor, this instigated the question of subservience to the record labels by means of an ironic *sign*ing away of one's proper name and proprietary rights by means of one's proper name and a *sign*ifying mark or *sign*ature. An additional irony is that through this performative act of signing away one's name (i.e., a testimony and a promise to abide by a legally binding contract), one's name/signature is also elevated to an object of desire by the public's para-religious desire for another "graph"—an autograph—connecting *fan*(atic) and *idol*(atry).[25]

Consequently, by turns marginal, eccentric, ostentatious, and brilliant, this strategic "footnote" in the storied time of Prince/S proves to be less a bizarre or tangential moment in his history than a philosophically ironic and crucial semiotic intervention into the identity formation of one whose identity and fame turned on the musical/auditory. Indeed, it was this non-musical, non-auditory "speech" act that, perhaps, "spoke" and "sang" the loudest about Prince. The very thing that made the artist formerly known as "The Artist Formerly Known as Prince" (once his contract ended and he could once again become what he had ceased to be . . . Prince) a musical legend—his musical voice—was subverted in favor of an inaudible sign[26] that, nevertheless, gave symbolic voice to this complex persona (Latin: mask) and allowed this multilayered persona (Latin: *per+sonare*) to "sound through" his music, characters, and signs as traces within this now iconic glyph.

Some say a Man ain't happy til a man truly dies
O why?
O why?
Times
Time
At a certain moment in time, Prince (Rogers Nelson) ceased to be
properly named (and controlled)
by a "proper" name by way of an "improper" speech act.
time
An unpronounceable and undecidable
Sign o' the Time that became a Time o' his Sign
S

If S symbolizes a conflation, conjunction, or copulation of gender, sexual, and racial identities, among other hierarchical binaries (through the conjoining of alchemical and/or planetary symbols),[27] it also signifies a fusion of musical traces of other artists that influenced Prince allowed him to hear and create beyond the borders of musical tribalism. His ability to fuse related but often disparate musical genres (e.g., rhythm and blues, funk, rock, dance, and rap, among others) with stylistic dexterity and creativity was evident in his ability to combine the fluid dance moves of James Brown with the cool rock swagger of the first guitar god/idol: Jimi Hendrix. Thus, his many musical influences and his love for those whose proper names have become metonymically associated with certain musical genres are also contained as traces within this instrumental non-musical symbol that, ironically, became an instrument of musicality. Its inscriptive materiality becomes the inspiration for the assemblage of matter that would become his equally iconic Love Symbol #2 purple guitar.

Moreover, we can honor the legacy of S bequeathed to popular culture and music history as a result of Prince's awareness and provocative implementation of the (post)structural and semiotic possibilities of language to signify in multiple directions simultaneously, which provided fertile ground for Prince's boundless lyrical inventiveness prior to, during, and after the creation and adoption of S. While this is rightly celebrated as one of the boldest moves in music history, in another sense it was nothing new for Prince whose playfully serious messing with signs and sexual innuendo to mess with our (dirty) minds was a consistent element of his lyrical creativity. His use of double entendres, puns, and substitutions of one semiotic unit for/4 its homophonic other (e.g., U for You, eye for I, and, of course, 4 for for, or is it 4 4 for?) changed the way fans viewed language and music by privileging homophony over "proper" semantic usage. Rather than some quirky eccentricity, his bold semiotic playfulness was a spill-over from his bold musical artistry that was not content with remaining boxed, compartmentalized, and segregated (as was the case early on in his career by the marketing strategy of the record labels that divided music in to white/Black).

Finally, the auto-glyphic gesture that became his name for a time provides the most fascinating and serendipitous parallel between Prince's performativity and the postmodern and post-structuralist linguistic turn that was the general ethos prior to and during his career. Without knowing, presumably, anything about these academic sensibilities, his consistent challenging of binary oppositions, his focus on the content of the form,[28] his "putting into question" notions of propriety or the "proper" (whether religious, political, musical, sexual, or semiotic), and his self-referentiality provide a lasting testimony to a keen intellect and creative imagination. Thus, Prince's semiotic interventions may be read as signs of and 4 our own postmodern time(s) that have witnessed the death of the author and the self. Interestingly, if the study of popular culture had been afforded some status among academicians during this time, this sign o' Prince's time could have served to mark the linguistic turn in philosophy and poststructuralism that had gained prominence and influence by the time that Prince decided to pen "Sign o' the Times" and put his own undecidable mark on the music world by means of this sign and symbol of undecidability; this double-coded symbol of may have served (and herein does serve) another purpose.

Time
At a certain moment in time, Prince (Rogers Nelson) ceased to be
properly named (and controlled)
by a "proper" name by way of an "improper" speech act.
time
An unpronounceable and undecidable
Sign o' the Time that became a Time o' his Sign
S

Prince's time may have ended on April 21, 2016, but the sign o' the times that he analyzed and transposed into a symbol—his S o' the Time—captured a moment in time by way of a symbol that also signifies, for some of us, the time(s) of a post-structuralist and deconstructive "putting into question." In "Sign o' the Times," a certain "apocalyptic fatalism"[29] takes on an interrogative tone and a general ethos read by various existential signs. It provides a lyrically apocalyptic diagnosis of contemporary life and death placed over a musical bed with a consistent sonic pulse that approximates the lyrical course (chorus) of Time(s), time(s): this sign—S—prophetically marks death(s) over time.

For instance, it marks the death and resurrection of Prince as S only to die and be reincarnated yet again as Prince. More broadly, it marks (or, perhaps, even inaugurates) the impending death of the record labels. This nominal (in both senses) self-sacrifice also instigated the death of musical gods/idols. As a reflection on signs, time(s), and death, then, it marked other sings of deaths, that, as with Nietzsche's prophetic articulation of the death of God, may have come 2 soon 4 our ears to hear and eyes to see. Ironically, by challenging the power of the record labels (and metonymically all labels), and even pronouncing the death of the record labels with the advent of the internet, there was also a concomitant death of the rock god/idol. Indeed, it would require much more time for this death of God pronounced by the madman to disseminate itself into the death of the musical gods/idols that had arisen to mythical proportions: as with God's "divine decomposition,"[30] rock gods/idols, too, decompose.

The control of the record labels and their myth-making machines have started to show signs of decomposition under the proliferation of music in numerous cites on the internet. These signs of our own times may be read as a partial fulfillment of Prince's prophetic utterances regarding the viability/ necessity of record labels due to the advent of the internet, which led to his own distribution of his music through this powerful medium. However, with the impending death of the very industry that created, elevated, and controlled artist musicians to the status of gods/idols, the reified nature of these musical gods/idols is revealed/unveiled as something other than a *sui generis* phenomenon of metaphysical genius. With the seemingly endless proliferation of unsigned musicians (i.e., the absence of marketing provided by myth-making machine), the carefully constructed mythos engendering and perpetuating the myth of the divinely inspired musician (viz., by the muses) dies, too. When everyone is a potential rock god/idol, no one is. Whether this is a happy or sad thing depends on one's (para-religious) desires for gods and idols.

Consequently, with the auto-glyph that graced that album and a became name, and with the passing of the artist-musician that set this chain of signifiers in motion, one cannot help but reflect upon these various names, identities, performative gestures, and their implications for a relationship between happiness and death when heard through the haunting lyrico-philosophical aphorism of "Signs o' the Times": "Some say a Man ain't happy til a man truly dies" and its interrogative supplement "O Why?"; indeed, "O Why" did Prince decide to "kill himself off" in order to be reborn by means of a mark or sign of undecidability? Why should we wait to call someone happy (as even Aristotle maintained) until one truly dies? What does it mean to truly die?

These intriguing questions and accompanying ruminations may provide some insight into the theological issues and cryptic religious lyrics evident throughout Prince's life and career.[31] Perhaps "Prince" had to "die" for the artist-subject S to be happy; to sacrifice himself, his "self," his legal name, his god/idol status, to which he had become a "slave," to be born again (not as Jehovah's Witness, at this time but) as an uncontrollable and, ironically, self-possessed and self-authorized creator for whom S was the "only acceptable replacement," substitution, or supplement for his name. Perhaps this "legal" "suicide" was symptomatic of a more profound religious "death to/of self" that would come later in his life.[32] Perhaps.

As with S, answers to these questions remain multivalent, overdetermined, and epistemologically undecidable. Nevertheless, perhaps it is better simply to memorialize the brilliant musico-lyrical performances that make us happy, while we are still alive. Along these lines, one might suggest that Prince's time o' the sign and the music created under various sign(ature)s functions not unlike Nietzsche's aphorism that "without music, life would be an error,"[33] as a musically performative response to the existential questions posed throughout the song and as a foreshadowing of the life and death of an artist whose life would have been error without the music that he gave to the world until his death.

In/conclusion: rather than providing some *resolution* to the song and the symbol in some musically and philosophically satisfying manner, let us be satisfied with the "unsatisfying" suspension of meaning and judgment—as in a suspended 2nd or 4th chord that awaits its triumphant conclusion/resolution by supplying its absent 3rd—in favor of a *revolution* in one's thinking and expectations that sees and hears aesthetic beauty in the suspension and undecidability symbolized by a (hiero)glyph[34] that became Prince's supplemental name for a *time* and continues to signify throughout our own *times* . . .

S

[The] Prince is dead, long live [the] Prince

Sign o the Times

Mess with your mind

Time

At a certain moment in time, Prince (Rogers Nelson) ceased to be properly named (and controlled)

by a "proper" name by way of an "improper" speech act.

time

An unpronounceable and undecidable

Sign o' the Time(s) that became a Time o' his Sign

S

Time

7 Choruses of Time(s) x 7 Years of Time as the Sign[35]

S

time

D.C. al Segno[36] S

Notes

1. Lyrical content and form based on "Sign o' the Times." Prince, "Sign o' the Times," YouTube, August 11, 2017, http://www.youtube.com/watch?v=8EdxM72EZ94.

2. "Prince Rogers Nelson Obituary," Legacy.Com, accessed February 12, 2018, www.legacy .com/ns/prince-rogers%20nelson-obituary/179702429.

3. One of Nigel Tufnel's famous lines from the movie *This is Spinal Tap* who said this about a beautiful melody he was playing on the piano for a song ironically entitled song "Lick my Love Pump."

4. On the supplement, see Jacques Derrida, *Of Grammatology*, trans. Gayatri Chakravorty Spivak (Baltimore: Johns Hopkins University Press, 1997).

5. Steve Douglas explains that the unpronounceable glyph on the cover of the album prompted fans to use the artwork copyright title "Love Symbol #2" as the album's title. He adds, "Accordingly, Prince's logo has a semi-official name of 'Love Symbol #2' (what, or where #1 might be is anyone's guess)." Steve Douglas, "The Prince Logo. Also known as Love Symbol #2," *The Logo Factory* (Apr 27, 2016). www.thelogofactory.com/the-prince-logo-love-symbol-2 (site discontinued).

6. On (constantive and performative) speech acts, see J. L. Austin, *How to Do Things with Words*, ed. J. O. Urmson and Marina Sbisà (Cambridge, MA: Harvard University Press, 1975); see also Jacques Derrida, *Limited Inc.* (Evanston, IL: Northwestern University Press, 1988) for his deconstructive treatment of speech act theory.

7. "The 25 Boldest Career Moves in Rock History: From Bob Dylan becoming Born Again to Panic! At the Disco dropping the Exclamation Mark, the Decisions that have changed the Music World," *Rolling Stone*, accessed February 12, 2018, www.rollingstone.com/music/lists/the-25-boldest-career-moves-in-rock-history-20110318.

8. Regarding Prince's abandoning his first name only status in favor of S, see the Prince interview conducted by Larry King on CNN (Dec. 10, 1999). CNN, "Prince Rogers Nelson's Entire 199 CNN Interview (Larry King Live)," YouTube, April 21, 2016, www.youtube.com/watch?v=m8mg7CxAYUM.

9. If you find yourself "singing" the melody inaudibly in your "mind," don't worry; as with Saussure's "signified," it should inscribe a non-auditory "sound pattern" (or sound image) and thereby replicate the music without, presumably, violating "proper" copyright permission: Prince/S was infamous for going after copyright violations. See Ferdinand de Saussure, *Course in General Linguistics*, trans. Roy Harris (Chicago: Open Court, 1983).

10. Prince's press release (i.e., his performative speech act); quoted in Rupert Till, "Pop Stars and Idolatry: An Investigation of the Worship of Popular Music Icons, and the Music and Cult of Prince," *Journal of Beliefs and Values: Studies in Religion and Education* 31, no. 1 (2010): 69–80.

11. Regarding this issue of the copyright ©, see Derrida's debate with John Searle in *Limited Inc.* **This is cited in note number 6

12. See Jacques Derrida, "Force of Law: The 'Mystical Foundation of Authority,'" in *Acts of Religion*, edited by Gil Anidjar (New York: Routledge, 2002), 228–98.

13. "Controversy," according to Matt Thorne, was one of Prince's favorite songs to perform live and one of his first attempts at a self-mythologization that "sees him spending seven

minutes emphasizing how hard he is to define" Matt Thorne, *Prince: The Man and His Music* (Chicago: Bolden, 2016), 69.

14. Thorne, *Prince*, 311.

15. Thorne explains that Prince's conflicts with Warner Bros. led him to "the paradoxical desire to hide in plain sight" and "that he'd even discard his own name, leaving 'Prince' to languish (temporarily at least) alongside Joey Coco, Alexander Nevermind, and Jamie Starr as one more abandoned identity." Thorne, *Prince*, 268.

16. Thorne notes this song's "symbolic significance" as "being the track most closely linked with his decision to retire his name." He adds, "In 3 Chains o' Gold, the number seven refers to both the assassins and the seven alternative Princes, whom he kills off one by one in the video, foreshadowing the "death" of Prince that would follow when he changed his name to S." Thorne, *Prince*, 292

17. Describing the press' difficulty writing (about) S, Douglas states, "The Prince camp were only too glad to help, developing a font for the symbol that was distributed on floppy disk to outlets—substituting the letter P with the now famous symbol (it was also thought that this was a way for Prince to figure out who he could trust in the press.)" Steve Douglas, "The Prince Logo." Our use of S comes from a similar downloadable font.

18. Regarding this symbol's asymmetry as symbolic of imperfection, see Margaret Rhodes, "The Fascinating Origin Story of Prince's Iconic Symbol," *Wired*, April 22, 2016, www.wired .com/2016/04/designers-came-princes-love-symbol-one-night/.

19. Regarding complex irony, see Claire Colebrook, *Irony* (New York: Routledge, 2004), 9-13.

20. On Prince's "deconstruction" of various binaries, see Nancy J. Holland, "Prince: Postmodern Icon," *Journal of African American Studies* 21, no. 3 (September 2017): 320–36.

21. On the proper name, see Jacques Derrida, *Of Grammatology*.

22. As with de Saussure's critique that "[for] some people a language, reduced to its essentials, is a nomenclature: a list of terms corresponding to a list of things. . . . It assumes that ideas exist independently of words . . . [and] that the link between a name and a thing is unproblematic, which is far from being the case." de Saussure, *Course*, 66. So, too, S subverts any essentialist notion of word, self, and name. And as with the *différence* in French between *difference* and the Derridean neologism *différance*—the "a" is seen but not heard any differently; written but not spoken—as inaudible as the inscribable but unpronounceable glyph: S. See Jacques Derrida, "Différance," in *Speech and Phenomena and Other Essays on Husserl's Theory of Signs*. Studies in Phenomenology and Existential Philosophy, trans. David Allison (Evanston, IL: Northwestern University Press, 1973).

23. Even though, as Thorne notes, "'Deconstruction' is not Prince's take on Derrida," the signifier "deconstruction" was and continues to be disseminated in popular discourse, regardless of one's knowledge of Derrida's philosophy. Thorne, *Prince*, 370. As with the all-pervasive signifier "postmodern," serendipitous associations or conceptual resonances without direct connections are not necessarily precluded. For instance, as Nancy Holland argues regarding Prince's status as a "postmodern icon," "The question remains of Prince's relationship to postmodernism as an academic movement. I concede that there was most likely no direct connection, but that in some way makes the relationship itself postmodern on a meta-level, a manner not of straightforward modernist causality, but of myriad, varied, and ever-changing currents of lived experience, images, words, and texts (including musical texts)

that have floated through the ether of cutting-edge thought and art in the thirty-five years since Prince was named *Rolling Stone* magazine's 'Rock Artist of the Year.'" Holland, "Prince: Postmodern Icon," 335. Indeed, about the importance of S, Holland states, "Independently of anything else about his music or the persona he created of/for himself, the glyph would mark Prince as a postmodern artist." Holland, "Prince," 321. See also her juxtaposition of Prince and Derrida, Holland, "Prince: Postmodern Icon," 330.

24. Or, as with Nigel's dull-minded confusion, is it "sexy" as in Prince's "Sexy MF"? Also, on the S album.

25. On pop gods/idols, see Till, "Pop Stars and Idolatry" and Rupert Till, *Pop Cult: Religion and Popular Music* (London: Continuum, 2010).

26. In interviews and movie scenes during the period, it was not uncommon for Prince to refuse to speak. His responses were often mediated or ventriloquized through another voice, whether that of a girlfriend or a puppet, Thorne, 109.

27. Till, "Pop Stars and Idolatry."

28. See Hayden White, *The Content of the Form: Narrative Discourse and Historical Representation* (Baltimore: Johns Hopkins University Press, 1987).

29. Thorne, *Prince*, 188.

30. Friedrich Nietzsche, "The Madman," in *The Portable Nietzsche*, edited and translated by Walter Kaufmann (New York: Penguin Books, 1976), 95.

31. Thorne, *Prince*, 193.

32. Thorne recounts one such religio-mystical reason provided by Prince: "According to his wedding programme, the decision came to him in a vision while visiting Mayte in Puerto Rico, where he saw the symbol, wondered what it meant and heard a voice telling him it was his new name. It was a nice attempt at a superhero-style origin story, but the symbol had been a developing part of his iconography for years, now gaining the extra horn from one of the alchemical symbols for soapstone (although some fans prefer the notion that the horn represents the fusion of man, woman, and musical instrument)." Thorne, *Prince*, 296.

33. Friedrich Nietzsche, *Twilight of the Idols or, How One Philosophizes with a Hammer*, in *The Portable Nietzsche*. edited and translated by Walter Kaufmann (New York: Penguin Books, 1976), 471.

34. "Papyrus" is a fitting font by its metonymic association with Thoth's undecidable "*pharmakon*" and Prince's Ankh-like (hiero)glyph. See Jacques Derrida, "Plato's Pharmacy" in *Dissemination*, translated by Barbara Johnson (Chicago: The University of Chicago Press, 1981).

35. Thorne, *Prince*, 296

36. Which *capo* [or head]? The one at the *capo* or title of this piece, Nigel's song? And for that matter, which *segno* (or sign)? The sign/*segno* o' the times in the title, or capo, which would leave one ensnared within the title? The superscript 12? The sign following the superscript? The sign o' the artist formerly known as S, the sign o' all the signs throughout this piece in an endless round of signification (i.e., from signifier to signifier *ad infinitum*)? So many *capi*, so many *segni*, so little *tempi*.

Chapter 10

MY POP LIFE

One Man's Journey to the Dawn

ANTONIO GARFIAS

All of this and more
is 4 U
With Love, Sincerity and Deepest Care
My Life With U I share

I've said it before and I'll say it again, that very short but very sweet almost-haiku is about the most perfect beginning of any music artist's life that I have ever heard. The man has work to do, but before that, here is his mission statement to the listener, just so we know his honest intentions. Granted, it can be interpreted as millions of other love songs, a promise to a romantic interest, but as the first song on his first album, I can't help but think that he was making a commitment to us as well as himself.

My Life With U
I share

Indeed, he shared his life with us, and up until his final days, he lived up to that promise made decades in the past. But just as he committed himself to us, there are millions of us that did the same for him. We didn't share our lives with him in the same way that he did, but the same sentiment was there. It started with the music but quickly evolved into something more. A lifestyle, if you will.

What you're about to read will most likely pull at very familiar threads, take you back to very similar experiences. Specific purple stories about how we were lured into that world by a lace-covered hand telling us of a place called Uptown. It's a story about me and Prince. It's a story about how we met (not literally, of course) and how he changed my life in small ways and large. It's about the lengths he drove us all to, the record stores we stalked looking for his material, the rumors we heard, the actions we took because of those rumors. I predict that it is, in large part, a shared story.

We weren't born Prince fans (were we?). We became fans through exposure and listening and personal tastes and, and, and . . . And yes, I know the preferred term in our circles is "friend" instead of "fan," but I will be using the latter for this writing. The former is a little too new-agey for my tastes.

Personally, my musical tastes and habits set me up perfectly for such a following. I've heard many fans proclaim their instant and devoted love of Prince after hearing whatever song they remember hearing, but that was not my experience. Mine was a gradual induction with crossroads and signposts along the way, guiding me to that mythical dawn. Lucky for me, I chose correctly at each step, listening to the beat of my own heart instead of the masses who were beginning, in 1985, to tell me that his time was up. I don't think so. He was just getting started.

To begin, I am a music junkie to the core. It's in my bones. My blood. My DNA. My elbow. To quote my first college roommate: You're the most-listening-to-music dude I have ever met. I listened all . . . the . . . time. Getting ready for class, walking to class, doing homework, going to sleep at night. But not radio. I, ultimately, had to curate what was going in my ears.

In retrospect, this was a major shift in my listening habits. As a young boy, you couldn't pry my ear from the radio. I was a product of 1970s AM pop. The infectious melodies swirled in my head, pumping colorful dopamines into my bloodstream. I consider myself to be firmly rooted on the synesthetic spectrum, "seeing" the song as abstract paintings. Most of the time it happens on a subconscious level, songs only revealing themselves if I start to focus on them.

As a nine-year-old (I was born in 1970), I would sweep the radio dial one last time before going to sleep, hoping to catch one last song that I wanted to hear before succumbing to my nightly slumber. No headphones at the time, so I pressed the small radio to my ear. Musical delicacies by Glen Campbell, ABBA, Andy Gibb, B. J. Thomas, Jim Croce, 10cc. I was particularly intrigued by the one-hit wonder. Strangely enough, I considered them the best of all. They usually recorded lots of other music that, largely, remained unknown. But for one breakthrough moment, they wrote a song that caught the world's attention even if that moment was brief. Ironically, these songs continue to travel with us during our lifetime as constant companions, peeking out every so often, reminding us of times past, the good ol' days.

I got my first silver/gray Panasonic boombox (along with a pair of brown/beige Koss headphones) in the early 1980s during my new hip-hop obsession phase. WBMX and WGCI were my stations. Nightly countdowns. Friday and Saturday night mixes. End-of-year marathons. I spent entire weekends in my room with my boombox on Record-Pause to quickly capture FREE SONGS to add to my collection. I remember wasting an entire Saturday and Sunday waiting for "She Blinded Me with Science" to be played to no avail. Men at Work's "Down Under" and Taco's "Puttin' on the Ritz" also had a similar attraction to me. I didn't merely like these songs. I needed these songs.

I love the idea of a "collection" and have had plenty over the years: comic books, Star Wars merch, books. I definitely thought of music in this way, too. Once I got that bad boy on a Maxell 90-minute, it was mine. I didn't start buying my own music until I was in my midteens, so until then, it was mixtapes. I labeled them, numbered them, dated them, filed them. They were my prized possessions, and each one of them became their own album. I knew which songs followed which songs by all the repeated listens. To this day, I can hear a song and know which song "should" follow it based on Tony Cassette #38, for example. Since most of the music was taped off the radio, I'd get DJ chatter, bits of commercials, contemporaneous timestamps which act as instant time machines. Bob Wall and Tom Joyner were as much a part of the tapes as any musical content.

These were my musical tendencies, my habits. To go into my tastes would take up way too many paragraphs so I'll spare you that indulgence. I've read so much *Rolling Stone* since the Run DMC cover issue and have seen the word 'eclectic' printed countless times over my still-current subscription that the word now sounds cliche. But at the risk of sounding cliche, my musical tastes are eclectic. I really did (and do) listen to lots of musical genres: classical, pop, R&B/soul, hip-hop, doo-wop, barbershop quartets, musical theater, classic country (I walk a tight line with country; some I love, some I despise), hard rock, blues. You get the idea.

It just boiled down to the song. Did it draw me in? Did it captivate me? Did I lose myself in it? I **constantly** lose myself in the music, awakening from a fog of intro/verse/bridge/chorus. My vision blurs at the edges, moving inward, until nothing exists but the song. This is when my synesthesia takes hold with melodic lines floating through the air, bursts of bass colors adding to the frame in a Jackson Pollock splash. It's a hypnotic experience. I find myself snapping out of a daze, as if slowly regaining consciousness after being drugged. Of course it's not always like this. That would be problematic listening to my iPod (I don't stream) in the car.

So that's my background in a nutshell. Pretty straight forward. I like music.

But where's Prince? you might be wondering. Lots of backstory for a piece about a lifelong Prince devotion. Well, Prince makes his first appearance in my life pulsating from the radio as I rode in the backseat of my aunt's light green Chevy Nova (her name was Betsy; the car, not my aunt). It was 1981/82. We were driving down Columbus Avenue in East Chicago and were stopped at a red light in front of a fruit market. The song was "Controversy." Lots of details, I know, but that's how my memory works.

Again, I must admit I am not one of those fans who was an instant devotee after hearing the first few seconds of a Prince song. Mine was a slower and more deliberate journey. I'm a little envious of the Facebook posts where people admit to being hooked from the very start when they heard "Soft and Wet" back in 1978, pouring from their radio speakers. They've been with him from the jump, and I think that's amazing. I'd love to be able to wear that badge of honor, the ultimate ride-or-die, life member. I'd imagine it's similar to the pride I get from telling younger people that I saw the first *Star Wars* on its initial release at the movie theater. I had nothing to do with it, but I was there, young Padawan.

No, that is not my Prince story. My experience was a slow drip forming a puddle on the floor which eventually gains motion and direction, obeying the laws of gravity and nature until it finds a larger body to travel with. As the metaphor continues, the river rages onward until it finds its ocean. I have found my ocean and the water is, indeed, warm enough.

But, oh, to go back to that drip. Tiny, inconsequential and quiet, I was alone with my source. It was he and I. No Big Bang. Instead, (R)evolution.

So on that day in the green Chevy Nova, Prince came. And went. I don't even know why that memory has stayed with me all these years. In hindsight, does it mean anything? Probably not. But maybe the memory was fresh enough in my mind to gain strength (drip) with my next exposure. "Oh yeah, that's Prince. I remember hearing 'Controversy' in Tia Josie's car last year." Drip.

That next memory comes in 1983. I had two best friends as a preteen: Tico and Artie. Lots of other kids were part of our neighborhood gang, but those two were my boys. Hanging out on the porch, boom box in tow. Listening to Artie's stories, he was the storyteller. Picking on Tico, he usually got the brunt of our adolescent horseplay. Not really getting into trouble, but rather, getting into mischief. Backyard self-rolled "cigarettes" (rolled newspaper and grass; not marijuana, actual lawn grass), dirty magazines, talking about the neighborhood girls, trying to make a soap box derby car out of Tico's doghouse (don't ask). The usual.

Artie's dad was a bass player in the area's biggest local band (at least I think they were the biggest; they seemed to have a pretty large following at all the church events), Together. All of that is to say that Artie's dad was a music dude, not just some guy who liked to listen to the radio. He bought music with his money. Grown-man music with grown-man money. He had albums and cassettes strewn across his bedroom floor. I'm not saying that we didn't buy music in my household. We did. She probably doesn't realize it, but my mom turned me into a *Soul Train* kid. We had Deniece Wiliams. Teddy Pendergrass. Barry White. The Gap Band. Slave. But there's something a little more alluring about outside influences, about seeing what made others tick.

"Hey, you gotta hear this. Follow me." Artie and I were doing our usual daily hang.

I followed him to his parent's room and he started digging around for something. After a little searching, he picked up a white cassette tape and popped it into his dad's radio. He pressed Play, listened, Stop, Fast-Forward a little, Stop, Play, listen, Fast-Forward some more, Stop, Play.

"Ok, listen."

Drum beat, synths, groove.

"What am I listening for?"

"Shh, you'll hear."

I want U so bad it hurts, it hurts

Uh, I wanna, I wanna, I wanna, I wanna, I wanna fuck U

"WHAT DID HE SAY???"

"SHHH! Listen!"

I'm not saying this just 2 be nasty

I sincerely wanna fuck the taste out of your mouth

Holy! Shit!

I looked over at Artie whose eyes were bulging, a distorted grin on his face that was trying its best to suppress a hysterical cackle. I was slack-jawed. Ol' boy ain't never heard anything like this before. This wasn't Teddy. This wasn't Barry. This was something else.

"This is Prince," he tells me through his giggles.

"Shh, let me listen!"

We let the tape roll, careful enough not to play it too loud so his parents wouldn't barge in to see what we were getting into, it being their bedroom and all. They didn't. So we sat there on the floor listening to the forbidden fruit. We knew we shouldn't be, but that made it more delicious.

People often talk about having their mindsblown after hearing something for the first time and, in that instance, I was no different. The music rules had definitely changed for me on that particular sunny afternoon. For me, songs were candy for the ears, endlessly pleasant and, for lack of a better word, fun. But "Let's Pretend We're Married" offered something new, something shocking, something unpredictable. I was still, basically, a kid with a limited musical knowledge. Sure, I listened to a lot of it, but I was still putting in my ten thousand hours. I didn't know if anything like this had ever existed. I only knew what I knew. And now I knew.

My teenage years continued their course. "Little Red Corvette" and "1999" made their radio impact, but I don't have any stories about them. They made my directly-off-the-radio mixtapes (Tony Cassettes 1, 2 and 5) for sure, but they were merely building blocks to my foundation. My drip was still a leaky kitchen sink. A potentially powerful leak if you don't get it checked out, but still a leak.

I need to preface this next passage with the acknowledgment that it is 1000% unoriginal. There is nothing particularly unique about what *Purple Rain* means to me that is not much different to millions of us, along with millions of not-us who are no longer on our particular ride. *Purple Rain* was huge. It was gargantuan. It was the gateway to many. It was the Pied Piper. And I gleefully followed that piper into the enchanted forest and got lost for decades.

The summer of 1984 was about three things to me: the Chicago Cubs (magical season!), football practice (I was about to be a high school freshman, and this was my first foray into organized football) and *Purple Rain*. That is one solid summer.

"When Doves Cry" was on constant rotation on MTV, and I was like a moth to a flame when those bouncy opening sounds issued forth. Everything stopped and I was drawn in. Movie clips from an as-yet-unreleased movie were scattered throughout, adding intrigue and mystery. Looks good, thought a fourteen-year-old Cubs lovin', football practicin' pre-freshman.

Was I out-of-my-mind crazy to see it? Was I foaming at the mouth, ready to break down doors to get my seat? Not quite. But it definitely made my mental rolodex. To reiterate, this was still my "pre" phase. It was these various Prince moments being slowly doled out over the past couple years that were quietly starting to boil. I apologize for all the water references.

It wasn't like today when you see a movie trailer, decide it's something you want to see, wait for opening weekend, get in the car, go see it. That's grown-up stuff. When you're a kid, it takes a bit more. At least for this kid, it did. "Maybe we can go this weekend to see it." "Hope we can scrounge up enough money for us all to go see it." "Wonder if anyone else in my family even wants to see it."

It turns out that, yes, other people in my family did indeed want to go see it. So much so that my sister and cousin went to see it before I did! Don't ask me about the specifics of how that took place, I don't remember. What I **do** remember is my sister coming home, gushing about the song "Purple Rain."

"And then at the end, he sings this song. It goes . . .

Purple Rain, Purple Rain, Purple Rain, Purple Rain, Purple Rain, Purple Rain . . ."

That's all she remembered. Two unresolved looped measures of the eventual quintessential rock anthem.

Finally, it was my turn. Having come home from football practice one day, legs seized with cramps, unable to get up from the living room floor (those practices were brutal), my mom saw my current state and decided better of her evening suggestion.

"Well, we were going to see *Purple Rain*, but we don't have to if you're that tired."

By that point, my anticipation was at a fever pitch. I had to see this movie. "I'm good; let's go!"

We drove to Griffith, Indiana, to a small movie theater and managed to get seats to the sold-out showing. Before the lights went down, the energy was unlike any other I have ever experienced in a movie theater. The closest that I remember was probably the opening of *The Empire Strikes Back*. The crowd was raucous. Loud. Excited. I saw a girl from my class there in the opposite aisle. When the lights went down, the crowd erupted. Had they all seen it already? Did they already know how great it was? It's hard to say. It was probably three weeks since its opening, so it was entirely possible that many were here for a second or third look. Whatever it was, I was caught up in it, too. It was very similar to the experience of climbing to the first drop on a roller coaster, the anticipation achingly growing until you reach the point of no return. Here, we gooooo . . .

My body buzzed with the opening extended version of "Let's Go Crazy" and it continued for the next two hours. The week before, a friend of mine gave me his mini-review of "Darling Nikki." "It's the baddest song you'll ever hear!" And it was. I carried the overpowering expectation of greatness to my theater seat that night, and Prince delivered on all the hype. What more can I say? *Purple Rain*. Amazing. We all know that.

My mom agreed to buy me the album ("Make sure it's the one that comes with a poster inside!") and it remained in constant rotation for months. Koss headphones affixed to my earholes, I absorbed it in on a daily basis.

I physically spun the record backward with my finger to hear the hidden message at the end of side 1. Yeah, a little creepy. But interactive! Cool.

My mom wasn't one of those parents who carefully curated what we watched and listened to, so listening to Prince wasn't considered taboo as it might have been in other households. Actually, it was probably me who was a bit more sensitive about the issue when my sister (two years younger) was listening with said Koss headphones and blurted out, "WHAT DOES MAS-TURBATING WITH A MAGAZINE MEAN???!!!"

"Be quiet! Give those to me!"

No, I didn't explain it to her. I just shut the situation down.

As previously stated, nothing original in my *PR* story. I'm sure thousands of us have, pretty much, the exact same story.

But what happened after the furor of its initial release? That's when my story starts to take shape, gains its direction, forges its way downstream. It was more than merely song, movie, soundtrack, end of cycle. Other tracks/events started to move around in the shadows, subtly calling attention to themselves. Psst, over here.

Like . . .

What was that amazing music during the love/sex scene?

I need to hear that version of "Let's Go Crazy" again!

You mean to tell me that there are NEW SONGS on the singles called B-sides?

You mean to tell me that there are new EXTENDED songs on extended, twelve-inch singles B-sides??

That fall/winter, as an inconsequential high school freshman, I somehow got invited ("showed up" is probably the more accurate term) to a Cool Kids house party. It was in the basement and it was jam-packed. Copped beer (that's what we called alcohol illegally-obtained-by-minors) was in great abundance and everyone stood shoulder to shoulder, the boys being boys, the girls being girls.

But then, I heard (felt) a bassline coming from the next room, the dance room. I inched my way to the door, trying to get a better listen. *What is that???* Emanating from the room was a red light, oozing out of the doorway to paint its threshold in an alluring tone. I could see the bodies in the dance room doing what they were doing, bouncing to that bassline, bathed in the red, red light.

We can fuck until the dawn . . .

It was the first time I heard "Erotic City," and I think it changed me as a person. I didn't want that song, I needed it. I needed to know where to get it. I needed to own it, to play it whenever the hell I wanted to.

Click. Something was permanently locked into place.

This was all too much. And I wanted all of it. But I didn't get it all. Barely any of it, in fact. I was still (kind of) a kid. I had no purchasing power to speak of. There was, it turns out, too much than I could afford. But now, my ears were tuned to its frequency. And knowledge is power.

Similar to the *Purple Rain* experience, I'm sure we all have our I-stuck-with-Prince-after-Purple-Rain-when-he-strayed-from-the-mainstream badge proudly pinned to our chest. We continued to support his latest album, our ears listening for the new single, knowing that it would undoubtedly come with a previously unreleased B-side with new artwork and new remixes. I'm not sure how prevalent unreleased B-sides were in that era, but there was a particular pride and excitement knowing that it's what my dude did. They were heartfelt little gifts, perfectly wrapped in a bow, that Prince regularly gave us, his devoted listeners. A little "thank you," maybe. In any Prince-related conversation, we instantly held the higher ground.

Sure, Raspberry Beret is a good single choice, but the B-side is sooo much better.

You haven't heard Hello? It's about the night he declined the invitation to the "We Are the World" session. You should check it out.

Maybe we were becoming a tad musically snobbish, but it was so satisfying. We were on the inside. Prince gave us the ammo and we sprayed that knowledge. Clack-clack-clack-clack.

Even though we didn't have the connectivity of current-day social media, we were starting to become One. The interactions weren't by the hundreds; they were by the ones and twos. I miss those days of one-on-one interaction with fellow Prince admirers. You would start talking to the local record store owner (my guy was the older gentleman at Taurus Records in Hammond, Indiana, who told me every time I came in for a particular song: "That's not on a single, you got to buy the album"). Or start up a conversation with a fellow record-bin hunter. Or form a friendship with a couple dudes at the Graffiti Bridge opening weekend (as I remember, we were the only three in the audience).

Or putting up a Prince flyer at college, searching for other people who were looking for people like me. Sometimes, it feels like I'm looking back on someone else's life, thinking about the lengths I went to for my passion. Did I really do that? Was that me? Was I really becoming that guy? Yes, I was becoming that guy, but this was only the tip of the iceberg.

Let me rewind the tiniest bit. Before I became the dude that started posting Prince flyers on campus, I was just another (admittedly huge) Prince fan, buying the albums, collecting the singles, discovering the B-sides. Normal stuff. I didn't know anything about record store "import sections." (I'd be curious to know exactly when Prince became a main fixture in those bins.) I didn't know about bootlegs, out-takes, demos, rehearsals, concert recordings. How could I? I didn't live in Manhattan or Los Angeles or the cool Chicago neighborhoods with the ultra-hip carries-everything record stores.

Growing up, my two main record stores were Taurus Records, an amazing R&B independent store, and Woodmar Records, another independent store that was housed in a local mall (Woodmar Mall).

On reflection, Woodmar's design was octopus-like, its body being the center of the mall, the wide-open area where Santa set up shop every winter, the main hub. From there, its tentacles branched out this way and that and at the tip of one of those tentacles was Woodmar Records at the end of a hallway where the mall lights seemed to either be dimmed or not working. "Woodmar Records" in blue neon, welcoming the musically curious. If the approach to the store was a bit darker than the rest of the mall, the inside of the store was even darker. This was no fluorescent-lit Musicland/Sam Goody joint. Sure, we were still in a mall in Hammond, Indiana, but this place definitely had its own vibe.

On every trip to Woodmar, I was allowed to walk the mall on my own, window shopping at the places that interested me, not my mom. As the years passed, the stores that interested me changed. Kay-Bee Toys, Woodmar Tees (a place where you could pick out the t-shirt you wanted and choose an iron-on from thousands and thousands of choices to be ironed onto it; I exaggerate, it was probably 100 choices), Woodmar Bookstore and ultimately Woodmar Records.

I was a browser 90 percent of the time, but whenever I had money burning a hole in my pocket, I went there to relieve myself of it. On one occasion, I set up shop in front of the Zine rack. I picked up various magazines, skimmed through them, put them back. But there was one that unexpectedly caught my eye. I thumbed to a page toward the back of the mag, and I saw an ad for 'bootlegs.' Hmm. Bootlegs? I didn't have specific knowledge about what they were exactly, but thought I had a pretty good sense of what they were.

The ad was from some guy in Portland, Oregon. His address was listed with highlights from his inventory. Led Zeppelin. The Grateful Dead. Pink Floyd. Prince.

!!!!!

You have my attention, good sir. It was one of those moments; I can still see the small black-and-white print of the small black-and-white ad. Just as there was a pre-*Purple Rain* me and a post-*Purple Rain* me, there was now a pre- and post-Finding-This-Magazine me. It cost two dollars to send in for his complete catalog. Whatever these "boots" were, I was going to find out for myself. Naturally, I mailed away for it posthaste. Done and done.

This is, undeniably, when my river evolved and became a force of nature. God help anything downstream of this. No dam could stand up to its power.

An envelope arrived a couple of weeks later (snail mail, am I right?) and the contents were not the glossy pages of a professional publication, no Grainger catalog for the music world. Instead, enclosed were about ten xeroxed pages stapled together. No typewriter or computer was used in the drafting of this document. It was all handwritten.

I skimmed the pages, passing over the Stones, the Who, the this-and-that's until I found it. On the lower portion of one of the pages, sectioned off on its own by the author's hand-drawn squiggly lines, was the Prince section. In current times, this section would easily need its very own catalog created just for Prince. But back then, it was a rather limited offering. Over the years, I have collected so much Prince material/literature that I need large bins to contain them. But oh, to still have that first catalog. I'd love to see what I saw for the first time. What I do remember is that these items were rather pricey. The cheaper selections were $25, but in general, they hovered around the $40 range.

Reading over the listings over and over, I seemed to be in a panicked state. What was I going to buy first? There's so much here! I can't afford all this, but I want it all! I contacted a Prince acquaintance that lived in Indianapolis (his "name" was X24, and it took me an embarrassingly long time before I realized that it was Christopher and not "ex-two-four" as I was calling him) and told him about what I found. We agreed to buy different things so that we could make copies for one another of what the other hadn't bought. You know, game the system. Split them costs in half!

Like I said, I don't remember everything that was in the catalog, but the first thing I ordered was *Charade*, a collection of bootlegs/unreleased songs from *Parade*. I thought the name *Charade* was quite clever. The order was made, fulfilled, and devoured in that order. "Little Girl Wendy's Parade." "Movie Star." "A Place in Heaven." "All My Dreams." "There's Other Here With Us." "Old Friends 4 Sale." This was gold. This was the stuff of dreams. I was now **on the inside of the inside**. Platinum member with all rights and privileges.

The remainder of that portion of my Prince life unfolded in an unsurprising manner. I collected and collected and collected, building my library, filling in the missing pieces of my soul. It was later that I read about Prince's disdain for these black markets, but by then, it was too late. There was no way I could turn off the faucet. I'm a weak man, and there was no way I could deprive myself of these gems. The temptation was too powerful, each unheard Prince song floating out there in the void, yet reachable. I just couldn't do it.

I found myself rationalizing my actions with many scholarly arguments. This was a "victimless crime." No one was getting hurt. I wasn't buying this music in lieu of buying the officially released offerings; I was just enhancing my experience. What could it hurt that little ol' me was hearing these vaulted tracks? To this day, I understand and see the validity in arguments against buying/collecting bootlegs, but I try not to be too hard on myself. I've cut myself a break over the years. It also eases my mind that I continue to buy just about everything the estate issues. I have never used the excuse of 'I already have that' to keep me from supporting the legacy. If I don't buy it, it's usually because I can't afford it (I'm looking at you, *Sign o' the Times* singles box set) or already own the official original release (*One Night Alone*; yes, I'd love it on vinyl, but did you see the price tag on that SOTT Super Deluxe Vinyl edition???). I have so many versions, both video and audio, of the *Lovesexy* tour, but if the estate ever officially releases that monster, I'll be the first in line to preorder it. I guess you could say that I'm paying my penance, making up for past sins.

I was now ready to operate at Next Level. My Prince card was stamped and current; I was ready to do battle. Time to put up my campus flyers. I was now That Dude.

I took out an 8×10 sheet of paper, drew out Prince's name in the classic Purple Rain font on the top third of the sheet and asked a very important question.
Prince fans

Are you looking for hard-to-find stuff?
Rehearsals, Demos, Alternate takes, Live Concerts
Call me at the XXX-XXXX

I made tabs at the bottom of the flyer for people to eagerly and uncontrollably rip off so they could run home, screaming down the street to dial my number.

To my recollection, only one guy called. His name is (also) Tony and he remains one of my very dear friends these decades later. He was a groomsman in my wedding and has an incredible Prince story of his own about how Prince was also a very strong and guiding force in his life. I am honored to be a small part of his story, and I'm proud of my part in it.

So like I said, he was the only person who called. And it was totally worth it. I wasn't disappointed that I didn't receive an influx of responses to my tacked-up fan flyer. I finally found someone who had the same uncontrollable and proactive drive when it came to Prince.

We shared music, of course, but more importantly, we shared stories, conversations, insights, opinions. We shared friendship. Born out of one man's music, this fascination was now affecting my life in real ways. It was bringing people into my inner circle. Because through Tony, I met Mark and Peter and so on and so on. We did this, that, and the other: going on a spontaneous high-speed trip down to Indianapolis when the rumor was that Prince was performing with Parliament/Funkadelic at the Black Expo (the rumor was false, but we met a new "Prince Guy" and got to see Parliament perform for about 4 hours!); huddling around a boom box in Tony's dorm room listening to Jesse Johnson or some other Minneapolis-sound band that Tony was more familiar with than I was; planning the ultimate Minneapolis sightseeing trip.

I'm 100 percent sure that you can now book a Prince sightseeing tour in Minneapolis (especially post-April 2016), but not so in the early 1990s. There was no Google, not even a widely used internet at the time. No, we had to put in the work to make it happen.

Jump cut to the Summer of 1993: Tony and Tony, packed up and ready to drive out west: destination, Uptown.

From what I remember, Tony made up our itinerary. He had a list of purple places that we planned to find, each of them with a check box next to it. You know, so we could mark them off the list, mission accomplished. It was the ultimate Prince scavenger hunt: the hospital where Prince was born; Prince's childhood home; Prince's high school; Flyte Tyme studios; the Glam Slam club; Paisley Park; Prince's house with the yellow windmill in front; Electric Fetus; the Purple Rain house; Pepé Willie's house (our itinerary went deep).

These are the types of things we felt compelled to do. We were always pushing forward, wanting to do things that went beyond merely sitting around and listening to the latest record. Something about Prince's aura and mystique took up large parts of our waking hours. I concede that we often glorify the past with bright and shiny colors, make it out to be times of wonderful happiness with no sorrows. Yes, there were sorrows. Yes, there were other things in my life besides Prince. But also, yes, those years were glorious in their discoveries, their awakenings, their experiences. I was in danger of evolving from That Dude into That Guy's a Little Crazy.

Example:

I'm not sure when it started, but at some point, I discovered the existence of a magazine called *Controversy*. *Controversy* was the absolute best. It was a beautifully put together Prince fan magazine that was published in Europe. Great in-depth and very specific writing, amazing color photos; this magazine was top-notch. My *Controversy* experiences go beyond this story, but this specific instance will best illustrate my latest transformation.

"Diamonds & Pearls" was about to be released, and *Controversy* planned a fan convention in Minneapolis that year. People came from all over the globe to finally meet face-to-face with their fellow Prince brethren. I walked into Glam Slam for the first time, decked out in a new Prince shirt, a silver Prince love symbol chain around my neck, eyes bulged to full circumference. I wish I could say that I remember what song was playing, but I can't.

My eyes were darting to and fro, trying to take it all in. *Is that really the Graffiti Bridge motorcycle? Yo, check out the Prince symbol on the dance floor! Is that Pops?!* (Pops was a guy I met at a local *Controversy* magazine party in Chicago; I told you, I have other *Controversy* mag stories.)

If you were to ask me, I'd probably say that I'm an introvert by nature. There's nothing comfortable about the thought of me walking into a night-club by myself in a mostly foreign city, ready to party the night away, come what may. But whether I knew it at the time or not, these were my people, and I was where I needed to be. I belonged there. Instead of finding a corner to stand in, I made my way through the crowd, making eye contact with strangers, throwing out head nods every couple steps. There was commonal-ity, fellowship, and at the risk of sounding corny, love.

My three to four days there were filled with some amazing experiences and memories (even a Prince sighting!!!), but I want to highlight a small side excursion to Paisley Park.

As with any event like this (the convention), cliques started developing, and people began to hang out in smaller circles. My group consisted of four other guys. I knew two of them from the Chicago party, and met the other two during the convention. We collectively decided to rent a car and drive out to Paisley Park to see it in person. During these earlyish years of Paisley Park, it was hardly the fan-friendly place it has come to be. You would think that a tour of the facility *might* be possible for convention goers, but in the early 1990s it was a hard "no." (The closest the convention got to Prince par-ticipation was an autograph session at Glam Slam with most of the NPG. No Rosie, no Prince.)

We found the address and directions out to Chanhassen in whatever fashion we did in those days and ventured out. (We were 'detained' by a Chanhassen police officer while we were trying to see Prince's house, but I digress.) Driving down the highway, the Big White Mansion revealed itself along the Minnesota skyline. This is where the magic happens, as they say. We didn't have any delusions of grandeur, thinking we were going to be able to hit the jackpot and make our way inside. We were just taking it moment by moment, seeing where the road led us.

We pulled into the front parking lot (no security), parked, got out of the car, loitered. I'm sure this was a common occurrence at the facility, but we didn't know anything about that. We were bold enough to stroll up to the front door, peer inside the glass windows, but not bold enough to take it any further. We didn't ring the doorbell, didn't knock to ask if we could be let in. We seemed to know our limitations and respected those boundaries. I say we respected those boundaries, but this next part will no doubt seem contradictory to that statement.

Before getting back in our car, I picked up one of the pink-ish rocks in front of the studio and put it in my pocket, a memento from my mecca. That was that. We got what we came out here for, to see it in "the flesh." But as we were about to pull out, I noticed that there was a way to continue driving to the rear of the Park. Again, no security.

There are times in our lives when we react on pure instinct. No thought is given to reason, rationale, or consequence. We just act. All five of us in that car were of the same hive mind, five acting as one.

Hey, turn left, see what's back there.

The driver turned left. Turning a corner, we saw a spiral staircase propped up against a fence. It looked old, rusted, and familiar. Was that the "When Doves Cry" staircase? I think it is! That is so cool!

Who knows? Maybe it was "the" staircase, maybe it wasn't. Sure looked like it, though. But then, we turned our eyes toward the studio and saw that it was the trash area. A large dumpster was there, sitting against the building. And what do they say about one man's trash being another man's treasure? Again, no thought, just reflex. Primal urges.

Let me out the car.

I am (sort of) embarrassed to say that I was the first one in. I didn't actually get into the dumpster like Morris's "girlfriend" in *Purple Rain*, but my upper body was hanging over the edge as I was pulling bags out of it. One bag. Two bags. Three bags. I don't remember how many we got, but we got bags.

Hey, there's a camera!

I looked up and saw a security camera mounted to the wall, looking down on our shameful actions. We didn't panic. We just decided that it was time to go. Bags in the trunk of the car, we drove to a nearby parking lot to divvy up the treasure. There was no arguing about who got what and how much each person got. It was, "Here, you get this stack. You get this stack. And you get this stack." Yes, I got some really cool stuff from that outing, but, more importantly, that was when I could now add dumpster diving to my resume.

He did what? Yeah, That Guy's A Little Crazy.

You can clearly see the path my life was now taking, the lengths that I was now willing (and able) to go through to satisfy my hunger. But shouldn't it be about the music, you might ask. And you'd be right to ask that. Yes, it was about the music. The music was and always will be the prime focus.

But there was something about following this man that made me feel I had to do more. I didn't just have to; I wanted to. I was extremely happy and fulfilled whenever I was doing whatever Prince activity I was doing that day, because, yes, I was doing something every day. Or close enough that that's how I viewed it. I was starting to develop a Prince lifestyle. Was that a thing, a Prince lifestyle? Didn't matter; that's what it felt like.

One day, I would work on my Prince lyrics binder. I sat at my college dorm desk, popped in a Prince CD into my standalone Kenwood CD player and hit Play. I transcribed each song to the best of my ability (some of those songs are really difficult to decipher). And not just the main lyrics, but every utterance on the recording. I titled my lyric folder "Prince, in his own words: Every ooo, ahh & baby."

Another day, I would work on my cassettes. My personal Prince 'import section' was growing by the month and, of course, it wasn't good enough for me to just label the cassette and file it away in my Tony cassettes system. No, I had to look for Prince pictures that 'spoke to me,' that were distinct. I would photocopy these pictures, cut them out to fit over the cassette labels, and then color each picture with color pencils and markers to create my own cassette cover. Prince with fire engine red lips, a light blue facial complexion, a neon green suit. You know, kind of like the real thing at times. The final touch came with a black sharpie when I would label the cassette in my own hand-drawn personal font: Purple Rain OT's. Or the Camille Album. Or Lovesexy '88. Titles like that.

Then there was the time I decided that purple would be the dominant color in my wardrobe. I started buying purple t-shirts, purple sweaters, purple turtlenecks, white Nikes with a purple swoosh. I don't think I ever told anybody about this decision, but after a while, I don't think I had to. My dad brought home some plastic safety goggles from work one day and gave them to me. They were purple. Where the temples met the frame, there was a plastic shield that acted as protection for the eyes. These were, without a doubt, safety glasses. That's okay, I told myself. I'll find some way to file them off, and I'll have some cool frames. I never got around to filing the glasses down but wore them around campus anyway. Mama, there goes that man.

All of this may sound extremely time-consuming, and it was. But I was also a full-time college student with a girlfriend and friends and college parties to attend. But if there's one thing college teaches you, it's time management. It just meant that there was not a lot of time to lounge around in bed. Or sit in front of the TV for hours at a time.

Was such an obsession (because that's what it was turning into) healthy? Was it detrimental? Dangerous? Could it possibly start affecting my personal relationships, the relationships outside of my Prince bubble? It might have had I crossed another few thresholds. But I never did. Where I landed up was, I suppose, good enough.

I had a serious girlfriend at the time, and there was only one time that I remember her suggesting that I might be taking it a little too far. I don't think her words were as harsh as that, but the implication was there. But that was it; that was all she ever said. She knew it made me happy, so I guess it was good enough for her, too. She wasn't a Prince fan, but that was okay with us; not an issue.

Then, there were my poor college roommates, all of whom had to endure the countless Prince pictures, album covers, and posters that blanketed large sections of our small apartment. It started off with the area immediately surrounding my desk, but would slowly creep its way, picture by picture, in a purple urban sprawl. The pictures made their way toward the ceiling and ultimately, yes, onto the ceiling itself (it was a huge European tour poster). But the guys didn't care. Didn't bat one eye. Didn't say one word. Oh, that's Tony, that's just his thing, do we have any beer in the fridge?

I was going to say that Prince was starting to become a large part of my identity, but that ship had already sailed many moons ago.

Hey, do you know Tony?

The Prince Guy? Yeah, I know him.

I was, indeed, the Prince Guy. Or, at least, the local Prince Guy as I'm sure that there were millions of other Prince Guys and Girls around the world, each with their own story, their own journey. And while this wasn't the goal, to become the Prince Guy, my chest swelled a little, my head held a little higher when I thought it might be true. That pride still lives in me as I realize that I am part of a very special group. A group that continued the journey after *Purple Rain* when Prince seemed to make a conscious effort to see who was really with him, who of us were really his Forever in My Lifes. The eclectic nature and diversity of his mid to late 1980s output seemed to be diametrically opposed to the mainstream glory of *Purple Rain*. He never wanted to be painted into a corner from day one and there he was, proving it album by album. He was in control. He made the rules. And the Purple Army loved him all the more for it. The army grew stronger by the year.

One other very important thing to remember is the time frame in which this all took place. I was a young and impressionable teenager when the cogs started to spin on this wheel, the age when the music you fall in love with tends to follow you your entire life. My canvas was mostly bare, and I was ready to splash new colors onto it. I was young, but I already knew that music was my thing, my passion. I didn't have the burdens of a job, of a family I had to support. I was able to be as greedy with it as I wanted to be. There were no repercussions. It was the pursuit of my happiness. So, I pursued it. I followed my bliss.

There's a large part of me that wishes I can say that these habits never diminished over time, that they only grew stronger and more ridiculous over time. But that's not true. I don't think my body would be able to take it if I continued that pace for the past twenty years. Instead, my Prince lifestyle, shall we say, evolved. Just as Prince majorly evolved over the years, so did I. I was no longer twenty-five years young. I no longer "didn't have a job." I no longer had the luxury of being as greedy and self-centered in my ways like I was back then. I now had a wife. I now had kids. I now had a dog, a mortgage.

But there's no less pride in my heart, no love lost for the man, the music. It all remains, strong as ever, continuing to bring me joy, happiness and satisfaction. No, I can't wallpaper our house with Prince tour posters and magazine covers. But I still have them all, tucked away safely, ready to be perused and gazed upon with loving memories: memories of music, of people, of experiences, of Prince.

I'm sorry if this reflection comes across as a little long-winded (I didn't even tell you about the time I outbid a local record store owner at auction for a Prince tambourine), but I wanted to acknowledge that so many of us share very similar stories. Sure, the details are a little different (swap "Erotic City" for "Bambi"; I was seventeen, not fourteen, etc.), but we share much of the same DNA. But oh, those details. They are the spice in this stew, the tasty stuff, the chili sauce.

Now if you will excuse me, I think I'll go throw on the Family's album. You know, that's the one Prince side-project that I wish he had kept for himself. But I digress.

CONCLUSION

JUDSON L. JEFFRIES, MOLLY REINHOUDT, AND SHANNON M. COCHRAN

It took a minute for the general population to take to Prince, back in the late seventies to early eighties, but once it did, he found himself the object of millions of adoring fans. He captivated America. He was different, everyone had an opinion of him. Was his music R & B, funk, pop, rock & roll or all, of the above? Was, he black or white, straight or gay are just a few of the questions that surrounded him. To these questions, Prince provided few answers, and that's just the way he intended it. There have been few artists around which so much mystique has swirled. Women found him alluring, some men didn't know quite what to make of him. He was unlike anyone we had ever seen. There have been musicians who have been just as eccentric, and controversial, but never quite so talented. Because of Prince's range of skills, it takes an equally talented and multifaceted group of writers to capture in words any one aspect of Prince.

This collective of authors, ranging from college professors to music teachers to musicians to clergy dives into aspects of Prince's work that few have explored. By examining both influences and rivals, the writers present to readers a more complicated and multilayered artist than perhaps previously thought. Many have argued that Prince was an original, to which the answer is, yes and no. Prince learned from others, borrowed from others, and was impacted by others. Some of those others are the subject of the chapters contained in this book.

That Prince chose not to credit Rick James with influencing his style and music does not change the fact that from James Prince appropriated a thing or two. H. Zahra Caldwell interrogates that dynamic better than anyone on the academic scene. Prince often dismissed those who saw the impact that Jimi Hendrix had on Prince, yet the similarities are glaring. One need only read Ignatius Calabria's work in order to understand the lengths to which

Prince patterned himself after Hendrix. These are just a few dynamics that the authors successfully tackled in this book.

In the end, in *Feel My Big Guitar* readers will find a space chock full of musicological analysis and memories about an artist whose work has touched and inspired so many people. With his myriad blend of genres that touch on some of society's most pressing issues, Prince has challenged the minds as well as captivated the hearts of millions of listeners. Ultimately, the authors in this volume have employed a blend of methodologies that offer a body of fresh, intriguing, thought-provoking, and mind-blowing work about Prince—an artist who is difficult to categorize, but easy to appreciate.

It has been more than seven years since Prince's untimely death, yet we can think of no artist (dead or alive) whose life, work and legacy continues to garner the attention of the academic community. Academic journals have devoted special issues to him; book chapters have been written about him, conferences, both domestic and abroad, have placed him at the center of analysis, and concerts and tributes continue to be held in his honor.

Readers will find that this book affords them a unique lens through which to view Prince, resulting in a richer and more nuanced understanding of one of the greatest musicians of the twentieth and twenty-first centuries.

ABOUT THE CONTRIBUTORS

IGNATIUS CALABRIA teaches middle school music at Woodland Hill Montessori School in North Greenbush, New York. He earned his BA in English from Muhlenberg College, his BM in jazz guitar performance, and his MAT in music education from the University of the Arts. Calabria specializes in teaching and arranging popular music, guitar education, jazz education, and the life and music of Jimi Hendrix. His forthcoming chapter, "People, Hell and Angels: The Socio-Cultural Contributions to the Rise and Demise of Jimi Hendrix," was included in the 2020 McFarland book *Popular Music in the Classroom: Essays for Instructors.*

H. ZAHRA CALDWELL, MA, MEd, PhD, is associate professor in the Ethnic and Gender Studies Department at Westfield State University. She is a historian, educator, and cultural commentator who teaches in the fields of history and Black and women studies. Her critical and academic work is focused on unpacking and expanding the definition of resistance within the long struggle for African American freedom, particularly as it relates to Black women and their cultural labors. She has published important work on cultural icons, including Beyoncé, Prince, and Hazel Scott.

SHANNON M. COCHRAN, PhD, is professor of African American studies, women's and gender studies, and English literature in the Departments of Interdisciplinary Studies and English at Clayton State University. She earned her doctorate from The Ohio State University. Her research areas include intersectional approaches to racial identities, body politics, popular culture, media culture, and gang culture. Included in her work on race and gender is the intersectional examination of how representations in visual and narrative cultures impact the lived experiences of people of the African Diaspora. She has published and presented her work both nationally and internationally. Some of her publications include the co-editorship of two special issues dedicated to Prince's life, work, and legacy—the *Journal of African American Studies* (2017) and *Spectrum: A Journal on Black Men* (2020). She is a native of Columbus, Ohio.

BRIAN JUDE DE LIMA is a racialized/Black jazz pianist with allegiances to the style of Teddy Wilson, Art Tatum, Bud Powell, and Thelonious Monk. De Lima holds a PhD in musicology/ethnomusicology, with research interests that examine the importance of learning the arts (particularly African American musics) as intersections of an interdisciplinary unified whole (music, dance, poetics, fine arts, theatrics), and a Master of Arts in classical composition. De Lima is currently a professor of music at Centennial College and the coordinator/developer of a new joint program between the University of Toronto Scarborough and Centennial College entitled Music Business and Technology. He is also the recipient of the 2017 KMB internship grant for innovative curricula design.

SABATINO DIBERNARDO is a senior lecturer in religion, philosophy, and humanities at the University of Central Florida in the Department of Philosophy. His primary teaching area is in philosophy of religion and popular music. His research interests are at the intersection of philosophy, religion, and popular music through the lenses of poststructuralism and irony studies. His publications include chapter contributions to the following edited volumes: *This Is the Sound of Irony: Music, Politics and Popular Culture*; *Music at the Extremes: Essays on Sounds Outside the Mainstream*; *The Ultimate Walking Dead and Philosophy: Hungry for More*; *Finding God in the Devil's Music: Critical Essays on Rock and Religion*; *Trumping Truth: Essays on the Destructive Power of "Alternative Facts"*; and *Cambridge Handbook of Irony and Thought* (forthcoming). He is also a guitarist performing on the Space Coast of Florida.

WILL FULTON is a musicologist and professor of music at LaGuardia Community College. He has contributed chapters to *The Oxford Handbook of Music and Disability Studies*, *The Oxford Handbook of Hip Hop Music Studies*, and *Beyoncé: At Work, On Screen, and Online*, and published articles in the *Grove Dictionary of American Music* and *American Music Review*. A former A&R director and record producer, Fulton produced and remixed recordings for Camp Lo, 2pac, and M.O.P. His coauthored monograph 33 1/3: Camp Lo's Uptown Saturday Night was released in 2017. He holds a PhD in musicology from the City University of New York.

ANTONIO GARFIAS, now living in Round Rock, Texas, is a former theater sound designer and audio engineer for Blue Man Group in NYC and Las Vegas. He considers his synesthesia a gift from the heavens. He shudders to think of the thousands upon thousands of dollars he has spent on music over the years but regrets not one red cent of that tally.

JUDSON L. JEFFRIES, PhD, is professor of African American and African studies at the Ohio State University. He earned his doctorate in political science at USC. He is the author, co-author, and editor of eight books. Additionally, over the past several years, Jeffries has put together two special issues devoted solely to Prince's life, work and legacy—the *Journal of African American Studies* (2017) and *Spectrum: A Journal on Black Men* (2020), of which he is editor-in-chief. He also teaches a course on Black Popular Culture where Prince is featured prominently. Jeffries's latest work is a three-volume encyclopedia titled *African American Culture: An Encyclopedia of People, Traditions and Customs* co-edited with Omari L. Dyson and Kevin L. Brooks, published by Greenwood Press.

TONY KIENE holds a BA in African American studies and sociology and an MA in American studies, both from Purdue University. He has spent the past twenty-four years in the Twin Cities entertainment and nonprofit sectors, which includes time at Penumbra Theatre Company and the Minneapolis Urban League. Kiene currently pens two Prince-related columns—"Purple Music: Musings on the Minneapolis Sound" published in the *Minnesota Spokesman-Recorder* and the PRN Alumni Foundation's "Alumni Spotlight: Stories from the Park."

MOLLY REINHOUDT earned her PhD in historical musicology from the Ohio State University in 2019 with a dissertation focusing on Spanish vihuelist Diego Pisador's *Libro de música para vihuela* (1552). For the past nearly eleven years she has served as managing editor of *Research in African Literatures* and *Spectrum: A Journal on Black Men* in the department of African American and African Studies at Ohio State.

The VERY REVEREND FATHER FRED SHAHEEN was born in Toledo, Ohio. He received his BA (1995) and MA (1997) both in English literature from the University of Toledo. Upon graduation, he spent three months in Paris, France, followed by one year in Montreal, Quebec. In 1999, he entered St. Vladimir Orthodox Theological Seminary in Crestwood, New York, and received his MDiv in 2002. Shaheen was ordained to the holy priesthood in 2004 and elevated to the dignity of archpriest in 2014. He currently lives in Iowa with his wife, Michelle, and their five children. He has been the pastor of St. George Antiochian Orthodox Church in Cedar Rapids since 2006.

In 2010, he contributed an essay to the collection, Arab Americans in Toledo. In 2018, his essay "Following Jesus, Finding the Muse: The Gospel According to Prince" was published in the Theology of Prince electronic journal by United Theological Seminary of the Twin Cities. In 2019 and 2020, he interviewed Prince associates Taja Sevelle, Estaire Godinez, James Bryant, and Matt Blistan and wrote spotlight stories on them for the "Stories from the Park" series by the PRN Alumni Foundation.

Shaheen has been an avid Prince enthusiast since 1982. Over the years, he has seen Prince perform fifteen times, the most recent of which was an intimate show at Paisley Park six months before the artist's death.

KAREN TURMAN is a preceptor of French in the Department of Romance Languages and Literatures at Harvard University. She earned her BA (2001) at the University of Minnesota and her MA (2008) and PhD (2013) in French Literature with an emphasis in Applied Linguistics at the University of California, Santa Barbara. Her interdisciplinary research interests include 19th-century Bohemian Paris, music, and dance during the Jazz Age, fashion and popular culture studies, community engagement scholarship, and topics of social justice and sustainability in the language classroom. Turman's publications on Prince include an essay on Josephine Baker, Claude McKay, and Prince entitled "Banana Skirts and Cherry Moons: Utopic French Myths in Prince's *Under the Cherry Moon*," and "Prettyman in the Mirror: Dandyism in Prince's Minneapolis."

INDEX

Printed in the USA
CPSIA information can be obtained
at www.ICGtesting.com
LVHW090951031123
762977LV00004B/28